Oliver St. John Gogarty (1878-1957) was educated at Stonyhurst, Oxford and Trinity College, Dublin. Gogarty was a fellow of the Royal College of Surgeons of Ireland and, like W. B. Yeats, became one of the first Senators of the Irish Free State.

His books, available in Sphere, include AS I WAS GOING DOWN SACKVILLE STREET, a racy tale of Dublin life in the 1920s, ROLLING DOWN THE LEA and TUMBLING IN THE HAY.

Also by Oliver St. John Gogarty in Sphere Books:

ROLLING DOWN THE LEA
TUMBLING IN THE HAY
AS I WAS GOING DOWN SACKVILLE STREET

It Isn't This Time Of Year At All!

OLIVER ST. JOHN GOGARTY

An Unpremeditated Autobiography

SPHERE BOOKS LIMITED
30-32 Gray's Inn Road, London WC1X 8JL

First published in Great Britain by
MacGibbon & Kee Ltd 1954

Published by Sphere Books Ltd 1983

TRADE
MARK

Set in Times

Printed and bound in Great Britain by
Cox & Wyman Ltd, Reading

Contents

Proscenium

Some years ago I was bowling along in a bus towards that Fairyland, Connemara, which is situated in the West of Ireland on the most westerly shelf of Europe far away from all the turmoil and grim realities of war. Outside there was rain, flooding and desolation. I turned away from the disheartening scene. Next to me I noticed a tall man seated. He wore a suit of navy-blue serge. I knew from the way his Adam's apple went up and down that he was tall. His moustache was golden and his blue eyes were looking straight ahead, fixed like all Irish eyes on futurity. In my best social accent I addressed him. I said, 'It is most extraordinary weather for this time of year.' He replied, 'Ah, it isn't this time of year at all.' He was evidently in the Fourth Dimension.

I have worked long at the enigma. I might have expected something like it so far away from all that is pedestrian and merely real. Suddenly, I thought what a magnificent title it would make for a book that dealt among other things largely with the past where it isn't this time of year at all.

Boys! O Boys!

O BOYS the times I've seen!
The things I've done and known!
If you knew where I have been
Or half the joys I've had
You never would leave me alone;
But pester me to tell,
Swearing to keep it dark,
What ... but I know quite well
Every solicitor's clerk
Would break out and go mad;
And all the dogs would bark!

There was a young fellow of old
Who talked of a wonderful town*
Built on a lake of gold,
With many a barge and raft
Afloat in the cooling sun;
And lutes upon the lake
Played by such courtesans,
The sight was enough to take
The reason out of a man's
Brain and to leave him daft,
Babbling of lutes and fans.

The tale was right enough:
Willows and orioles,
And ladies skilled in love;
But they listened only to scoff
For he spoke to incredulous fools,
And maybe was sorry he spoke,
For no one believes in joys
And Peace on Earth is a joke
Which, anyhow, telling destroys;
So better go on with your work:
But Boys! O Boys! O Boys!

* *Marco Polo.*

1 *5 Rutland Square, East*

It isn't this time of year at all. And why should it be? Why should a free spirit be subjected to a calendar? Why should there be workdays and holidays? Why should my winged ankles be thrust into a pair of jack boots? I did not come down from Olympus for that.

Gyroscope yourselves up into a region of calm and I'll tell you something. Days are the time it takes a planet to revolve on its axis and even that is not constant; our earth had once a four-hour day, twenty-eight days a week, enough to satisfy the most exacting labour leader; but there were no men upon earth then; the tides were over a hundred feet high and the moon was much closer. Perhaps before you are done you will think that it's close enough anyway. Between the stars it is all eternity. The universe had no beginning. It was always there. It will be there for all eternity.

All this stuff is as old as Kepler, who was a few hundred years before Einstein. If you have not heard of him, don't blame yourself but his lack of publicity.

I am not done yet. What about the years? There are none between the stars; but here they grow, cheer you, change you, age you and finally lead you to the slaughter, that is, into Eternity, where it isn't this time of year at all. That is the standpoint, it is said, from which Life should be surveyed, an interstellar standpoint; but while we are depending on the sun, let us, like a sundial, record only sunny hours. Who wants to read about misfortunes except when they are not his own? Misfortunes are part of character; so is Good luck; and when it comes to Good Luck I have a very good character indeed. But, in spite of my good character, do not think that I have not revolved upon my axis: 'Is it not fine to swim in wine and turn upon the toe?'

It may be a pity that this book is not in the modern mode of writing, that is, without a hero, without any serial sequence, without meaning and without unity except the unity of whatever comes into the writer's head. That is the modern or open-air lunatic asylum method. The 'thought chase' or the stream of consciousness. I will eschew that even at the risk of making myself the hero; using myself as the subject. This is no congenial task to me.

As 'I am a part of all that I have met' you can judge me on the principle of 'show me your company and I'll tell who you are'. Show you my company, that I will gladly do; and if I cannot keep myself altogether out of the picture the blame will be on you, for I am satisfied to sit in the proscenium, that is, the part of the theatre between the orchestra and the stage, while my company is acting: men and women some of them dead and gone but all ever present in the communion of memory; portions and parcels of the past who still guide us and carry us on. We are part of what has gone before. The past is more powerful than the present, for not only did it form us but nothing in it can be altered or destroyed. What we call the present is only a suburb of the past.

One of the most remarkable men I met used to say that to talk about evil spirits is to bring them about you, a variant of 'talk of the Devil and he will appear'. From this I concluded that it is an unhappy thing to talk of rogues, cowards, self-seekers, bullies, men obstinate in their vanity and other scoundrels. I have come across them all. If I name them, it is only because I want to anticipate history and to put what I knew of them in life on record. Some of them are heroes at the moment, heroes to the unreflecting masses, the 'common men', who are the heroes of the hour. Conversely, it is a wholesome thing to speak about the good if you wish to have them about you. That is what prayer is for; and though this history of sorts is far from being a prayer, it will be filled more with the good and the brave than with evil men. And it will be all the pleasanter reading because of this. At least, I hope so. I have met more good than bad men. I have met men who had in them 'translunary things' and yet were not so extra-stellar as to lose human interest. After all, there is such a thing as being superior to mankind, like Holy Willie. There is no welcome, salvation or housing for such here.

No one can tell where he was born even though he was there. The mother of the Duke of Wellington gave birth to him in a coach on the way from Mornington to Dublin. A coach is not a place within the meaning of the act, so it can be argued that the Duke was born nowhere; and yet he won the Battle of Waterloo, with Blücher's indispensable help. The future Duke was nursed in Merrion Street on the wrong side of the river from Rutland Square.

Had I been born in those days, I would have looked down on the Duke's family, the Wellesleys, for where I was born is only a few doors from the Marquis of Ormonde's town house and the houses of many worthies. I am a bit of a snob and that's not on account of my Olympian origin either.

It is better to be born lucky than rich. My nurse used to say that good luck was poured on me at my birth. She did not make me lucky or happy-go-lucky, but she foretold it, and she was right; to be lucky means to have a cheerful temperament. You never see a melancholy or a tightfisted fellow lucky, and it isn't that that makes them melancholy. It's the other way about; it's because they are melancholy, they are unlucky. So a cheerful temperament means a lucky one. It means far more. It means a happy one, and 'To be happy is the chiefest prize'.

It is sad to think that there must be more melancholy people in the world than merry ones. More influential ones, else why should there be this dismal outlook on life, 'Vale of Tears' stuff, and so on? If you take life too seriously, it will make you serious about everything, trivialities included. Life is plastic: it will assume any shape you choose to put on it. It is in your power to take things cheerfully and be merry and bright even though you are surrounded by melancholics who cannot imagine anyone being good unless he is unhappy. They equate goodness with unhappiness, as some ladies in great cities equate culture with seriousness. To these snouts you will always be bad; and it's no use trying to appease them. They all are paranoids and there is no bottom to their private hell. Have nothing to do with them if you want to lead a good life that is a merry one: 'For only the good are merry.' I prefer to think of life's great optimist, Brian O'Lynn who, when he fell into a river, exclaimed hopefully, 'There's land at the bottom!' Tell that to the bluenoses.

But why anticipate the gloaming and the end? You cannot appease Death, not even by dressing up in black. Maybe, all gloom comes from such idea: placation by anticipation. Whether it does or not is not such a problem as how to live merrily surrounded by gloom.

Five Rutland Square, East, was a good place in which to be born. East is more promising than West. I was probably born in my mother's room which looked out east at the backs of the houses in North Great George's Street which, though not so good an address as Rutland Square, held many distinguished persons including the great Sir John Pentland Mahaffy, afterwards Provost of Dublin University or Trinity College, as it is also called; John Dillon, the patriot, had a house there and there dwelt Sir Samuel Ferguson, whose poems and influence are responsible for the so-called Irish Renaissance.

The Sun, I was told, dances on Easter Sunday. I watched and saw it dancing on the ceiling; and that early memory remains with me, for divine control was about and Heaven was signalling. The hard fact that there was a cistern near the bedroom window from which sunlight could have been reflected makes no difference; now is now and then was then.

In the garden behind our house were flowering wild

currants. I played there with my sister under the long pink blossoms. Dark evergreens stood in the black earth, walled up from the 'area' on which the servants' bedrooms looked. The house was built in a century when there was no provision for the health of servants, let alone for their comfort. The men for whom the houses were built were ignorant of the fact that the servants' health might affect the masters. Had that been common knowledge and had social consciousness moved along with it, servants would not have been buried underneath the street, and their bedrooms would have had at least one window by law.

An ornamental iron vase stood in a plot all to itself in the middle of the garden. And then the stables. Sometimes a horse would be led out and I would be mounted and held upon it. This is an early memory.

There is a hinder one of a green wave over my head. That must have been when my mother dipped me in the sea at Salthill by Galway town where her father lived. Could I have been more than a baby in arms then? I cannot compete with one of Dr Sarnac's patients who not alone remembers herself in her mother's womb but in her father's testicle! John Kiernan, even if he tried, could not compete with that.

I have gone back as far as I can and I am beginning to wonder how can my early memory interest anybody, seeing that it bores me. What does interest me is my forgetfulness of whole periods of time. But for sanity's sake don't let us become philosophical; that way smugness and madness lie. You all know what happened to Plato's Mr Dooley, who had to drink the hemlock because he bored people to death. And you all know what that dirty carbuncular character, Karl Marx, who hated mankind, did to mankind with his *Das Kapital.* These men lacked humour.

Had Plato had his way the country would have been filled with motherless morons, just as Russia is filled with people who cannot call their souls their own, for in them individuality is annihilated. Plato was sold at Aegina by the Spartan Ambassador to Syracuse; but Anniceris bought him and loosed him, before he had a chance to see life steadily.

Karl Marx's carbuncles are festering all over the face of the earth in a kind of chain reaction and debilitating masses of mankind. Philosophy? Cut, shuffle or deal have nothing to do with it. Philosophy is the result of a bitch of a wife or none at all. Socrates is an example of the former, Plato of the latter; but we must hand it to Plato for endeavouring to endear himself to us by his mistress, Archianassa, as George Moore credited St Augustine with doing through his mistress and his illegitimate child.

Philosophy appears in the decline of a nation; in Greece after Plato, in Germany after Karl Marx. I will not mention France after Bergson. It is expostulating yet.

Until they have philosophers, or too-smart alecks, there will always be an England. They should be warned to stop theorising now. In the United States there are no philosophers, so there is no decline. I trust that you will not mutter as an aside, 'There is no civilisation either.' Just you wait and see.

Philosophy, though you would never suspect it, is what makes superior people call poetry 'an escape'. The real escapers are not the poets but the punctual, the commuters, the philosophers and all who seek to impose a rule and a regimen on Life. Regimenting Life is precisely the role of the philosophers: they seek by 'rules' to shackle thought; and they call their rules 'logic'! They dare not emerge from the fane they have erected to save them from the outer darkness wherein may lurk monstrous and frightful forms such as are seen in the gargoyles of Notre Dame. Imagination and mysticism they fear to face; and yet some intrepid artist faced them and carved their images. What is worse, these normals have had the audacity to call the glory of their race mad. It is high time that the tables were turned and that the prosaic were looked upon as morons, and those races that held madmen sacred came into their own. Poetry can climb Heaven and harry Hell. Philosophy is an air raid shelter for old men.

It is with the unruly, the formless, the growing and the illogical I love to deal. Even my gargoyles are merry and bright; my outer darkness by terror is unthronged. My thoughts are subjected to no rules. Behold the wings upon my helmet and on my unfettered feet. I can fly backwards and forwards in time and space.

2 *Green Thoughts*

Michael answered the doorbell. 'Your father got Fairfield,' he said. There must have been a lot of talk between Father and Mother which Michael had overheard. About that I knew nothing; but, judging by Michael's excitement and the serious scraps of conversation to which I was not supposed to listen, I felt that there was achievement in the air.

'Fairfield, I know; but where is it?'

'An old house on seven acres, about. Just to the right of the road before you come to the Botanic Gardens.'

I knew the Botanic Gardens. They were never crowded; in fact, there were few visitors so it was a safe place for nurses to wheel a perambulator and to talk with the gardeners or the man in the Gate Lodge. Some years back I had escaped from my nurse, who was thinking less of children than of grown-ups, and I had made for a boat moored to the bank of the Tolka, the river that borders the Botanic Gardens and flows between it and the gentle slope on which the Convent stands. The boat slid away and but for an attendant who pulled me out I would be keeping silence now.

'Don't let on I told you anything,' Michael said.

I flung my satchel, the one made of pigskin of which I was so proud, on the back hall table and rushed upstairs. Mother said, 'Your father's bid for Fairfield has been accepted. You will have a better place to play in than the Square.' Mother did not like Rutland Square, for though it was reserved for householders who lived beside it, there were gangs in it, and statements scrawled on the Bandbox, 'Molly loves Gerry', and disparaging remarks about O'Duffy, the dentist, and ribaldries about old Corney Walsh. Mother may have resented the remarks about the dentist, for he was the first to assure the neighbours that her complexion, the talk of the town, was not artificial but perfectly natural. As a girl she was called 'The Flower of Galway', and it was not only because her father was John Oliver, the miller.

Fairfield lay in an unfashionable neighbourhood to the north of the city on the road that went past the Botanic Gardens and the Tolka Bridge where the two tram horses rested while a third was harnessed and the climb to the tram terminus begun.

If you went beyond the terminus you came to the Model Farm. There were no 'ribbon buildings' in those days, that is, buildings that followed the water, gas and sewerage pipes, and so lined the roads, without depth. Open fields surrounded the town. There was the Bull Field even before you came to Fairfield, and fields with walls built of mud before you reached that. Behind St. Joseph's Crescent there was a field which stretched behind Kincora Terrace and Oliver Mount, all of which my father built opposite Fairfield's boundary wall. Now, with Fairfield, he owned fields on each side of Botanic Road.

The old name of Fairfield was Daneswell because of a stone-roofed well that rose beside a mound at the farthest corner near the Bull Field. A little stream bordered by enormous willows trickled from the well into a little pool which was to be my heart's delight. There is something about water which allures me even though it nearly pulled me in. Let psychiatrists make the worst of that!

The Tolka is my earliest memory of a river. By its banks, on its island and in its water I spent many happy days. Its north bank was bordered by a hedge of hawthorn and a green field that sloped up to the Teachers' College. It began with the waterfall under Tolka Bridge. Its source, of course, was farther away, in Clonee or Ashbourne probably. I often wondered if I dived from the bridge would the water under its white roof be deep enough to save my neck?

From the island near the bridge small boys, including myself, could fish for gudgeon with bent pins. You could see the gudgeon turning on the bottom, under three feet of water, with their sides flashing as they rolled. Schools of minnow swam over them and in the stiller places 'pinkeens', with their back fins spread and their gills highly coloured, could be caught. But the gudgeon were the prize; they were four inches long, or four and a half; the minnows, more numerous, were hardly three inches and the pinkeens never so long.

In the long reach before you came to the ruined mill with its dangerously deep millpond, an odd trout would dart by in the clear, slow-moving water. Very rarely a kingfisher flashed, a blaze of bluish green, to disappear in the high bordering hedge. I can see that sudden turquoise flight quite vividly now.

Carey, the Gate Lodge keeper, groundsman and general helper, showed me the knoll where King Brian's tent had stood near the well during the Battle of Clontarf in 1014. One of the berserk Danes entered the tent where King Brian was on his knees giving thanks for victory. He attacked the King who, though over eighty years old, cut off the Dane's legs with one sweep of his mighty sword. But the wounds he had received were mortal. He is said to have died in his tent which was pitched on the mound beside the well. Yes, the place was rustic enough to have legends and the legends were probably as true as legends are. We found a pit with human bones at the edge of one of the fields, and the millpond in which King Brian's grandson was drowned with a Dane gripping his hair was less than half a mile away. Fairfield House was two stories high with a gable in the middle and a hall door in a rounded tower at one end.

Another tower half as high led into the garden. The hall was level with the ground. Behind the house was the most wonderful garden I ever saw. A huge yew hedge many hundreds of years old separated it from the kitchen garden. Fully grown yew trees sheltered it from the north. The yew hedge was mysterious: there were tunnels in it where you found hollow eggs. Blackbirds nested in it, and in the big yews at the end of the garden low down in the branches little birds slept 'all the night with open eye'.

In the middle of the garden was a circle of hazels, and in each of two smooth plots near the house stood an ancïent mulberry tree patched with zinc where the branches had fallen. On the top of the garden wall to the east foxglove grew and wallflowers; they must have been used for simples in the days when foxglove was prized for its digitalis. Lily of the valley and mullein, for heart disease and rheumatism, were to be found scattered here and there. Diseases were cured from garden simples then, and these were not advertised.

Two rustic seats under the yews showed that the garden was planned for a restful place where you could sit and gaze on the smooth grass or let your eyes wander to the hazel circle of lighter green while at intervals a blackbird would dive cackling from the great hedge of yew.

The front of the house faced south. To the right its boundary wall was fenced with old elms. There were rows of elms in the fields and one, a magnificent specimen, stood solitary and symmetrical in the middle of a low hedge on which the maids spread clothes to bleach. Who would dream, as he walks the cement pavement that covers those fields now, that once a splendid tree stood there, with spreading roots that held fast when the Big Wind of 1902 laid low many a stately tree? This great elm had horizontal branches evenly spaced that sheltered many a country bird.

There had been large elms in Rutland Square too. The one that sailor McVeagh climbed, and won every small boy's heart, was tall; but it was black with city soot and it housed many sparrows and starlings but no country birds. No maids spread clothes to air beneath it.

My love of trees is a late trait, later than my love of water. Trees had a practical value for me then, particularly those that stood beside the gate. The upper part of one had been blown across the roof of the old coach house and had knocked off many of the little slates that roofed it, long before slates from Wales roofed more than half the town. The bole of this broken elm was hollow. That is what made me value the tree. Into this hollow I used to lower myself and shoot with a peashooter quite impartially all who rang the gate bell. The most dependable visitor was the rural postman; I must have learned punctuality from him. He called morning and evening. He would turn his florid face inquiringly at the welkin and the walls. He never suspected an innocuous elm five yards away. It was not until his spectacles were hit that he lodged a complaint. The son of the gatekeeper was blamed, but his alibi was waterproof so I had not to yield myself up.

To the fields and the stream and the trees of Fairfield I owe all that makes me feel at home in the country and restless in the town. To this little early touch of nature my love of solitude is due. I could lie for half an hour under the great elm and stare up into the green world of the branches and watch linnets and finches hop, or a single blackbird fly about in this unconfining cage. The pond was the scene of many an adventure with a heavy raft I made of pine logs that could hardly float. In a tin bath you could drift down the Tolka until you came, nearly came, to the millpond. I used to listen long to the stream from the well before I realised that streams have spoken through the ages to millions in unchanging tones, no matter what language the millions spoke. 'Water, first of singers, The sky-born brook'; and mine was only a trickle from a well.

True, I used to be taken to Kilbeg, the home of Farrell O'Reilly, my father's friend, for they both came from Royal Meath. But that country place was too large for a child. It had a river of dark water bordered with reeds but its invisible flow and its blackness were repellent; besides, it was forbidden. If I did not promise to keep away when the grown-up men were out shooting I would have to remain with the maids indoors. There was a wood but its trees were evergreen and all the same.

The liss, or fairy palace, was another matter. I would listen avidly to the men in the yard who talked about it, far too seldom for me. It was hard to get word of it except in a way that was meant to frighten but only made me all the more curious because I could see that they were frightened of it themselves. It stood in a field in front of the house, a raised square with a few twisted thorn trees on it which no man dare cut down. It seemed harmless; 'Ah, but just you wait till night.' But I was sent to bed long before that.

Kilbeg had a garden with many beehives. There was a well in the middle of the yard, but the door of it was always locked. The joys of Kilbeg were restricted. It had many fears; Fairfield had none. The Tolka, 'the stream that overflows', was not repellent. But both country places put a soul into me that is made of waters, fields and trees, with background of fairyland not too far away.

3 *'And Then The Schoolboy'*

Richmond Street School was about two miles away from Fairfield. Strange to relate, it was no pain to go to school. You could walk citywards up the slight incline until you came to the canal bridge with the long Whitworth Road to the left and the sunken railway parallel to it beside the canal. If you had time you could go by the canal bank and charge down the slopes as Robert the Bruce charged on De Bohun; or, loitering, wonder how long you would have to wait before you were big enough to jump from one side of the stone-edged lock to the other.

Over the bridge was a tavern, the Cross Guns, of which Mr McGuinness was the owner. In the little garden at the back you could see two young poplar trees yellow in the light of spring. It was disappointing that there was no signboard to show why it was called the Cross Guns. The right name may been the Crossed Guns. Who knows? But the Brian Boru to the right and behind you on the cemetery road before you come to the bridge had, and still has, the best signboard ever seen outside any public house. It shows King Brian of the Tributes advancing with his army to the Battle of Clontarf. He is surrounded by warriors but with little discipline, for they had not much discipline in 1014. Though he looks more like a crusader than an Irish king, the customers, who for the most part consist of mourners, mutes who drive the hearses and the more cheerful gravediggers, are not offended, for their thoughts are not on far-off kings and battles long ago. So Brian's banner flies uncriticised.

Only one of the boys came to school in any kind of a vehicle; that was Tom Kettle, who came in a governess cart, a little pony carriage with a door at the back. Two people including the driver, who sat sidewise, could sit on either side. The Kettles were originally a Danish family – all Norsemen are called Danes – and they had dwelt in the district around the village of St Margaret's long before the Battle of Clontarf.

'We came out of the sea along the Black Beach. We won all before us. We won it with our battle-axes. We hold it still. We have been in the neighbourhood ever since.' That is what Tom Kettle told me. The Black Beach is now Baldoyle, a name that conceals the Gaelic name, Baile dhu Gall, the settlement of the Dark Strangers.

Tom Kettle was dark. He had eyes like the eyes of Robbie Burns, the eyes of genius. He wore dark grey clothes with three buttons on the sides of his knee breeches such as all schoolboys wore. He would not hail any of the other boys when he came to the school, although his eyes looked here and there. It was as if he already had things in his mind that were beyond the school. He moved about in his governess cart, not to gather his books but because his energy made him restless. We were not in the same form, for he was my junior, and I don't remember seeing him in the playground at lunchtime; but I used to see him when he was called for to be driven home. His home was a gloomy house of dark stone two stories high with a northern aspect in the village of St Margaret's. It was the house of a strong farmer, Andy Kettle, who had crippled himself financially supporting Parnell.

My father never drove up in his mail phaeton with its two horses to call for me. He knew better than to differentiate his son from the sons of others who were, for the most part, working-men.

Richmond Street School was run by the Christian Brothers, the only native order Ireland has produced. 'Chisel your words', Dr Swan the president, used to say. They were the best educators in the country and that is why my father sent me there. They taught Irish long before it became a political shibboleth. My copy of *The Youthful Exploits of Finn*, interlarded as it was with pencilled translations, fascinated me with its opening sentence: 'Cumhal left pregnant his wife.' What did that mean? I knew that it referred to Finn mac Cumhal, the bald father of Oisin, grandfather of Oscar and great-grandfather of Diarmuid, the Irish Hector, the first gentleman in Europe, Diarmuid who never lied.

I knew none of the boys well; but I did know well the propositions of Euclid and to their clear unambiguous style I owe whatever smatterings of unequivocal English I may possess. 'The angles at the base of an isosceles triangle are equal.' Euclid called his fifth proposition 'The Bridge of Asses'. I am indebted to him for bridging for me the gap between geometry and English. To him, and to the fact that there were essays set once a week, I acknowledge my indebtedness, and to the men who taught so well.

There was an essay to be written about a country fair during the writing of which I had a vision of sorts: I could see a plain with banners and many-coloured pennons waving over white tents; some dim association perhaps with the sign of the Brian Boru. I saw, although I did not realise it then, that all writing depends on seeing and then projecting the scene graphically. It is not without significance that the Greek word for knowing is the same as the word for having seen: 'I saw, therefore I know.' Do you see?

4 *The Tipperary Hounds*

'To break the rainbow on the briar.'

The Master of the Tipperary Fox Hounds was in the study. It appeared that his underlip had become transfixed by his teeth as the result of some accident in the hunting field. My father was attending him. Mystery surrounded the Master as it did all my father's patients. This was a necessary precaution to prevent the children, by which I was meant, from telling about the patients to other children in the Square in the hearing of their nurses.

It must have happened about Christmastime because I remember many presents which were sent to us by the Master, Richard Burke. My sister and I got more presents that year than in all the years before put together. One present, a large board brightly painted, allured and disappointed me, a forerunner no doubt of disappointments to come later on from brightness and paint. The board, which was about the size of a small tombstone, oblong with rounded shoulders, was fitted with holes with nets behind. Into these you were to throw a ball. Whatever game it was escaped me, for I was able only to take in the bright colours without being able to appreciate the game. It was the beginning of my acquaintance with that very remarkable man, Richard Burke, Master of the Tipperary Hounds for forty years.

The Tipperary Hounds are unlike any other Irish hunts

in that they hunt in the season five times a week instead of the weekly runs of the Royal Meath, the Kildares and other hunts. And the Tipperary Hunt was exclusive; it had few members but all were devotees. Its headquarters were at a small hotel in Fethard which kept an excellent chef. Dr Stokes lived in the hotel and he was a fixture, an authority of some kind, probably a veterinary surgeon. Next to the Master, the chief member was Dan Maloney of the well-formed body and the ruddy face. When he blew his nose it took about sixty seconds to regain its deep purple hue. The Master lived at the Grove and there were hunters by the dozen in the stables as well as the pack in the kennels. All the members had to be endowed with independent means, for it costs money to hunt and to do nothing else. The Master had lots of money; so had his neighbour Lord Waterford, another leathery man and somewhat of a rival with his own pack.

I must have been about ten because I did not count when the Master was 'constrained by love' (it was the questing love of some rajah whom he had invited to the Grove) to make the rounds of his house after midnight. He stood with his riding crop in the doorway of my bedroom. He was gone in a moment.

Next day I was mounted on a horse called the Sweep. It belonged to his eldest daughter and was worth, so the groom said, eight hundred pounds – about fifteen hundred pounds in those days. They may have told me that by way of a caution. The value of the horse made me far more nervous than the intermittent gallops over the countryside. My ignorance saved me from timidity; I did not know, so I did not care, that my face might be broken by a horse baulking at a fence or by a fall over a low hedge with a quarry on the other side. Some such accident must have befallen the Master when he was delivered to my father by special train.

I learned some of the things that become a member of a fox hunt: not to overrun the Master of the hounds or to get in other members' way. I found out some of the mysteries that horsemen keep to themselves; for instance, all this about gripping with your knees. You can get a much better grip on the saddle by the calves of your legs with your toes turned out a little. That may be what all the mystery is about. You may leave it to the horse; he will know whether you know how to ride or not. And it is understood that the best seat on a horse belongs to the Master.

The morning was early. It must have been a cub hunt. There was no fear of my running over the Master; I could not see him, much less catch up with him. But there was a danger of my getting in some member's way. So I went off by myself and lost touch with the hunt. There were only eight or nine members out and no ladies.

What a lovely thing the country is! Underneath the springing turf and the softly breathing horse and the jump through the hedges that had not altogether lost their green. The dark, dull leaf of the bramble rose that looked so well with the dew on it and the red withering. Out from the hedge, the open country with the rounded outline of Slievenamon, the Hill of the Woman, far away in the brightening weather. They told me that Slievenamon was the scene of a competition among the women of Ireland and that some hero on the top of it was the judge. Slievenamon is in the heart of Tipperary, the Golden Vein. The country that Cromwell gazed on and exclaimed: 'A land well worth winning.' There is nothing to equal it in England, for the light there is different for one thing, and for another the land in England is not so fertile.

By riding over about twenty square miles of it I got to know the Golden Vein. Perhaps I had been riding over Fanning's farm (but it was years after, many years after) and the wretched land that, in spite of all geology, lay beside it. 'Is it in good heart?' I asked Fanning, the tall tavernkeeper who had in his veins Cromwellian blood, that is, the blood of the sour, jar-nosed humbug's troopers who settled in the Golden Vein. It was easy to draw him when it came to a question about his farm; or it may have been his brother's farm, and that of his brother's mother-in-law hard by. 'Fertile, is it? Many's the morning I had to get up early and give the sheep a kick in the rump to remind them to go on grazing.' 'And the land beside it?' I inquired innocently. 'Now I know nothing about it, nothing whatsoever.' When an Irish man wants to denounce you he knows nothing whatsoever about you. 'But I'll tell you one thing,' he continued. 'If it's as mean and meagre as the old wan that owns it, a blackbird would have to go down on his knees to get a pick out of it.' There was nothing mean or meagre under hoof in Tipperary of the blue limestone when I galloped over it.

I tugged my bowler hat hard down. Hats are worn, tall hats and bowlers, to act as crash helmets in case of a fall. No, I had better not go any farther. It will be hard to find my way back or to explain to the all-seeing Master at dinner before the guests, before the amorous rajah, if he is still there, why I deserted the hunt. Taking care of the Sweep will be no excuse. I wonder now if she knows the way home? 'Gone away!' The fox, or I?

Under a clump of trees I saw two stableboys with four horses. Remounts of course, one horse for the Master and one for Dan Maloney. At first they thought I was bringing them a message. Soon they realised that I was lost. 'They'll be here in half an hour if the run was west.' I was not interested. I was in a quandary; what hunting etiquette do you break if you are caught talking to the boys with the remounts instead of following the hunt? 'If you keep the hill to your left and walk the Sweep we will overtake you in about half an hour.' 'Thanks,' I said; and slowly turned, determining not to let them out of sight even at the risk of being sighted by the farseeing eyes of the Master or his friend. 'The hunt has left me,' I added; but you can't fool a groom any more than you can fool a horse. However, I imagined that it was much better than confessing that I had left the hunt. 'Walk the Sweep.' Have I been overtaxing her? It will all come out when I get back. This is certain: that a newcomer can do nothing right in a hunt. It would lessen the lore of the old stagers if such a thing were permitted.

The truth is that fox hunting bores me. If it bores me in informal Ireland, what must it be in formal England? The fact is, fox hunting, like horse racing, is a ritual, a religion in itself, the religion of the plain as opposed to that of the cave; and I have no vocation.

Why is it that people must have a purpose before they assemble? I cannot imagine Dan Maloney getting up and in the saddle at five in the morning in order to gallop over the fields while the dew is still in the hedgerows. Can you imagine people going for a first night to the opera if there were to be no interruptions from the stage? And yet everyone knows very well that people go to an opera chiefly to see how others are dressed. Then all this interesting assessing is interrupted by men in exotic costumes shouting in foreign tongues on the stage when the curtain rises.

Alas, there must be an ulterior motive for every activity. There must be hounds to ride to or leave. It may occur to you that it is somewhat roundabout and elaborate to go through all the ceremoney and ritualistic vestments prescribed for the killing or running to earth of a fox. Yet the 'best people' are right about one thing – they don't go in for abstract ideas. In fact they set their faces against anything of that sort. Have they not had warning enough in philosophers, politicians, idealists and so forth?

Businessmen! That brings up the thought of how a rich and retired merchant of London endeavoured to improve his social status; well, let us say status although there is no status in society if you mix with commerce in a direct way. He determined to join one of the exclusive hunts, to meet the 'best people' and be accepted by 'county' in the end. With this in mind he paid his subscription and sent down a dozen horses to one of the hunts. Somebody told him that a dozen horses was somewhat *outré*, even though times were hard and the fifty guineas a horse would not be an unwelcome addition to the hunt funds. He listened to advice and reduced his horses to five. He rode to hounds. He had not been long in the field when he realised that if he were to make an impression on the best people he had to make the county hospital first. That's where the flowers were and the sympathy. So he broke his collarbone. He was carried to the hospital; but no one called. Perhaps a collarbone was not enough? When he recovered he remembered that he had the other bone intact; if he were to break that and add concussion of the brain to his fall, he might become an object of concern. He developed concussion of the brain. No one took the least notice. He had overlooked one thing – the better classes are born concussed.

There is no doubt about it, some sort of limitation is necessary if you are to become an accepted, that is, a successful, member of a fox hunt.

5 *'But O, The Heavy Change'*

My father died in the same year as Parnell. I had seen crowds assembled to hear 'The Chief' speak from a house about eight doors above ours on the same side of the square. It belonged to a Dr Kenny who must have been a friend of the Chief because it was from a balcony of his house that Parnell addressed the crowd. All are gone now, crowds and all, 'without a fame in death' except the Chief. Dr Kenny is forgotten, for all his intimacy with Parnell. He must have felt important when he housed the Chief, though the crowds who make fame knew not, or little cared, from whose house the Chief spoke. So Dr Kenny got as little credit for housing the leader of the Irish People as is given to the manager of a hotel. Yet the entertainment of the aloof and cold man was apparently its own reward.

The death of a breadwinner is rarely a change for the better. In my case it was a change to misery and servitude. I was sent to a third-rate boarding school. The prospectus read: 'situated on a gentle eminence rising from the Shannon'. The name in Gaelic means 'the Sedgy Morass'. I will never forget that 'gentle eminence'. It was the only thing gentle in the situation, and even that was fallacious. However, the word 'gentle eminence' had a strong appeal to my mother, to whom words ever had a strong appeal, else why did she send me there? My brother never went to such a school, and now he is much taller than I. I was stunted; no wonder I am but five foot nine. I was starved; undernourished in body and soul at a most susceptible age. We were herded into chapel in response to some discipline of our disgruntled jailers at hours unsuited to a growing child. We were fed on what the boys called 'cow's udder', for there was no bone in that insipid flesh. I became so emaciated after a few months that I was not sent back but was bundled off to England where the routine was much the same, but the food was somewhat better and the school was cleaner. I never complained, for I imagined that no school could be otherwise and that all schools were miserably similar. It seemed I was right when I read about the Eton of fifty years ago. Yet Protestant schools as a rule were better. For one thing, they taught better; any 'public school' boy could outwrite us in Latin verses by fifty to one. We were taught to compose Latin verses like jigsaw puzzles, irrespective of ear. We used a 'gradus' to check the quantities of the vowels. The result of our labour was futility. Hexameters meant nothing to the teacher; there was no appeal to the ear, for he was deaf to 'The stateliest measure ever moulded by the lips of man'.

We read Xenophon in his Greek: the 'paradise', with game of every kind, and the words 'nobody caught an ostrich'. I could see the bird, with his short wings aiding his speed as he outdistanced the arrows. Yes, that was a relief!

But why was I not told that Xenophon was a man about town in Athens and that he added himself to the army to do a bit of reporting like another Winston Churchill? The invitation of the Persians to all the officers of the Ten Thousand mercenaries and the treacherous slaying at a banquet was withheld. And also how Xenophon refused to head the leaderless band unless he were (here the resemblance to Winston ends) chosen unanimously. That passage about his stripping off his clothes and marching ahead of the grumblers in freezing weather would have won my admiration, and my interest with it. Why was I not told what it was all about? 'It was all in the Introduction, so why did you not read it?' you will say. Perhaps it was; but it was no concern of small boys to add to their task, which was to pass their examination with as little addition to the 'terms of reference' as possible. Anyway, who ever read an introduction?

By the time I was ripe for 'the sweet and pleasant reading of old authors' the sparks of fervent desire for learning were extinct with the burden of grammar. Maybe I was 'hard to handle'. That I will concede. I will concede, too, that teaching such as me was no pleasant task. Nevertheless, traffic with the lads in black made life so uncertain that it seemed fruitless to learn. For instance, if you had the temerity to say to one of them, 'It's a fine day,' he would be sure to draw in his breath and answer with a sigh, 'Ah, well!' It put me in mind of the condemned Irishman who was standing on the trap door with a noose around his neck, when the padre asked him if he had any last request. 'Would you mind telling me if the floor is safe?'

They nearly took the mercury out of me. I will be fair; it may have been fifty-fifty, a 'fair shake'; but they should have known better than to expect anyone to learn that which the teacher hates. It gave me pleasure to underline in my translation of Plato: 'Knowledge which is acquired under compulsion obtains no hold on the mind.' I must have been docile. When I think of the uncomplaining and unquestioning way I suffered in two of my three boarding schools I know that I was docile, and a fool. I had done nothing to be treated as a criminal is treated, with dislike, suspicion and distrust. Walking in Indian file along the wall, which we had to do in each corridor! What was that for but to make you feel servile? Well, the sons of wealthier parents than my widowed mother had to submit to that treatment. When I got to understand it afterwards I realised that all this hardship was intended to wean boys from their homes. Homesickness was a part of the discipline. The school instead of the home.

I was experiencing a medieval discipline, the rule of some fourteenth-century monastery on the Continent. The Middle Ages were about us with their fears, discomforts, and their superstitions. Though it was in England it could not be called an English school. It was a religious jail. There must be something resilient or devil-may-care in me that saved me from becoming embittered and resentful for the rest of my life. The only result was a recoil from all they practised. I was thinking all the more of getting out from all that was going on within. In spite of three grave accidents I was saved by the gymnasium, the swimming pool and the playing fields. And, I must add, the pride I felt each time I saw my straight young brother walk down to the dais to take a prize.

When I returned to Ireland I had to mark time before I would be old enough to join a medical school. So I was sent to another boarding school. The best of the lot. There I met Tom Kettle again. He was about fifteen and as big as the biggest boy and his limbs were longer and better boned than most. Under a low broad forehead, which a lock of hair made lower, glowed those dark eyes of his which held always a playful smile. His restlessness revealed his courageous, liberal and unchained soul. His was the terse and graphic phrase. I remember his description of a racing cyclist entering the straight and preparing to go all out: 'he put down his head.' There comes under my eyelid a moving picture of his grey-clad figure scorching round and round the gravel cycling track of the school, his long legs pushing power into the pedals, his brown face bright with exercise, and a glow in his dark eyes that could light a room.

Though I was two years older I took to imitating him. I am easily influenced by those I admire. His honesty and enthusiasm could have influenced one less susceptible than I. The successes of his older brother Andy on the cycling track added to Tom's glory.

Very few had bicycles at our school. I got one for a present; and I got my heart's desire. Though it was a roadster I converted it, as much as such a heavy machine could be converted, into the semblance of a racing bicycle. The transformation was effected by lowering the handle-bars, changing the saddle and removing the guard that covered the chain. I imagined myself equipped for racing, though the amount of road work that poor bicycle had to do would have worn out any racing model. I thought nothing of riding thirty miles a day to play football for the Bohemians in Dublin, and the same distance back after dark. I took no credit for this performance, for it caused no fatigue; but I regretted every mile that was not on the racing track because it detracted from the raciness of my machine.

The school authorities let me out so that I might decant my energy, lest it burst the staves. In summer I played cricket in the First Eleven. The only thing I remember is that I bowled out Captain Bonham-Carter of the garrison with the first ball. All in all I enjoyed this school, which was a great relief from my English education. They fed us well. They did not try to break your will and leave you spineless. There were fine trees about the place; and there was the Liffey, black and bright; and one of the prefects came from an old Galway family well known for their eccentricities, the mad Dalys. James Augustine Joyce was at the same school but, as he was four years younger, he was in a different grade, so I did not meet him there. It was not until later years, when we were at the Royal University, that we met. Then 'we two were nursed upon the selfsame hill', as Milton called the plain of Cambridge.

6 *'Faire And Softly'*

Doctoring was in our family, so off to see Dr Bermingham my mother took me. He was registrar of the Catholic University Medical School. His want of manners was so evident that, at the end of the inverview, when he pattered out: 'Here's a pamphlet in which you will find the answers to all your questions', holding out the pamphlet as he kept on writing, there was no one to take the extended brochure. I was driven out of Cecelia Street, up Dame Street, to be entered in Trinity College!

There, the registrar was Dr Traill, afterward Provost. Though he hailed from the North of Ireland his brusqueness did not make him rude. He was considerate of others, and therefore a gentleman. He won my mother's approval at once because he asked, 'Won't you be seated? And may I ask if you are related to my friend the late Dr Henry Gogarty?' After that it was Faire and Softly. As we drove away my mother said: 'Now that you are entered among gentlemen I hope that you will never forget to behave like one.' A large order among the wild medicos of those days! A hope that could not be fulfilled if I had to satisfy my aunt, who had not only the Almanac de Gotha by heart but Burke's Landed Gentry as well. Yet it must have gone hard with my mother to enter me in a Protestant university. The fact that it had been my father's intention to do so may have consoled her; and it was not then a matter of excommunication to enter Trinity.

Scholastically the time spent in the Royal University availed me nothing. I had to begin all over again in Trinity, but the rigours of examinations in the examination booths of the Royal stood me in good stead in a university which went in more for educating its students than in filter-passing them as if they were so many bacteria.

The time at the Royal was not altogether lost. I met a less disciplined class of student in the Aula Maxima: 'Citizen' Elwood, James Joyce, Cosgrove, and Joyce's friend Sheey-Skeffington, an opinionated, bearded little theorist in knicker-bockers. We had great fun during my short time in the Aula Maxima. Dr Campbell, the Professor of Chemistry, was a lean old gentleman who wore an old-fashioned full-skirted frock coat and cuff links as large as a lady's watch. He would ask: 'What are the Halogens?' and answer the question himself, 'Chlorine, Fluorine, Bromine and Iodine, never found free in Nature, always combined.' When asked to repeat we would chant: 'Dolan, Hegarty, McCluskey, and Dwane, never found free in Nature, always combined' – the names of a quartette of students who would have nothing to do with us, being earnest and hard-working.

Surgeon Blaney lectured on surgery. We soon discovered that he was merely repeating the textbook on Surgery by Rose and Careless. He had a huge scrotum and a huge memory.

Our Professor of Zoology was Dr George Sigerson, the famous author and scholar. He practised psychology, and he was a friend of the famous Frenchman scientist, almost of the eighteenth century, Charcot. He had a mane of white hair and a snub nose which showed his Danish origin as much as did his name. Our textbook for the course was Thompson's *Zoology*, which contained every species of animal, fish and insect in the world. It was far too long to learn. None of us could expect to memorise all its contents except, of course, the Halogens, so we divided the book into boroughs or constituencies and elected representatives for each set of three of the animals or 'orders' in the book.

I was the member who represented snails, anodons – crayfish, lobsters, etc. – and the common earthworm. Simon Broderick a student from Youghal, stood for the crustacea, oysters that have their reproductive apparatus in their feet, spiders and jellyfish. Christian was the member for insects of all sorts. Cheers hailed the man who could get through the most patter before he was ordered out. If a man were asked about an animal not in his constituency the member for that animal hastily would rise to answer and rattle off sentences from Thompson by rote.

'I have noticed,' said Professor Sigerson, 'that those who are most noisy in class are most silent at examinations.' Then he would put on his tall silk hat out of which parts of the specimens that had been handed around class were sure to fall. Of more than thirty in the class, only five passed: the Halogens and Simon Broderick. Just think of his luck! He got every animal he represented and the result was honours, though he knew nothing about zoology but the three orders in his bailiwick.

The only specimen that came my way was Nautilus, the giant Norwegian lobster; and though I wrote word for word, 'The male seizes the female in his great claws, throws her on her back and deposits the seminal fluid on the ventral surface of the abdomen,' it availed me nothing. I failed dismally; and I also failed to get an *ad eundem*, which is credit for the exams which you had already passed, when I left the Royal and entered Dublin University. This goes to show in how little esteem the Royal was held by the older university. I lost a year or whatever time it took to matriculate in the Royal, pass its First Arts examination, and attend lectures on chemistry, surgery and zoology. I must have lost more than a year; yet what matter? I met many people whom, as I said, I would not have met had I been only in Dublin University.

Joyce lived in my direction; he lived at Cabra and got out at Dunphy's Corner while I stayed on in the tram until it reached Fairfield, about a mile from Joyce's home. He used to walk down to visit me and we would go back and forwards under the apple trees in the kitchen garden, for that garden had the longer paths. Perhaps it was when the blossoms were in the air that he got that first of his lovely lyrics in *Chamber Music:*

> My love is in a light attire
> Among the apple trees.

His lyrics were as spontaneous as those of the Elizabethans whom he admired so much.

One morning as we walked in the garden, shortly after I had entered Trinity, he asked me if I would lend him my .22 rifle. What he, who to my knowledge had never handled a gun, wanted my rifle for was a puzzle; but I obliged. I continued to puzzle until one day he said, 'You are eligible to compete for the Gold Medal for English verse in the Royal.'

'But I am a student of Trinity College!'

'You have passed First Arts in the Royal; I tell you that you can compete.'

'Why don't you go in for it yourself?' I asked.

'I am thinking of your rifle.'

When I had untangled the cryptogram I realised that he had pawned my rifle and was proposing that I should redeem it by winning the Gold Medal for English verse, then pawning that and regaining my rifle with the money. The credit for pointing out the way was to go to him. I won the gold medal, which duly went into the pawnshop for something like eighteen pounds, but my rifle never came out.

Another member of the Aula Maxima whom I would not have missed was John Elwood, called the Citizen to ridicule his advanced views. He was an ebullient fellow who always had a quizzical smile in his eyes and around his shapely mouth. In the semicircular portico of the National Library we would meet every morning when I was not at lectures in Trinity College. Opposite to the library, in which the bookless students used to forgather, was the National Museum; it also had a pillared colonnade. Its hall was circular and decorated by nude plaster casts, somewhat larger than life, of the famous statues of antiquity. One morning Joyce arraigned Elwood. He assumed an air of great gravity, as he was wont to do when about to perpetrate a joke.

'It has come to my notice, Citizen, that this morning, between the hours of ten and ten-thirty, you inscribed your name in lead pencil on the backside of the Venus of Cnidus. Are there any extenuating circumstances that may be cited in your defence?'

'He's terrific,' said Elwood when he recounted the tale. 'A great artist!' 'Artist' in Dublin stands for a practical joker or a playboy; someone who prefers diversion to discipline; a producer, an 'artifex'.

If I were to draw a Parallel Life between then and now there would be only the sad difference which a Frenchman has expressed better than I could ever do, no matter how hard I might try: 'When we grow old we think that we have taken leave of our vices, whereas the truth is that our vices have taken leave of us.'

7 *'The Craft So Longe To Learn'*

Dublin has more than a dozen hospitals. Vienna, a much larger city, has but one; but then disease in Dublin is a *modus vivendi* and it therefore assumes a religious aspect. There are Protestant, Catholic and Presbyterian diseases in Dublin. The Adelaide; Sir Patrick Dun's; the City of Dublin, commonly called Baggot Street Hospital; the Meath; and Stevens; these are all Protestant hospitals. Stevens deals largely with the police 'who also serve' but are liable to contract venereal disease while standing and waiting – on point duty! In the Adelaide only respectable diseases are treated. There are two 'hospices' which are not teaching hospitals though they are called by inviting names: the Hospital for Incurables, and the Hospice for the Dying. One would think that the latter might be a very good teaching hospital, for its students could make no mistakes unless, peradventure, somebody recovered.

The Richmond Hospital, which was chosen for me, is nearly neutral. It is in reality a chain of hospitals, the

Richmond, the Whitworth and the Hardwick; surgery is taught in the Richmond, medicine in the Whitworth, and fevers in the Hardwick, separated from the other two. The Richmond has more knights and Presbyterians than all the other hospitals in the town. There were Sir Thornley Stoker, his brother-in-law Sir William Thompson, and Sir Thomas Myles: Protestants all. The Catholic 'balance' consisted of Dr Coleman and Dr O'Carroll; Sir Conway Dwyer was afterwards introduced.

The Richmond Hospital stood at the head of Red Cow Lane and looked south over Smithfield market to the mountains beyond the Liffey. It was an old building reached by a transverse set of granite steps which an iron railing protected. Beatty, with his large beard, his hollow chest in its dark blue brass-buttoned uniform, was the hall porter. He interviewed the incoming patients and tipped off the medical students as to the proper manner to adopt with each. His recommendations were possibly influenced by monetary considerations – what profession is entirely free from such? – but this is mere conjecture. There were other porters about the place who recalled pre-anaesthetic days, days not far off from Beatty's powerful youth, days when porters held strong men down on the sinister table of dark oak and stifled their struggles until the surgeon's work was done. Dublin resisted anaesthetics, for disease in Dublin is religious, and has the Book not said that women must endure the pangs of childbirth, and so on ...?

In the external clinics or dispensaries, as they were called, varicose ulcers were dressed with red oxide of mercury, but never cured; running ears, eyes with trachoma and cases of tertiary syphilis were attended to day by day. This was a part of the medical student's training and could not be omitted. Another part, also indispensable, was to 'walk' the hospital and listen to the lectures delivered at the patient's bedside by the visiting physician or surgeon. We were taught to use our ears and eyes, that is, to be observant to an extreme degree. For instance, a certain physician would walk through the ward hurriedly at the head of his class and, when he had passed through, turn and snap, 'How many in there will be alive in the morning?' You were supposed to judge by the position of the patient in the bed (decubitus): a dying man makes no bulge of the bedclothes.

As we got hardened we used to count the faints when the newly come students saw a catheter passed through a stricture or an abscess opened for the first time. 'What and why is there such a knife as a bistoury?' the surgeon would ask. 'It is a curved knife, curved so that its converging edges will cut more rapidly.' That was the answer, and it brought back the days before there were anaesthetics, when speed was one of the prerequisites of a surgeon.

I was Sir Thomas Myles's clinical clerk, or intern. Sir Thomas was a powerful man with a flowing golden moustache, large blue eyes and regular features, a very handsome but childless man. My mentor in Trinity, Dr Yelverton Tyrrell, the wit and diseur, commented thus, 'Now if Lady Myles had selected some little croquet-playing curate instead of this Adonis, she might have had a dozen children.' Sir Thornley in his turn was supposed to be in love with the matron of the Hospital, Miss McDonald, who was very strong-minded, as indeed she had to be. Sir Thomas showed his magnanimity by quashing the rumour and adding, 'Every allowance should be made for Sir T. He has hell at home.' About Sir William, Sir Thornley's brother-in-law, there was no scandal. He was one of those whose grandeur depends on silence. If a grand manner could cure disease, Sir William would be the world's benefactor.

One of Sir Thomas's ward rounds led, most indirectly, to a night of scandalous outbreaks in the hospital. Sir Thomas was transilluminating a hydrocele, which is a tumour caused by serum collecting between the tunica vaginalis of the testicle and the testicle itself. This is usually the result of an injury. There were two lady students present, both Presbyterians, breastless, defeminised, with dry hair. They stood with their arms folded at the edge of the class, a class in themselves.

'Take a look through that and tell me what you see,' said

Sir Thomas to me as he handed me the transilluminating tube.

I gazed. 'The light that never was on sea or land,' I said.

'This is not exactly the consummation of the Poet's dream,' Sir Thomas said. 'The question is. What is the etiology of hydrocele? Dr Fulton is about to enlighten us.' Every medical student is called 'doctor' by his seniors, out of some kind of satire. The medicals don't object, for it carries immunity in the dangerous places in town. Fulton was tall, heavy and somewhat stooped, as if the weight of his face were too much for him. He had a large pale face, wide-eyed, small-nosed, with a long upper lip which a little fair moustache did nothing to diminish. We called him Clinoclaustes, which means Bed Breaker, for the story ran that his weight and vigour contributed, with his partner's aid, to the collapse of a bed in the Kips: 'The tailor fell through the bed thimble and a'.'

The Kips can wait for an explanation; the man with the hydrocele is getting cold in the bed. Fulton knew; his heavy utterance gave his answer weight. 'Good, Doctor. Now Lamb will give us the differential diagnosis between hydrocele and hernia. Dr Lamb?' While Lamb was gathering his wits, Tom Myles, as we called him familiarly, told the class how Gibbon, the author of *The Decline and Fall of the Roman Empire*, suffered from both hernia and hydrocele. From time to time his doctors used to draw off quarts of fluid from his hydrocele until one day his hernia also pierced and he died from peritonitis. Therefore the differential diagnosis cannot be over-emphasised. Lamb knew his work and when his answer came, Sir Thomas congratulated him in such a way that Lamb became, if possible, all the more studious.

Charlie, an outpatient, was a syphilophobe, and that is an almost incurable condition. You can contract it without getting syphilis, which Charlie probably did. Now we used to say that we could cure syphilis but not syphilophobia, that is, the fear of syphilis. It was a cheering statement because it implied that the patient was not to permit his misfortunes to depress him. That way suicide lies. Charlie told me that he had so much mercury in him that he couldn't stand with his back to the fire because the column of mercury in his spine would bump against the base of his skull and knock him out. I saw in the harmless Charlie a way of getting my own back on the inoffensively studious Dr Lamb.

First I must find out what were the doctor's hours of duty. 'He goes off every night at twelve,' Beatty said. Then he added, 'Thank you, sir.'

'Charlie, if I give you a prescription to clear out that mercury you must follow instructions to the letter. What time is it now? Let me see. It's half past twelve. Yes; you will want twelve hours. By the time you get home to take my medicine it will be, say, one o'clock. Very well. One o'clock. Say one-thirty to be safe. You will take these three tablets and in an hour or two your urine will turn green, a dark blue-green. Take plenty of fluids. You might even drink a few pints of Guinness; but the point to bear in mind is not to let any of the urine out of your sight. Preserve it in any vessel that can hold it and no matter how much there is – the more the merrier – bring it up here immediately for analysis before it gets stale. No matter what time of night it is: any time after twelve hours. Ring the night bell; ask for the house surgeon. If there is any delay say you are just up from the country with an urgent message for him. Understand? Got that?'

Charlie said, 'God bless you, sir.' There were tears of gratitude in his eyes.

That night, or rather in the small hours of the next morning, I was wakened by a cursing and damning and a crash of crockery. 'What the hell do you mean, Beatty?' It was Lamb's voice cursing. Someone had wakened him from his sleep – and he was a heavy sleeper – with an urgent message from the country and when he opened the package – he probably expected to find something like the package that came for me at Christmas – he was confronted by a large night jar or pot, full to the brim with a green fluid.

'Lamb, I am surprised at you. Using such language in the middle of the night; wakening the whole dormitory.' The voice of Richards, the student from Wales piped up. 'What has happened? Whatever . . .' It sounded frightened. But the expected roar did not come from Clinoclaustes. Where was he? Experimenting somewhere?

Lamb's loud outrage continued: 'That damned scoundrel, Charlie, sends me up a pisspot full of urine stained with methylene blue.'

'I certainly would expostulate with him,' said Richards.

'Expostulate be damned! What's the use in talking to a madman? I'll report Beatty for wakening me when I'm off duty.' But Beatty was, according to Boss Croker's definition, an honest man, that is, 'A man who, when he's bought, stays bought.'

It was turning over in my mind, 'What's the use of talking to a madman?' and thinking that words are only the symptoms of certain diseases; and we are taught that you must not treat symptoms: you must not treat words with words. The disease causes the words. Words in this case were accessories after the fact. Treat the disease and the words will take care of themselves. What's the use of talking anyway?

Another noise. This time raucous laughter and cries came from the ward beneath mixed with snatches of bawdy song. The time for such singing was right but the place was not. What was that? Water? There may be a fire raging and that noise comes from the Fire Brigade. But firemen don't laugh while on duty. We pulled on a few clothes and went down to investigate. There was the clever Fulton, Clinoclaustes, drunk as a lord and wielding a fire hose. Some strange rowdies, apparently companions of his evening, were chasing a goat which leapt over the beds dangling a length of chain. One patient, a paralytic awaiting operation, jumped from his bed and fled to shelter.

For the amputation stumps cold water was not the proper treatment. 'There was a dozen of stout in my locker before I went off duty, where is it now?' Clinoclaustes asked angrily as he turned with the hose held like a rifle over his shoulder. Plaster from the ceiling was coming down in flakes. Some nurses, thoroughly alarmed, gathered at the door. Clinoclaustes stared drunkenly at them. A young nurse still in her teens, with her hair fallen in disarray, fled from the doorway.

Dr Lamb screamed, 'Call off your friends, Fulton. I won't be responsible for this.' After an interval the lights went on fully. Wet bedding and mattresses were removed.

As dawn was breaking quiet was restored. I thought that it was time to avail myself of my privilege of going home once a week.

Next day there was an atmosphere of foreboding: an extraordinary meeting of the Board. And we were all up before it. Lamb, as senior, and responsible for law and order, testified first. He said nothing about Charlie but he acknowledged that he was awakened by a noise. He said that he was a light sleeper (oh!), which made the noise lighter as it were. Some men whom he did not know were tampering with the fire hose. He, as responsible house surgeon, though off duty, put them out. Richards, the squeaky little Welshman, was only a spectator. 'Of what?' asked Sir William. This took a lot of floundering to explain. 'And you, Fulton, what have you to say for yourself?'

'I cured a case of paralysis. It was not a case of brain tumour but hysteria.'

'That will do.'

Fulton was, as they say in the 'varsity, 'sent down'. Dr Robert Woods, laryngologist and otologist, recently elected to the Board, had me to examine. I was at home. He did not ask what hour I went there. Maybe he forebore deliberately; but he had to administer a rebuke. I explained that, as one living within walking distance of the hospital, I was permitted to take my meals at home when off duty and to sleep at home once a week.

'And that was not too often,' said Dr Woods.

There was no mention of the goat. Beatty restored it, for a consideration, to its owner in Red Cow Lane.

Where were my wits when we were up before the Board? They were there all right but they were in abeyance, for I did not realise at the time that the reason for such outbreaks and such loose living among medical students arose from what would be called now 'occupational neurosis'. The young nurses, finding themselves confronted daily by dirt, disease and death, grew tough. Medical students went wild as a reaction. Youth betimes confronted with Death: The outcome of this unnatural juxtaposition was outbreaks of wild licence among the men, and callousness among the young nurses, most of whom were in their early twenties or younger.

And what about the demoralising effect of the way in which we were housed? At least I could have said that; but would they have been prepared for it? An old loft, with rafters showing above, in which we slept fitfully: dying men and corpses below, and groans arising to our sleeping place in the darkness. Is it any wonder that we had occasional outbreaks? Had you yourselves, our mentors, been always models of propriety? What about Tom Myles's brother, who used cops as castanets? What about Tom himself? Though they had endeared themselves to us by lawlessness in their student days, such arguments could not be proffered. Yet I must have sensed the connection between conduct – not to mention disease – and housing. Years after, I wrote that slums breed diseases and demoralisation. For example the incidence of tuberculosis falls fifty per cent when the family has two rooms instead of one.

How Tom Kettle abetted me in my campaign for better housing and the abolition of slums will be recorded further on. This is no place for a homily, nor am I given to homilies. If you catch me giving out a homily, shout 'Author!' as the unpaid 'ghost' is said to have done to the politician.

8 *Fugax Erythema*

Instead of being sacked, as Clinoclaustes was, we, that is, Lamb and I, were promoted from surgery to the medical part of the chain, the Whitworth Hospital. Medicine came before surgery, so it was a promotion to the older branch. There was a time when the barber-surgeon followed humbly at the heels of the black-garbed, triangular-hatted, cane-carrying physician, to let blood into his brass basin, curved like a new moon.

The Whitworth was an old building but clean. Its visiting physicians were Dr Travers Smith, Dr Coleman, and Dr Joseph O'Carroll, called 'Joc' on account of his initials. Travers Smith had married the daughter of Professor Dowden of Trinity College, author of *Shakespeare, His Mind and Art*. She was so homely and he so good-looking that, contradictorily, her homeliness broke up their home. Dr Travers Smith went to Cavendish Square, London, and married a widow after his divorce. Dr Coleman had also an unfortunate experience with matrimony; his wife, though a Roman Catholic, took divorce proceedings against him. He was always unobtrusive; we found him so. The scandal, because it was not of our making, but that of an unbalanced woman, did not stick.

Joc was such a martinet that he made his children send him letters written in French when they were on their so-called holidays. He took even the slightest thing seriously.

In the middle of the ward, on the floor, seated on many cushions and surrounded by mattresses, was a case of trichinosis. He jerked and fell off his cushions every few minutes because the worm acquired from measly bacon moved in a motor area of the brain. Had he been a clown in a circus, he would have been comical; but in the Whitworth under Joc he was indeed a tragic sight. The effect of the spasms on the other patients apparently never occurred to Joc, who exhibited his authority by upsetting the ward and making a central show. It was a characteristic projection of the little man.

Joc was lecturing. We all stood about the bed in respectful attention. In the bed was a young country girl with rosy cheeks. Joc ordered the nurse to pull down the bedclothes. There is a special way of pulling down the clothes so that a patient may not be exposed indecently. The nurses know it.

There are no gynaecological cases in the Whitworth. When the time comes for gynaecology you must go to the Rotunda Hospital, the Coombe or Holles Street.

Joc signalled impatiently. He wished to lecture on a red spot, or rather, on two red spots, that had been found by a nurse, a novice most likely, earlier the same morning. At last the knees were shown to Joc's liking.

'Gentlemen, you will notice two red spots on the inside of this girl's knees. Let us approach the problem scientifically and we shall thus be enabled to solve it. Now, first of all we must define the disease. We notice two red spots. What is the medical nomenclature for redness? No one answers. Must I send for Dr Lamb? No, I will not interrupt him. He, doubtless, is engaged on his duties. I will tell you: redness is known in medicine as "erythema". Now we will proceed to define the erythema. What gentleman will palpate it? Mr Kirby, take your hands out of your pockets and oblige me by palpating this erythema. No, no! You must palpate with two fingers of different hands or with the two hands, not one; and not with one finger! Is it smooth? You say that it is slightly rough. Have you asked the girl what is its history? No. Tell me, girl, how long have you had this trouble?"

She does not answer. She is overcome no doubt by being surrounded, with her legs half naked, by so many young men. 'Let us proceed. Nurse, did you notice this skin eruption yesterday? No. Now what do we have at our disposal? We have an erythema that appeared since yesterday: it is slightly rough, not smooth. Now, Mr

Kirby, press the erythema gently, and quickly remove your fingers. What do you observe? The redness disappears and returns quickly. Now with all these facts in our possession let us call some great foreign dermatologists into consultation. Suppose we are sending an account of this to Paris – we will take it that this girl is some lady's French maid . . .'

A voice from the bed. 'I am only a dairymaid.' Tears, silent tears.

'Silence, young woman! We will write, not in French, but in Latin, with its vocabulary of words derived from the Greek. We will write thus, having saluted your colleague in Paris, "We have here a case of erythema, *recens, fugax, nodosa*." That is: it wasn't here yesterday; that makes it *recens*; it disappears on pressure, *fugax*; it is slightly rough, *nodosa*. To a communication such as that we should expect an enlightened reply. Now, my good girl, you may speak. Tell us how long have you had this ailment and how can you account for it?'

'Oh, Doctor, is it any harm? I always waken up with it if my knees are crossed.'

9 *Pulver Olympicum*

It would not be fair if the impression were conveyed that a medical student's life was all work. There were many hours of leisure when off duty. Was not Isodore McWilliam Burke champion cyclist of England, while a resident in St George's Hospital, London? No wonder he was champion with such a dominating name: first in the field. My venture in the field was in the twenty-mile Junior Championship of Ireland.

The Amateur Athletic Association controlled, through its committees in the different countries that made up the

United Kingdom, all amateur athletics. It certified records, fixed the rules and suspended or outlawed all offenders. Larry O'Neill, a dark, serious, tubby little man all in black, black knickerbockers, and black-a-vised – but there was white cotton wool in his left ear – was its president in Ireland and he presided over the race to be held in the Pheonix Park, which, with its nineteen hundred acres, is the largest walled park in the world. It was walled to protect the residences of the satraps who represented the King in Ireland and were called Lords Lieutenant and Chief Secretaries. These, as a rule, were noblemen wealthy in their own right, sportsmen very often; but they knew nothing about the humble sport of cycle racing. Polo and fox hunting were more in their line.

The Phoenix Park was chosen for the twenty-mile Junior Championship not for its connection with the Lords Lieutenant but for its good roads: the better the roads the better the race. A four-mile lap was marked off to the south of the central highway past the Castlenock Gate, the Knockmaroon Gate, round the dangerous corner at the Furzy Glen, down the winding road, until the hill at the Hibernian School was reached. When the toiling cyclists climbed that steep they had the flat road east of the Fifteen Acres – about two hundred acres in fact – in front of them before they turned to the left and entered the central highway from which they had started. There were twin oaks on the left of the roadside about a hundred and fifty yards from where the finish would be.

Crowds already were assembled by the time I cycled up. Here and there the bright caps of the different cycling clubs could be seen in the crowd. There were competitors from the Al Fresco, as 'posh' as any club of its kind could be. Charlie Pease belonged to it; and not only was he the one-mile champion of Ireland but the winner of the Blue Riband Championship of England, which was also the mile. Charlie Pease was a gentleman and kept himself aloof, except in competitions, from the other members. Aloofness, for the most part, constituted a gentleman *in diebus illis*. Yes; by its members and its victories the Al Fresco was the outstanding club in Ireland. I was a member, though that would not placate my aunt!

The National was far larger; it had Tom Goss and Cockey Meade, the fifty-mile champion, among its members, and Alex Sweeney of the Carpenters too. There were competitors from various clubs in the North of Ireland; but as all the North was discounted and discountable by the men of Leinster, and that included Dublin, their competition was not taken seriously except for the hidden feeling of the gravity of a disgrace if any man of Dublin should be beaten by a fellow from the North. So, barring a wholesale accident such as that lamentable one that occurred during a ten-mile handicap which I won at Ballinafeigh near Belfast in Ulster, when all but four of a field of forty fell at a corner during the first lap, there was not a hope for the venturous sons of Ulster, whose hardihood merely made the championship more representative.

Old Blunden, a pompous member of a firm of attorneys – probably he was its head clerk – officiated fussily. He it was who would fire the starting pistol. Quite an official? Yes. The only serious rival, though I say it who shouldn't, to myself was Christy Dodd, the son of a wealthy 'potato factor' of Smithfield near the Richmond Hospital. His form was well known to the hospital porters as he scorched round and round Smithfield when it was empty in the evenings; and his form was relayed to me. He was a bigger fellow than I but he had not half the experience nor the speed, on a smooth track anyway: and the finish in the Phoenix Park was smooth enough. I felt that I could take on Christy Dodd. Who was he anyway? He had never showed up at the fast-run races on the sand track at Ballsbridge.

'Bang!' The explosion so frightened old Blunden that he nearly shed his silk hat. We were off. We had twenty miles to go and the principal thing was to avoid being spilled or elbowed down the steep at the Furzy Glen. The men of

Ulster, full of suspicion, were leading in a knot. How could they know the terrain? All right. Let them lead and set a pace that would mean a record to the winner, who I intended to be. It might do no harm to warn them, for the simple reason that they would never believe me but rush all the faster because of the warning, to be careful at the corner or – crash!

This pace is terrific. And the worst of it is that you dare not use any of the competitors, except perhaps a club mate, for a pacer because you never could tell when he might wobble off and bring you down. It was therefore something like a consolation to think that at this pace there was sure to be a spill in the first lap, when the bunch rounded the corner at Furzy Glen.

We were going past the Castlenock Gate now at a hell of a lick. Another few hundred yards and we would be at the dangerous bend. It was now time to shout, 'Be careful, boys! Go slow!' I knew it! they started sprinting. I knew that they would, that they would take my warning for some Dublin jackeen's trick. What was that? I couldn't see, for I was riding last. I could hear the branches of the furze crunching. I could hear the shouting; and the groans of the spectators who had gathered at the spot. 'Geordie, are ye dead, mon?' Well, they would not take my advice. Was the race to stop for a dozen men from Ulster? Not by any means. Now let us begin in real earnest. Where is Christy Dodd? Right ahead. He was too good a rider to precipitate himself down at the Furzy Glen corner, which must have been known to him well.

Once the men who were strung out for the better part of a quarter of a mile were passed, they were passed once and for all. They never could catch up again. It's a very fast run downhill to the big climb at the Hibernian School corner. Very fast. There were no free wheels then, nor brakes either. There were places where it was necessary to backpedal. A pity? True; but it is better than a smash; and there would be the very reverse of backpedalling when it came to climbing the hill. I did not feel much distress. I must have gotten what is called your 'second wind'. Oxygenated thoroughly, as Sir Thomas Myles would say. We were cheered when we entered the straight for the first round. Possibly the cheers gave us credit for the absence of the North. For having survived them anyhow.

Charlie Pease and the Maggot, Gibson, agent for the Osborne bicycle, stood ready with a tandem to act as pacemakers after the first four miles. What a pity that the Maggot fastened himself to such a cyclist as Charlie. I was hoping to shake off Dodd as the pace behind the tandem increased. How could Charlie go fast with the Maggot behind?

To get the pacemakers you had to take the lead, so in the second round I came into the straight first. 'How are you feeling, laddie?' 'Fine, Charlie,' I answered. The tandem got into its stride. 'Where's Dodd?' The Maggot said, 'You can forget him.' 'More pace,' I yelled to the Maggot. That shut him up.

On the grassy borders of the road were half-clad men, limping along. Some of their cycles were badly broken up. The ambulance from Stevens took care of the rest. 'Bit of a spill?' Charlie said, turning his small well-groomed head to look at me. Round and round, at what seemed too slow a pace for one sheltered as I was by the bodies of the two cyclists on the tandem, round and round we went. I did not like to offend Charlie, handicapped as he was by the Maggot, to ask for greater speed. He guessed what was passing in my mind. 'We're well within record.'

At last the pace was called off. 'It's up to you now,' the Maggot said as the tandem rolled away. At my side was that really dark horse, Christy Dodd! I resolved to start a murderous pace when I should reach the double oak tree. 'Not all the potatoes in Smithfield will help him when I really get going.' I said that to arouse my soul. I was really rather nervous when he showed up at my side after the punishing pace for twenty miles. 'Now!'

I must say that he did his best and it was very good but he was too big and somewhat lumbering when it came to really fast work. I hadn't time to look behind me. I won by fifty yards. Old Blunden tried dignity and taking it for granted. He attributed what I thought was a personal triumph to the club. He pushed officialdom too far. I dived into a pond beside the club's marquee. That night I couldn't sleep a wink.

At breakfast my mother saw it as she turned over the *Irish Times*. Inwardly she may have been proud but she certainly concealed it. 'Your professors in Dublin University will hardly find your exploit a matter for congratulation. If you must indulge in athletics, why not play cricket for the university, or join the Rowing Club?' If cycling appeared to her to be an ignoble pastime, the silence in which I received her rebuke was most noble. I was about to say, 'Don't I play football for them?' But I remembered how I played against them for my old club, the Bohemians, and the disparaging remarks in the weekly paper, *T.D.C.*: 'His game is that of a professional.'

Until I brought the conversation round to Charlie Pease I could not rest. I made it clear that he was a member of the Al Fresco Club and that he came from a distinguished Yorkshire family, one member of which, Sir Something Pease, was a member of Parliament. 'If your friend is a member of that family, he must be of a cadet branch, very cadet,' my aunt remarked. Then to soften it she said, 'God has blessed you with a robust body. Youth must find an outlet for its energy. If you can spare the time from your studies, you might join the Ward Union Hunt.' The stockbrokers, barristers, wheel-chair stag hunters – Saturdays only!

Morning was melting into noon as I walked down Sackville Street. The Dublin Corporation had not as yet changed the name into 'O'Connell Street'. The Doric column rose darkly, with Lord Nelson standing on its top, his sword touching the ground like a walking stick beside him; his right arm in an empty sleeve. In beautiful letters lined with gold were recorded his victories: Copenhagen – one would think that the less said about that the better; the

Nile; Trafalgar. They call his column 'Nelson's Pillar'; from it all the trams in Dublin start. I thought it the best of all the columns I had seen; and I think so yet.

When you crossed the head of Earl Street, you reached Clery's big shop. It was just as well that I looked into its windows, for in one of them I saw a poster advertising a coming cycle meeting to be held at Ballsbridge. 'Gogarty v Time' it announced. Before my mother sees that, I said to myself, it must be removed. I went in to speak to the manager of the shop. 'It will be in other places,' he explained. 'So why object to this?' I explained, and it was taken out.

I looked up and down the Liffey as I crossed its bridge. It is only fifty yards wide; but it bears no mean city on either bank: the Seventh City in Christendom. Guinness's great brewery stained the sky with its smoke to the west. To the east the red funnel of one of the brewery's cross-channel steamers brightened the Custom House by which it lay. The green dome of the Custom House shone on high. The light broadened as the Liffey neared the sea. Masts rose on the right. It is a merry morning. I wish that I had not had a restless night.

A few stragglers were standing outside the Ballast Office, which is what the Port and Docks Board Building is called. They were waiting for the ball to rise on its pole on the roof. That would mark twelve o'clock, and the time was exact because it was sent in from the Observatory at Dunsink: sidereal time by which people set their watches. Why I cannot say because no one in Dublin cares whether the time is exact or not and those who were watching the ball did not look as if they owned a watch. Perhaps it gave an air of earnestness to the day.

I met Alfred coming along Westmoreland Street. He was the only son of the Professor of Chemistry in Trinity College, Professor Emerson Reynolds, who had for factotum Clancy, the stepfather of Cockey Meade. Alfred wore a dark serge suit. On his shoulder he carried a light brown overcoat folded like a flattened tube. He was a fashionable and impressionable youth; that's probably what brought him to the café district where young ladies and waitresses would be about. He said that he was just strolling along. I said so I thought. He looked at me shrewdly, but my air of innocence must have reassured him, for, 'I have to congratulate you,' was his next remark. 'Yes. Thank you. I didn't sleep at all last night, I dived into the pond after the race. I blame that for my want of sleep.' He looked astonished. 'I was not talking of any race. Do you not know that you have won the Vice-Chancellor's Prize for English verse?'

That will balance things for me at home, I thought rapidly.

'The Vice-Chancellor's Prize is twenty pounds,' Alfred said. 'We should celebrate.'

'It'll have to wait until I am paid. I haven't got any money now.'

Alfred pointed with his thumb down Fleet Street. 'What about Weldon at the Back of the Bank?'

The Back of the Bank is the name of Kelley's pawnshop, which is managed by the over-astute Jimmy Weldon, a friend in need of medical students, and of most other students.

'One of your medals?' Alfred said encouragingly.

'No. No. I cannot celebrate now. I have to try for the mile record at Ballsbridge next week.'

I felt that my excuse was a little lame but I was glad to get Alfred away from Weldon's before he learned that my gold medal for English verse from the Royal University was reposing in Weldon's care. However, Alfred assured me that he would be the last man to urge me to break my training.

We walked on to the front of *T.D.C.*, that Palladian front which makes Dublin, with its other buildings, the most beautiful city in the country, though other towns have better sites. Cork for instance, on its island in the river Lee. I often wondered why there was not more talk about the beauty of Cork. I asked a Cork man. 'No buildings,' he said. That explained everything. The only building in Cork is the university and that looks like a convent or a reformatory.

In the case in the entrance hall of Trinity College was a notice giving the names of the winners of the Vice-Chancellor's prizes. I could see my name; but I could not very well stand gazing at it, not with the hall porters and students hanging about, so I assumed a blasé attitude and passed into the quad. From a door on the right a gowned figure with a beard like that of the poet Chaucer, carrying a bundle of papers, emerged. It was Professor Dowden. He was Professor of English in the university, and didn't he surround it with dignity? When he died they made a Plymouth Brother Professor of English. At least that is how the father of W. B. Yeats described Professor Trench.

A gloom hung over the place. I could sense it. What had happened? One of the students told me that my friend Bird was in trouble and up before Mahaffy, the vice-provost. He had shouted a well-known couplet at him the night before. Mahaffy was the best known of all the scholars whose industry had sent the fame of 'The Silent Sister', as Dublin University was called in Oxford and Cambridge, over all the world. Mahaffy's textbooks, *Lyric Poets of Greece; Dramatic Poets of Greece; Rambles and Studies in Greece*, taught Oxford and Cambridge Greek. So it was all the more heinous for poor Bird, drunk or sober, to shout,

> 'Yclept Mahouf by those of heavenly birth;
> But plain Mahaffy by the race of earth,'

and to wave at him familiarly.

Bird at last came out through the narrow door in the wall that led to Mahaffy's rooms. He would tell nobody what had happened. To the anxious question, 'Are you sent down?' he shook his head. He looked moved, and no wonder. We left him alone to commune with himself; but it was not long before the whole incident and what had happened came out. Mahaffy listened to Bird's humble apology. Bird confessed that he was drunk. Mahaffy said,

'No one takes the least notice of what a gentleman says in his cups.' So Bird was a gentleman in Mahaffy's estimation; and that was the reason why Bird at first would tell nobody what had happened. Bird felt overcome by emotions of respect and gratitude. The apology had done it – if you ask me.

Mahaffy was the greatest don I ever met. The examination for fellowship, which leaves its successful candidates text-drunk and good for nothing but to draw the salary that goes with what is a lifelong appointment, and take a few pupils, had not the least effect on him. He had taken it in his stride as a matter of course. He had taken much more in his stride: long before Egyptology had become a subject for research workers, Mahaffy had written a book on the subject which after all these years has not been found wanting. He had a perfect musical ear, and that, they tell me, is a thing that appears only once in a century. He was a sportsman: he had with his single-barrel gun shot a snipe at Sir John Leslie's shoot in Glaslough, County Monaghan, at ninety yards. Sir Shane, who is now Sir John's heir, measured the distance and Sir Shane can be called as a witness if anyone doubts me, for happily he lives and rules Glaslough. I am usually accurate when it comes to sport. When Sir Shane's brother at the same shoot accidentally loosed his gun and blew the hat off Mahaffy's head, Mahaffy merely looked at the shattered garment and remarked, 'Two inches lower and you would have blown ninety per cent of the Gweek out of Ireland.' He could not, or would not, pronounce his *r*'s correctly. Maybe it was because neither the Earl of Fingall nor Lord Talbot of Malahide could pronounce their *r*'s except as *w*'s. From this you may have deduced that Mahaffy 'dearly loved a Lord'. But it would not be accurate to dub him a snob, for snob means *sine nobilitate:* Mahaffy had nobility and made it a point to associate with noble men. Also a snob is defined by Thackeray, who knew what he was talking about, being a snob himself, as one who worships mean things meanly. Too slick! And to such a great man as

Mahaffy quite inapplicable. He was as omniscient as the scholarship and science of his day permitted. Now people grow tired of omniscience.

It is related how one night the dons of the college conspired to get the great man on some subject on which he was not an authority and so could not talk. After a consultation they selected Chinese music as the subject that they would bring up, as it were, accidentally at dinner. They discoursed on Chinese music, traced its origin and its effect, and expounded the difference in the Chinese conception of music and the European attitude. Mahaffy said not a word. The dons, inwardly delighted, kicked each other under the table. When they had exhausted the subject, Mahaffy said, 'Gentlemen, you have fallen into two errors that I myself nearly fell into, and you know how I hate to do anything foolish, when I wrote the article which you have been discussing; for the Encyclopaedia Britannica twenty years ago.'

The man I loved most in Trinity was Dr Yelverton Tyrrell. He was a Senior Fellow, Professor of Greek, and on occasion an examiner for the B.A. degree. We called him 'the Divine Doctor'. He was a very liberal and genial wit. His close friend was Henry S. Macran, Professor of Moral Philosophy, for whom allowances had to be made; and Tyrrell made them. Tyrrell it was who awarded me the maximum ten marks in my examination for English in the B.A., but that was merely a preliminary reason for my love and admiration. He was the wittiest man of his day and what a day it was! Tennyson, George Meredith, Wilde, Browning, Swinburne, George Wyndham, Jebb and Jowett flourished then.

10 *We Ourselves*

Why could I not imitate Alfred Reynolds, who, even though he was aware of waitresses, conducted himself respectably? He was studying to be an engineer. But the life I led as a medical student, when you had to deliver fourteen babies before you could qualify, brought the slums about me and the Kips, as the redlight district of Dublin was called. It is true that there are few births in a red-light district, for grass does not grow on the beaten track; but the Kips adjoined the miserable dormitories of the city whose denizens were poor and prolific, and children crowded the gutters. Here on the mothers the medico could practise to fulfil the requirements of the curriculum.

To look at the different roles I played in what may be called different incarnations is like looking into an aquarium and watching the highly coloured fish swim by like bubbles flattened or made long.

One of my incarnations, which began long before I studied at the Royal and Trinity, was as a politician – it began innocently at the Stad, and inevitably ended at a tavern called the Bailey.

The Bailey is in Duke Street, off the fashionable shopping Street, Grafton Street. It is nicely situated; so is Davy Byrne's, which is a tavern opposite to it. Upstairs in the Bailey is the smoking room; in this room Parnell and his followers were wont to meet. That was the reason why Arthur Griffith chose the Bailey and had a few 'large ones' with his friends of an evening, twenty years or so before his unswerving purpose freed Ireland, and Ireland made him its first President. I knew him since the days when his first movement for freedom began in An Stad, Cahill McGarvey's little tobacco shop opposite Findlater's

Church at the corner of North Frederick Street. That was about 1899.

His friends were George Redding, the solid man from Guinness's Brewery; Jimmy Montgomery; Neil – all wits and rhymers in their way. Griffith never discussed politics with his friends or with anyone; but there was an awareness that if you were not true blue, that is, a Sinn Feiner, and Sinn Fein means 'We ourselves', you had no right to be in the smoke room with Arthur Griffith. Sinn Fein implied that you were in agreement with the principles laid down in Griffith's pamphlet, *The Resurrection of Hungary*, and the application of the policy outlined therein was to keep the Irish members of Parliament away from Westminster; make them stay at home and boycott Westminster. How successful was this plan, which was attributed to Hungary, history now can prove.

I remember one night at the Bailey, like hundreds of others ... Arthur was there, so was Jimmy Montgomery. Arthur had almost as high a complexion as Montgomery; he was shorter and stockier than his friend. He wore tight-fitting pince-nez which indented the sides of his nose in two red grooves. When he took off his glasses to polish them these grooves showed. His rolling gait gained for him the nickname 'Cugaun' or 'dove', from the Kaffirs over whom he was overseer when he worked in a mine in South Africa. This roll was caused by a shortage of both his *tendo Achillis*. Actually he rolled rather than waddled when he walked. He apparently did not dislike his nickname, for he used it as a nom de plume in the weekly paper, the *United Irishman*, which he edited, and which he wrote nearly all himself. He wore glasses, because his blue eyes were short-sighted.

Neil arrived and announced that it was Sunday and so he had to leave any minute now to relieve, at 6 p.m. prompt, his father who played the harmonium at a local chapel. I am always uncomfortable when people announce that they must leave at any hour. I like to think of such meetings as permanent. I dislike the transience implicit in such remarks. You never see a clock in a well-regulated tavern or if there is a clock it is an antique and in any case it never strikes the hour.

George Redding came in and hailed us with a kind of grunt as he hung up his hat. Lewey the waiter rushed in with a large one for George. 'Ah,' Griffith called Lewey, and he made an inclusive sign by circling with his finger. Then turning to George, he asked, 'Any news?' George is slow to answer. He felt in his waistcoat pockets and produced a cutting from a newspaper. 'I cut this out this morning. I think that it is an excellent piece of prose.' Then he read something about a prize fight on a windy heath, and waited for our remarks. Griffith said, 'Hum. The best prose writer and the one I take for my model is Dean Swift.'

That was news to me. It is only because I don't know much about prose that I missed the explicitness of the dean's style and that of Arthur Griffith. Both are unequivocal and clear. I take very little interest in prose. I can hardly remember the Lord's Prayer; but when it comes to poetry it is quite a different matter. That I can remember because of its rhythm, without which there is no poetry. If you cannot remember what is called poetry perhaps it is because it is not poetry; or you are not a poet.

The people I know have good memories. Neil can recite and write; so can George Redding, and as for George Russell, Æ, he is the man with the memory for both prose and poetry. How can you be a poet without a memory, seeing that Memory is the Mother of the Muses? This quotation cured Yeats when he was affecting forgetfulness.

It is a fact that in Scotland Calvinism produced poetry in the person of Burns, and many others, by recoil. Neil owes to pedestrianism his recoil into poetry, for poetry is a recoil from ugliness and decay. In Ireland the recoil from English injustice made poets of us all.

Recoil made Arthur Griffith the author of a ballad very hard to come by now, *The Thirteenth Lock*. As for George Redding, in spite of all the respectability of the brewery behind him, he can bend a verse with the best and shoot his arrow straight to the mark.

> Oh, Marie Stopes, I never knew how far it
> Was wise to mingle love and faith until
> I saw the holy brother of Boyd Barrett
> Lead his full quiver up Killiney Hill.

'The holy brother of Boyd Barrett' was one of three brothers whom an overpious mother ruined. The holy brother spent his days in church kneeling and his nights begetting children. His wife was redheaded, and his quiver full.

Lewey came rushing in with a round of whiskeys. Someone remarked that it was half past six. As the whiskey and soda slid under Neil's moustache, he put down his glass and, sighing, said, 'And therefore, ye soft pipes, play on.' Obviously his father would not be relieved at six to play heard melodies; but as those unheard are sweeter than the harmonium of any chapel, the defection of his son can be condoned.

When Arthur Griffith started to leave no one tried to dissuade him. He was inflexible even in little things, so off he went. When he was gone a certain restraint left with him. Jimmy Montgomery opened with a story about the down-and-out who rushed into a grocery store, slammed down two pennies and ordered 'Two pennyworth of soup powder!' then he turned with a knowing look and remarked, 'If you're living with them, you've got to feed them.' That he would not have told us had Arthur been present, not that Griffith was a prude; but there was about him something that made levity seem out of place.

I had been talking to Neil a day or two before about Friar John, one of the characters in Rabelais, who saw in one of those outlandish islands the Two-backed Beast, the merriest animal that exists. Neil, who has a fluency in rhyming unapproached by any living poet of my acquaintance and by few I have since read, started with a ballad about the too well known wife of a Professor of Romance Languages who in one of her exploits went off with a native Irish speaker, that is, one of the few who learned Gaelic in their cradle. He was a very near approach to a tramp, hobo, or gaberlunzie man, and he affected that role much to the discredit of the language:

> The song I heard and the song I sing
> Are one and the same and the self same thing:
> This is the story and thus it ran:
> She's away with the gaberlunzie man!
>
> That two-backed beast of which you speak,
> He wears no horns upon his beak,
> And the reason is not far to seek:
> It needs strong back where a back is weak.
> There's wisdom yet in the ancient rann:
> She's away with the gaberlunzie man!
>
> Then guard your foreheads whatever befall
> For the tallest forehead amongst you all
> And the wisest scholar that ever was born
> He yet may wear the cuckold's horn.
> 'Twas ever thus since Time began:
> She's away with the gaberlunzie man.

When Jimmy gallantly suggested that the lady in question was 'more sinned against than sinning', Neil instantly remarked, 'Like the trees on the canal.' There were wits in the Bailey even though James Stephens seldom came in. He has described his own impressions, so I will leave them to him.

As I left the Bailey I met O'Leary Curtis, tall and thirsty, with a skin so smooth that he seemed to have been carved out of ivory. His voice was sweet and sad. We called him the 'Japanese Jesus' even though he wore a black goatee. He brought back another of Neil's quirks, a parody on 'The Wearin' o' the Green'. Neil has it this way.

> I met O'Leary Curtis and He took me by the hand
> Said, 'How is poor old Ireland; and who is going to stand?'

He was persuadable if someone stood the drinks, no matter what time it was. He told me that he was selling electricity for the Dublin Corporation and asked if I thought the

Church would help by having its altar bread prepared by an electric toaster. I could not hold out any prospect of comfort because I was not in the confidence of the executives. I told him where his friends could be found. His eyes brightened: hope of another kind would not be long deferred. I just saw Arthur Griffith in the street and the Bird Flanagan, so I came along. The problem of 'Who is going to stand?' would soon be solved.

Any mention of Bird Flanagan makes me uneasy. He is one of three brothers who would be better had they remained in Turgenev. Characters such as these are to be found both in the Russian author and in Dublin's fair city. Who is the Bird? Well, let me try to tell you. He went to a fancy dress ball at the Earlsfort Terrace skating rink dressed as the Holy Ghost and supported by two of the Holy Women. In the middle of the floor he laid an egg about the size of a football. The management interposed; he and his supporters were expelled. He went out clucking. But the name 'Bird' stuck to him since the incident of the egg. His father, an alderman of the city and a much respected man, sent the Bird to Australia twice but he flew back. Then he was sent to Canada, but he was a homing pigeon. The last we heard of him was from a friend who returned from Buenos Aires. He said that there was a large hole in its principal street. Looking down, he saw a man with a broad back and a red neck plying a pickaxe. He recognised the ensemble. 'In the name of God is that you, Bird?' he called. The Bird looked up. 'For God's sake get to hell out of here! It took a lot of influence to get me this job.' He spat on his hands and resumed his work. He was done with bad companions. A great 'artist'.

Dr. Johnson says – and I thoroughly agree with him – 'There is nothing contrived by man by which so much happiness is produced as a good inn or tavern.' I agree; but would my mother? Very doubtful. My aunt? Certainly not; and she would be very much upset if she knew of the 'low' company I was keeping.

11 *'And That Sweet City Of The Dreaming Spires'*

Why did I go to Oxford and when? If you must know – and I hate dates – it was in 1904. Much good may that do you. Now for the 'Why?' There were two reasons and many subreasons. Here's one of the principal reasons coming this way: wall-eyed in cap and gown over trousers of light grey stripes, my tutor, Smyly, came from his rooms on the north side of the Front Quad of Trinity. His trousers matched the colour of his eyes. I could see him on the opposite side of the big holm oak that stood in the centre of its square plot. Reason enough, you would say if you had met him. He never once tutored me, never once spoke to me: disapproved oozed out of him. That is why I rejoiced in the company of the Professor of Moral Philosophy, Henry Stewart Macran.

In Macran's rooms I met R.W. Lee, Fellow of Worcester College, Oxford. He was my second and sufficient reason. Good will and urbanity flowed out of him. You felt it, for all his reserve and self-possession. The personality of the man was an invitation. Time was no objection, I had plenty of time, so off I went for a few terms to Oxford. It is better to be educated beyond your means than to have means beyond your education.

One of the subreasons was that I could no longer compete in cycling races. Larry O'Neill, the little fellow in black knickerbockers and the lump of white wool in his left ear, who was president of the Irish branch of the Amateur Athletic Association and, afterwards, chronic Lord Mayor of Dublin, had suspended me for bad language at the Furzy Glen corner where all the cyclists from Ulster crashed. It is remarkable how gloomy fools impress the Irish public.

It was night by the time I reached Bletchley on my way to Oxford. A falling star streamed down the blue vault. I am superstitious, especially when I am feeling taut. Was the falling star an omen? If so, an omen of what?

Worcester College is the only one of the colleges of Oxford that had athletic fields in its own grounds. It is famous for its gardens and its lawn, where *Comus* is played in the summer under the trees. Worcester or Wuggins, as it is called in the slang of undergraduates, is at the end of Beaumont Street, a rococo façade dark and uninviting. But when you pass through the forbidding portal you come on a charming sight. In front is a sunk lawn. On the right, houses of sandstone three stories high stand in a row which ends at the house of the Provost. The flowery wall of a water garden closes the view straight ahead. To the left is a row of little two-storey fourteenth-century cottages. When I was admitted to Worcester I dwelt in the third one in the row from the Pump Quad. In the Pump Quad was the famous Daniel Press, called after the Provost. This was the private press that printed the poems of Robert Bridges, afterwards Poet Laureate. I owed much to H.S. Macran, and the friendship of R.W. Lee was not the least of the debt.

So to Worcester I went.

All the men at Oxford were between eighteen and twenty-two. I was a year or two older than the generality; but as I had come to Oxford to sample the place and to have a shot at the Newdigate, which is a prize for English verse, it mattered little. I was not reading for a degree. In fact I was not reading at all. I should have been studying medicine, but that is a subject which is inclined to pall, particularly on a bright summer day.

Instead of reading, I played a little soccer. I hired one of the earliest motor bicycles, an Indian, from an agent who is the present Lord Nuffield, the Henry Ford of England, and ran it to taverns in the many villages that adjoined the university. I met a Buck or Beau from New College who was as free as myself. He accompanied me and often drove the motor bicycle, which had a trailer that was really a trailer, for it trailed behind, attached to the bicycle by a metal tube. One a day when the driver turned too sharply I was thrown out and forgotten for miles on the road.

One morning there approached me, coming through the Turl against the light, a youth who could not help being comely – I judged by his walk, for his face was against the light; when he came level I found that my guess was right. He had auburn hair, hazel eyes and a pointed sensitive face. He was almost tall. It was Compton Mackenzie coming from Magdalen College probably to look into Blackwell's bookshop. He it was who wrote *Sinister Street*, a novel about the equivocal time of youth. It was a marvel how such a young man could have so much wisdom. His book was a 'best seller', and reader too. That was a long time ago; but long as it is, he has never fallen from the high distinction of his early book and this in spite of many books. He couldn't be looking for Christopher Stone, Scholar of Christ Church. I left Stone not ten minutes ago and he said that he had a lecture to attend. He said nothing about Compton Mackenzie. They were friends. Mackenzie became Stone's brother-in-law later, for he married his sister.

I might as well tell Mackenzie that Stone had gone to a lecture and tell him of the sonnet which Stone composed on the depravity of the age. Sir Somebody – I remember only his title – and the Hon. Mrs – that will do – had been the principals in a divorce at which all Oxford was laughing, for had not Slater, the venal detective, given intimate and amazing evidence? Slater would photograph your wife, or anybody else's who could pay, in the most compromising positions and give evidence that was most telling in any divorce proceeding. He would also do it vice versa. His magnifying glass and what it saw was the decisive factor in the famous divorce trial. Stone affected to be envious of the notoriety of Sir Something and to be blasé as befitted an undergraduate of the university, for it was the proper thing to be blasé before you began life. So he testified to his prowess before Jeune, who was Divorce Court judge. 'It needs not June for beauty's heightening.'

> My name is written on the mirrored brink
> Of Love by rosy-filleted finger tip
> Jewelled with perfidy. Mine amorous lip
> Sucks the dull stain of passion like the pink
> and blushing blotting paper starred with ink.
> This is mine heraldry: a trouser clip
> Found on the bed beside a bodice slip
> That dropped unseen while amorous draughts we drink.
> The slanderous cuckoo in the apple tree
> Fluted his horned unforgotten tune;
> Later, oh, Slater, on the ambrosial bed
> Spied a moon-glimmering spot misdirected;
> And all unmellowed plucked me, gloriously
> Before the summering up of pitiless Jeune.

It was stuck in my head because it is some of the cleverest, if not the very cleverest, writing I have ever come across. That cuckoo in the apple tree, for instance, and the epithet 'slanderous'; 'Cuckoo, cuckoo, a word of fear.' And 'apple tree'. Stay me with flagons; comfort me with apples. I am sick of love, as the character in Stone's sonnet was supposed to be 'sick and very sick'. And then, 'the summering up' of pitiless Jeune! Is it any wonder that I have never forgotten it? 'It needs not June!'

I made a few discoveries at Oxford. One was that it was not exclusively a home of learning; in fact, learning was bad form; for any exhibition of it at table you were liable to be 'sconced' – that is, dared to drain a five-and-a-half-pint tankard, and fined if you could not make it. I found that 'good form' was *de rigueur*. Conduct was the rule at Oxford, not scholarship, and this had been the vogue long before Matthew Arnold's father, who was an Oriel College man, invented 'the old school tie', which as everyone knows is the outward sign of devotion to a code. Good Form taught young men to hold their drink in silence; it prescribed the cane you took to church on Sundays; and it took for granted that any culprit should come forward and acknowledge his misdemeanour rather than have the whole college 'gated' and the innocent locked in with the culprit.

From what monstrous complacency came the cult of stupidity? It is fostered in the country's schools and universities where the country's leaders are educated. It is a dangerous thing and requires to be exposed. As I have pointed out, it began when the father of Matthew Arnold, an Oxford man and Headmaster of Rugby School, preferred character to brains. Rugby is not one of the leading public schools but it is one of the best known. From it the cult of the Old School Tie, that is, loyalty to the boys of the Old School (which means loyalty to the Empire) spread to every school in England, even to the jails. Character may be preferable to intellect; but this cult of character instead of brains presupposes a settled and unchanging civil service which in return presupposes an Empire. With the disappearance of Empire and the colonial appointments that went with it, the Old School automata of the civil service were out of a job. They were incapable of adjusting themselves to change. Their brains were atrophied when learning became bad form. The Empire has melted away and these men have become a clog on progress, so much so that witty Winston Churchill, who, as a wittier commentator remarked, spent the best years of his life preparing his impromptus, is said to have exclaimed, 'England is a Laocoön strangled by the Old School Tie.'

In Arnold's time the Empire seemed to be everlasting and unshakable. He is not to be blamed because he did not foresee the inherent suicide in the stupidity he so assiduously promoted.

I made another discovery, or rather I had my eyes opened to a fact that was unaccountable hitherto. There was a conceited, mulish, mediocre fellow who was the *most popular* man in our college. I often wondered why. It was not until F.C. Crawley told me that as nobody would take the trouble of putting him in his place he was made 'popular' instead. The principle was the same whereby mankind calls the Black Sea the Euxine; and country people call the fairies the 'good people' when in reality they are mischievous and vindictive. This was very valuable information. It explained why people accept certain politicians. To hold the skunk in them would raise such a 'stink' that it was long ago decided to let them alone.

But the Newdigate, which is an annual prize for English verse, was my aim. The verses, in that time, had to be in the heroic couplet, the metre of Alexander Pope and of all the bores of the eighteenth century, Oliver Goldsmith always excepted.

The verses which I sent in did not win the Newdigate. They obtained a *proxime accessit*, which, being translated, means runner-up. I was disappointed because, with every Vice-Chancellor's Prize (I got four of them at Trinity College, a record, they say, since the prize was instituted) and with the gold medal for English verse in the Royal, I had begun to think of myself as a professional as opposed to an amateur. I was disappointed, until I read the prize poem written by George Kennedy Allen Bell, now Bishop of Chichester, with its

> Only I
> Hear the lank eagles crying up the sky.

Then I knew that a better man had won: 'lank eagles.'

George Kennedy Allen Bell was a fine poet with a whimsey when the mood was on him. In Dublin he met Macran, and he learned that his ideas of philosophy – Moral, of course – were sometimes a cause of anxiety to his wife. This he recorded:

> You could be all things but a good
> And wifely man;
> And that you would not if you could,
> We know, Macran.

And the parody on Swinburne's *Félise* is not unbecoming

to one who wears a mitre. He shows the power that is in him with his straight

> Ilion, city of Troy
> And the tall grey towers thereof
> Fallen, and gone from joy
> And out of the hand of Love.

I am sorry that Chichester is so far away. I would like to hear its bishop preaching. Of one thing I am certain: I am sure that the reference in the last line of one of the best limericks in the language, which describes the effect of the attendance at matins of one of the citizenesses on the bishop, does not refer to the present incumbent.

> There was a young lady from Chichester
> Whose curves made the Saints in their nichesstir
> One morning at Matins
> The heave of her satins
> Made the Bishop of Chichester's breechesstir.

The next year the rule as to heroic couplets was changed. The Newdigate can now be won by any form of verse, even blank.

I had not won what I set out for, but quite accidentally I performed a feat at Worcester unprecedented in the history of the college. I drank the sconce. I have already told you what a sconce is. It is a silver tankard that holds more than five pints. It is called for as a punishment on those who transgress at meals by making a pun or quoting from the classics. As a rule I do not make bad puns, and I would hardly have tried a tag from the classics in such society. I sometimes resort to the classics to prevent my ignorance in other fields from being shown up, hoping that a change of language will change the subject. It was the resentment of the abominable Bamburger who sat next to me at table that was to blame for my being sconced. He knew that I was supposed to be reading medicine and because I forbore to answer his endless questions as to what was good for training in the way of food he hated me. He was to represent Oxford as a lightweight in the annual inter-varsity boxing competition, hence his questions about what he should eat.

Bamburger called for the sconce.

'Now, Bamburger,' I said, 'you know the rules: if I drink the sconce without taking it from my lips, I am privileged to sconce every man at this table. I will sconce only you and that won't do you and your training much good.'

He called to the butler, 'Bring in the sconce.'

Again I protested: 'Look here, Bamburger, you don't know what you're up against. I am not referring to the Cambridge lightweight but to myself. I can drink as many pints as my pals put up. I was weaned on pints.'

It was unavailing.

There was silence in the hall when the butler with due ceremony bore in the sconce on a salver. It was full to the lid with cold ale. I felt 'mortified' as they say in Dublin. All eyes were on our table; and at the high table, where the dons were, conversation ceased. I received instructions: I was not to remove the tankard from my mouth until I had drunk it dry, otherwise I would acknowledge defeat.

I planted my elbows firmly on the table and raised the silver tankard to my mouth. I took a deep breath. I began to drink. The first two pints went down pleasantly enough. It would have been enjoyable if there had not been so much depending on the draught. You would never guess what affected me most. Not a feeling of repleteness. No. You could never guess. It was the awful cold that hurt me on both sides of the throat and went up into my ears. Don't believe them when you hear that the English don't know how to cool their ale. They keep it in the wood in a cellar and that does not conduce to conduction. (A pun! Enough to sconce any man.) I held on, conscious still. If this goes on I will pass out; but on it had to go. I suppose it took two or three full minutes, and two minutes are enough to die in. Look at the second hand of your watch to realize how long two minutes can be. To me, whatever time it was seemed ten times longer. At last I reached the bottom and I put my head back to drain the thing so that it would not drip when I held it upside down. Cheers broke out all over the hall; even the imperturbable butler permitted a gleam of admiration to enliven his countenance. The dons on the upper table looked down at our table. I tried to get the conversation going again and off myself.

'Bamburger, I warned you. Now you can take on.' There was little sign of approval for that because all the table was afraid of the pugilist. Next day he was knocked out in the first round by an accidental blow of the blond Cambridge man's head. No one pitied Bamburger and no one blamed me, for he was too ugly to win even a boxing match.

On the whole, I'd rather have drunk the sconce than won the Newdigate. Oscar Wilde won the Newdigate and landed in Reading Gaol. G. K. A. Bell won the Newdigate and became Bishop of Chichester. And, latterly, it was won by a woman who, I am sure, could never have achieved the sconce. The way I was treated from that day on, you might think that I had seen the Holy Grail.

To shed distinction on your college fills you with a lasting elation. I put up a record that puts Worcester ahead of all colleges when it came to the bibbery. Whether the dons appreciated my effort or not, I cannot tell. It would have been just like them to have preferred a winner of the Newdigate. I could not have won the Newdigate. Had not a star fallen over Oxford?

There is a gap in the sandstone ledge of the library roof. It gave way as I jumped from the library to the roof of the Georgian row of buildings, on the right as you enter the college. The gap is still there (if they haven't repaired it) to show that an Irishman can drain the sconce and still jump across a gap sixty feet up in the air, and leave his mark upon the college. The Provost had a leaden chimney about eight feet high which attracted attention one night. Next day it was found embedded in the sacred lawn of the quad. All were to be gated. I came forward.

At Oxford they practise the Greek adage, 'Nothing too

much.' Boasting and ebullience are bad form. Hence it becomes one to become blasé. I am ebullient on occasion, I admit. I hope that I am not boastful. The Provost forgave me. Like Bird of Dublin, I was 'in my cups'. The Provost blamed the sconce. Perhaps it is just as well they take thought of nothing but conduct in Oxford. It is the only form of education, and what more do you want? Is it not, after all, better than taking dejectedly a seat upon the intellectual throne? Some men never recover from education.

12 *Tancred*

Where did I first meet Dermot Freyer? I say it is a poor friendship that can trace its beginning. I must have met him during one of my frequent visits to London. After all, London was but sixty miles away and I could get an *exeat* easily.

When I met Dermot Freyer he was impatient to introduce me to his friend Tancred. 'But who is he?' So there were people who had not heard of Tancred? 'Well, Tancred is a poet who is very particular about *le mot juste*. He will stop lifts, if he happens to be alone in one, until he gets it. My father's house in Harley Street has an automatic lift and it has been so often out of use to the household, because it was so often in use to the poet, that I have been forbidden to invite him again. Let us meet him tomorrow in the Café Royal.' Now I don't like the Café Royal and never did. It is the meeting place of all self-conscious people, pseudo artists and real ones. Would he meet us in an ordinary pub, say in Tottenham Court Road?

Enter a knight just taken out of his armour. I have never seen an armoured knight except in museums, and Tancred looked jointed, as if he were accustomed to move only in armour. 'Ha! And how are *you*?' he said. 'Been roebucking lately?' It was Dermot Freyer who urged him on in spite of himself before one who would have been a stranger save for what Dermot had said in my favour. We had a few drinks before getting on to the subject of verse. It must have been winter because the piece Tancred read had just been composed and it was about a New Year's Resolution. There is no need to go into the delay, the forgetfulness of the subject, and the interruptions, common to a public house. I have not forgotten the lines. I guessed that 'reticule' and 'misrule' must have put many lifts out of commission. Here is the result:

New Year's Resolution:

My assets shall not gild the reticule
Of any rose-lipped daughter of misrule.

And there were many more but I cannot remember them now.

I do remember a poem of Dermot's; one about a little child. I remember it because when I went searching the corpus of English literature I could find only very few poems about children, and none of them as good as Dermot's. But it was long afterwards that I came across the lines in one of those privately printed brochures such as Blackwell publishes for enthusiasts.

Little Dolly Dimplekin
Has dimples on her cheeks and chin,
And dimples on her knuckles too,
Which show that Dolly's years are few.

Tancred knew every word that Herrick had written. He had some mysterious theory about one of Herrick's friends, Shadwell. According to Tancred, Herrick had locked up Shadwell in his *Hesperides*; and here and there you could hear Shadwell calling through the bars of Herrick's verse. He was probably calling for help; but it was all so mysterious that I did not inquire so I could not be sure. It would not have cleared the matter because Tancred was incoherent about the dark mystery and Freyer laughed and laughed whenever I showed interest in Tancred's theory. I saw no symptoms of lunacy in this theory; no more than I saw signs of latent lunacy then in Joyce.

Freyer was a Cambridge man. Tancred, all I could find out about him was that he worked in the Stock Exchange. That is, he had to wear a bowler hat. A helmet would have suited him better. He was a close friend of Dermot Freyer, and that was enough for me. He knew literature and he wrote verse. So we three had something to talk about. Too much probably, because one night I nearly missed the 'Flying Fornicator' back to Oxford. It reached the city of the Dreaming Spires a few minutes before midnight. If you are not in college before midnight – an *exeat* is no help – you have to tell where you were and bring witnesses.

I don't know how the train got its name. It was used a lot by the dons and that, added to the irreverence of the undergrads, probably christened it.

13 *Chamber Music*

> I saw and hearkened many things and more
> Which might be fair to tell but now I hide.

James Joyce said, 'Do you know that we can rent the Martello Tower at Sandycove? I'll pay the rent if you will furnish it.'

Sandycove is about seven miles from Dublin on the south side of its famous bay. It lies a little to the east of the harbour which takes the mail boat from England early in the morning and late at night. The water between Dun Laoghaire and Sandycove is called Scotsman's Bay and is bounded by the east pier of the harbour and the two-storeyed, thick-wall Martello Tower, with the Battery close by the Forty Foot, a resort for strong swimmers.

The Martello Tower is one of the many towers which the English built along the southern coast of England and the south-eastern coast of Ireland *after* Napoleon's threat of invasion. Some say that these towers got their name from a sculptor's mallet, others from the name of the man who designed them. They all look like the muzzle of an old-fashioned cannon, ringed around the top. They have very thick walls with two little windows for each storey. The entrance is on the side away from the sea.

The rent for the Tower at Sandycove was only eight pounds all inclusive per year, payable at Dublin Castle. We took it; and Joyce kept his word and stumped up the rent from a prize of twenty pounds that he had won in some examination. I did the furnishing from unmissed things from 5 Rutland Square. 'It's a poor house where there are not many things superfluous.' I learned that at school from the poet Horace.

Well I remember how we went out to inspect and to take possession, for Joyce had an uncle who was a clerk in an attorney's office from whom we had probably heard that possession is nine-tenths of the law. He was careful to leave some article of his as a symbol of possession before we moved in. The only movable thing he possessed was a roll of manuscripts which contained a score or so of poems written in his clear handwriting. Later these were published in a little book he called *Chamber Music.* How they got their title remains to be told.

The Tower at Sandycove is built of clear granite. It is very clean. Its door, which is halfway up, is approached by a ladder fixed beneath the door, which is opened by a large copper key, for there was a powder magazine in the place and the copper was meant to guard against sparks which an iron key might strike out from the stone. There is a winding staircase in the thickness of the wall to the side that does not face the sea. On the roof, which is granite, is a gun emplacement, also of granite which can be used for a table if you use the circular sentry walk for a seat. Over the door is a projection from which boiling oil or molten lead can be poured down upon the enemy. Beside this is a furnace for making cannon balls red hot. There were no shells in the days when it was built, but the red-hot cannon balls could burn a wooden ship if they hit it. Happily these towers were never used, though they were occupied by coast guards until quite recently.

We lived there for two years, greatly to the anxious relief of our parents. Joyce had a job at an adjoining school. I had some reading to do for my medical degree. When the weather was warm we sun-bathed on the roof, moving around the raised sentry platform with the sun and out of the wind. In the evenings we would visit the Arch, kept by watery-eyed Murray, soon to become a widower, or go into the Ship in Abbey Street in the city to meet Vincent Cosgrove or 'Citizen' Elwood, our friends from the Aula Maxima.

To get into the city 'depended' sometimes; it depended on our being in funds. We could go either by tram or train provided that we possessed the fare. Early one day we wandered off in the direction of the city. We were certainly at a loss, a loss for fares or for the subsequent entertainment if and when we reached Dublin.

Joyce saw him first, a tall figure coming rapidly in our direction. I looked and recognised 'old Yeats', the father of the bard. He was out for his morning constitutional. As he came nearer he appeared an uninviting figure, old, lean, and very tall. His dark eyes burned brightly under shaggy eyebrows. 'It is your turn,' Joyce whispered, 'For what?' I asked. 'To touch.' Reluctantly, and with trepidation, I spoke to the old man, whom I hardly knew. 'Good morning, Mr Yeats, would you be so good as to lend us two shillings?' Savagely the old man eyed me and my companion. He looked from one to the other. At last he broke out: 'Certainly not,' he said. 'In the first place I have no money; and if I had it and lent it to you, you and your friends would spend it on drink.' He snorted. Joyce advanced and spoke gravely. 'We cannot speak about that which is not.' But old Yeats had gone off rapidly. 'You see,' said Joyce, still in a philosophical mood, 'the razor of Occam forbids the introduction of superfluous arguments. When he said that he had no money that was enough. He had no right to discuss the possible use of the non-existent.'

We quoted and parodied all the poets. Joyce could parody every prose style and get an equivalent sound for every word. It was chiefly the Collects or the New Testament he chose to parody, for that blind, bitter antagonism towards the teachings of his childhood – an antagonism which finally broke his mind – had already begun.

He could be very solemn about it.

Vincent Cosgrove was another mother's boy. He was cynical and amusing, pensive at times, and cynical with himself. He caused jealousy by walking out with Nora Barnacle, who was the girl with whom Joyce eloped to Flushing before he married her. She had beautiful auburn hair. Vincent came to an early end. He inherited a few hundred pounds on his mother's death and in a fit of remorse, after a few weeks in London, jumped off one of the bridges over the Thames.

To the Tower, on Sundays, Arthur Griffith would come, and sometimes he would come out for the weekend. He would not let himself be outdone by anyone. It was my custom to swim to Bullock Harbour from Sandycove before breakfast of a morning. You skirted along by the granite rocks, but about halfway to the harbour the rocks receded and you entered a round extent of water from which the shore was equidistant on two sides. There was no landing until you turned and swam again along by the shore.

One morning, as I swam back from Bullock Harbour, I missed Griffith. He had been beside me, between me and the rocks. Then I saw him under the water but even then I forebore to go to his assistance because of his anger if he found out. Things got too alarming so I pulled out that determined man. Though his body was scraped as I pulled him up the rock, no allusion was made to the incident when he recovered and walked back to the Tower. I desisted from going for an early morning dip after that.

Joyce very rarely bathed and never in the Forty Foot, which was below the Tower. Once, when we took a tram to Howth on the other side of Dublin Bay, he did get into the swimming bath at the north side of the Hill. I forget if I saw him in the water, but I remember seeing him naked on the side of the bath, carrying a sweeping brush over his shoulder and deliberately staggering along. I was about eight feet up the rock at the side of the tank trying to get a foothold for a dive.

'Jesus wept; and when he walked, he waddled,' Joyce announced.

I studied the naked figure. 'So that's what his uncle wants to make a half miler out of,' I said to myself. 'He'll never do it with that physique. Why, his knees are wider than his legs. He has lost his faith. Now what is to become of his form?'

One morning back in Sandycove I was shaving on the roof of the Tower, because of the better light – it is a good idea to shave before going into salt water – when up comes Joyce.

'Fine morning, Dante. Feeling trancendental this morning?' I asked.

'Would you be so merry and bright if you had to go out at this hour to teach a lot of scrawny-necked brats?'

Touché! He had me there: not a doubt about it. Why don't I think of other people's problems? I must develop a little sympathy: suffer with them; realise their difficulties. I am glad that he has a job, though it is only that of a teacher.

The golden down that would be a beard on a more robust man shone in the morning light. Joyce did not need a shave.

'Yes,' I said, 'that is enough to obscure the Divine Idea that underlies all life. But why be atrabilious about it?' He gave me a sour look. He turned and stooped under the low door.

'I suppose you will bear that in mind and attach it to me

when you come to write your *Inferno*?' I said.

He turned and made a grave announcement: 'I will treat you with fairness.'

'Put a pint or two in fairness and I won't complain.'

He was gone.

What would be the use of sympathy with a character like that? He would resent sympathy. He is planning some sort of novel that will show us all up and the country as well: all will be fatuous except James Joyce. He will be Judge Joyce, to whom Judge Jeffreys, the hanging judge, won't be able to hold a candle.

I knew that Joyce was incapable of writing a *Paradiso*, but little did I think that *Ulysses* would be a masterpiece of despair. And all the worse because it represented the *disjecti membra poetae*: the scattered limbs of a poet. Joyce was the most damned soul I ever met. He went to hell and he could not get out. He could not help it, and no one could help him; he was stubborn and contemptuous. He could not follow in his father's footsteps, for they were too zigzag. His father was an alcoholic, an old alcoholic wag. His mother was a naked nerve; and Joyce himself was torn between a miserable background and a sumptuous education. My cavalier treatment did nothing to help, nor did the attitude of his friend, the lighthearted 'Citizen', who insisted on seeing in Joyce 'a great artist': a droll.

Presently I heard him climbing down the ladder. I went into the overhanging balcony and called down, 'Don't stop at the Arch on your way back.' He never looked up but he raised his stick in a grave salute and loped off.

Added to the grievances of his upbringing, and they were many but unavoidable, was the outrageous conduct of 'Maunsell's Manager'; that is what he called an illiterate fellow from Belfast who, when he was not selling ladies' undies, managed – and ruined – Maunsell and Co., the publishers of nearly all the work of those in the Yeats circle. Maunsell's manager burned the whole edition of Joyce's *Dubliners* with the exception of one copy on the plea that the book contained an offensive reference to the King or

Queen. You may wonder why that should be any concern of a Dublin firm. Ah, but Maunsell's manager was a Belfast man who travelled in ladies' undies, wholesale, and some Belfast men are professional loyalists, combative only in times of peace!

I do not wish to pose as a blameless observer of my contrary friend Joyce. If in spite of myself I do, you will perhaps forgive me, though I confess that I aided and abetted him. I drank with him, lived with him, and talked of many things. I was called by one of his critics 'An accessory before the fact of *Ulysses*'. That, of course, is an extenuation of the truth. To know a man intimately does not make you an accessory to his subsequent action. I did my living best to cheer him and to make those thin lips of his cream in a smile. Very seldom I succeeded. I tried to show him by example how unnecessary and absurd was a seedy hauteur. Maybe I was wrong to try to make him genial. He must have regarded my efforts as the efforts of one who wanted to master him and shape him after the figure and likeness of the would-be mentor. He had the formal and diffident manners of a lay brother in one of the lower orders of the Church. But I was living with him and his constant air of reprobation and his reserve and silences annoyed me, for I took them to be a pose; and I detest humbug in any manifestation.

Joyce had 'a nose like a rhinoceros for literature'. From his appreciations and quotations I learned much. From Dowland's *Third and Last Book of Songs and Airs* he would quote, 'Weep no more, sad fountains,' and caress the end of the last stanza, 'Softly, now softly lies sleeping.' 'One lyric made Dowland immortal,' he would say. Another favourite and model of his was Ben Jonson's 'Queen and huntress chaste and fair.' Clarence Mangan's 'Veil not your mirror, sweet Aline' was often recited to show me what a poet Mangan was. Vergil's '*procumbit humi bos*' he would compare to Dante's '*Cade como corpo morte, cade*'. He tried not unsuccessfully to reform his style on the precision and tersity of Dante. That and his intensity, self-absorption and silence caused me to call him 'Dante' just to rally him from being 'sullen in the sweet air'.

I should have known better, for I was studying abnormal psychology under Connolly Norman, in Grangegorman Asylum who was one of the best teachers I ever met. But it is one thing to study lunacy in an asylum, another thing to recognise it in a friend. Had I succeeded in ministering to a mind diseased, Joyce would not be the greatest schizophrene who ever wrote this side of a mental hospital: he would never have been famous, and Dublin would have been less.

We are all more or less schizophrenic, divided as we are between good and evil, belief and disbelief, reason and emotion, and the conditioning of our childhood and the real experiences of maturity. That is the normal condition for which perhaps the word 'schizophrene' is inappropriate, for that word is associated with a pathological state of mind.

After all, who am I to talk about sanity? Out of four of my friends, two committed suicide, one contracted syphilis and the fourth was a schizophrene. Show me your company! I am showing them to you, for I would not have you think that I wasn't as good or as bad as any of them, but it was 'after my fashion'. In that lies a saving grace.

If I hate anything, I hate humbug or what appears to be humbug. That is why I preferred the Citizen to Joyce. The Citizen was as free as a bird. He was not inhibited. He laughed easily. Joyce had a grim sense of humour; he never laughed at all. He guffawed; but it was his way of being scornful.

Apparently it was payday at the school; for when Joyce returned he had evidently dropped into the Arch to see Mr Murray, who kept that tavern. He invited me to go to Dublin. He had a purpose in going to town but he would not tell me what it was and I knew it was useless to try to pry the secret from him. He liked to act mysteriously of set purpose. We hid the key of the Tower and walked to Sandycove station. We got out at Westland Row. Now the secret will be divulged, I thought.

Joyce said, 'They meet on Friday nights.'

'Who?'

He laughed at my want of understanding. 'The Hermetics.'

'Oh, Æ's crowd?'

'Precisely.'

He led the way to Kildare Street. We went up it to Molesworth Street and thence into Dawson. Joyce stopped before a large shabby office building and proceeded down the lane beside it for about thirty yards. He stopped at a side door and beckoned me. 'This is where Maunsell's Manager has an office. He lends it to the Hermetics on Friday nights.'

I knew that they met on Thursdays; but I said nothing.

'The Hermetics sound like nonsense to me.'

He bowed his head gravely. He was determined on some outrage, joke or insult and he assumed a pontifical air before it, as was his way. We ascended a stairway that was perfectly dark. He paused and listened at a closed door. No sound. Brazenly he opened it. The dark room was empty. After a long pause: 'Got a match?' he asked.

I lit the gas bracket. The room was empty but for a dozen folding chairs heaped against the wall. On the floor was a suitcase. The gas went out. We had no shilling to waste in the meter so we left.

In the street I noticed that Joyce was carrying Maunsell's Manager's suitcase. Larceny, I suggested. He said something about himself having been robbed by Maunsell's Manager. In the Ship we found that the suitcase contained a gross of samples. All were ladies' undies. We had a few pints. Joyce suggested a tour of the Kips – the red-light district – to distribute the undies to the various ladies. The proviso with each present was that the lady would write to thank the Hermetic Society. For all the ladies would know, the Hermetic Society might have been one of those rescue societies which were such a source of laughter in the Kips. Fearing that the bruit of an adventure in the Kips might reach home, I suggested that we visit the mistress of Sweeney the greengrocer, whose vocation kept her constantly indoors. This constancy was her only virtue.

We found her at home in Rutland Street, which runs down to Richmond Street from Mountjoy Square. Jenny produced some bottles of stout, then sent the one-legged girl who lived with her out for more. Joyce, with increasing dignity, suggested that she try on the undies. 'Belfast's best.' Jenny obliged with such zeal that Joyce gave her the dozens of underwear and threw the suitcase with them into the bed. As he did so, his toe struck the night jar or 'chamber' and it rang musically. I never saw the letter of thanks she promised to write.

Our sufferings, it seems, were caused by Mrs Murray, or rather by her wake, at the Arch. She was the wife of the big-headed, thin little publican who kept the nearest licensed house to the Tower. As old customers we were expected, if not invited, to attend. Entrance was by the back door because Murray evidently did not wish to bring any trouble on the house that would be disedifying at such a time. The local police, however, were aware of the bereavement and they sent the constable on duty to pay his respects *en passant* to the dead. Mr Murray himself served libations; such service for the living was a habit with him which he did not turn off, now that it had become almost a rite.

'Here's how!' said the local constable, then, remembering the gravity of the occasion, said innocently, 'Here's mud in your eye.' In the eyes of Mr Murray there were tears, their liquidity overflowed, for there was always a watery film on his dreary blue optics. It had been raining and the probability was that the earth of Dean's Grange cemetery would be muddy; but in the toast of the constable there could have been no allusion to that. His was a well-known expression, the meaning of which, if any, escapes me. Kirke and Lyons, the two fishermen who sold us lobsters, were among those present. The other mourners were habitués, that is, pensioners, and one ex-conductor of the Dalkey tram. There may have been others. I am sure there were but I cannot remember them. I do remember Joyce's gravity as he intoned a ritualistic parody which was his form of joking: he recited Milton:

> 'She must not float upon his watery beer
> Unwept.'

There was a hiatus after that and we wisely did not attempt the unguarded stairs of the Tower. The potato patch was much safer and drier than its occupants.

What a pattern leaves can make, or rather what a pattern can be made out of leaves. Wonderful, wonderful! The window by Burne-Jones in Mansfield College, Oxford, for instance – is it by Burne-Jones? These are potato leaves, leaves of the potato plant. By Jove, I am lying in a potato ridge! I lift my gaze. Above me is the Tower. Where is my companion? I found Joyce in the ridge next to me. He was wide awake and staring up through the potato leaves. 'I have the title for my book of poems – *Chamber Music*.'

14 *Imported: A Patriot*

During the Long Vacation from Oxford, the length of which is a reminder that in the days of old students were released from their studies to work at harvesting, I invited to the Tower Samuel Chenevix-Trench. His given name was Samuel but he had it changed to Dermot by deed poll. He was of Cromwellian stock and the son of a colonel in the British Army, but when he got infected by the Gaelic Revival he became 'more Irish than the Irish themselves'. When you come to think of it, the Irish themselves care little about patriotism; for them it has memories of despair, so all our patriots are imported and Dermot Trench was no exception. When he was at Balliol, and there are no fools at Balliol, he would round up men from Ireland or with Irish propensities – remember Oxford is the home of lost causes – and teach them Gaelic in his rooms in Holywell.

His forehead was wide, with that level space across it which Lavater considers an indispensable mark of genius. His eyes were grey and set wide apart. His legs and feet were as long as those of the men who govern England secretly. His long legs were slightly curved; not curved enough to be bandy but they deviated ever so little from the straight. He was not our guest at the Tower for long before he removed all the oil-lamp shades because they were not manufactured in Ireland but made of Belgian glass. As a result of his patriotism the place was filled with smoke. He refused to use boot blacking until it was produced at home. His shoes grew a mould of verdant hue; 'The Wearin' o' the Green' on his feet! He refused to smile at the jape. 'Not another grim character?' I asked myself. 'One is enough for me.'

Joyce was greatly impressed by what he took for Trench's Eton and Oxford accent. With formal courtesy he gave him his bed at the right-hand side of the entrance door and slept in a bed under the shelf which ran round the room. It was where the number two is on a watch dial. Immediately over his head was piled all the tinware of the Tower – pots, pans, plates and a fish kettle.

One night about one-thirty Trench awoke from a nightmare screaming, 'Ah, the black panther!' As he yelled, he drew a revolver from under his pillow and fired two shots at the hallucination before falling back exhausted. Quietly, I took the revolver away. Again he woke screaming. 'Leave the menagerie to me,' I said; and fired the remaining shots into the cans over Joyce's head. One by one they fell into his bed. He scrambled out, dressed, took his ash plant, and left the Tower never to return.

Trench is Haines, the Englishman, in *Ulysses* and there is an allusion, which may read obscurely, to a black panther, about the middle of the book. Joyce had a great respect for Haines the Englishman. I was blamed for all the shooting. Had Joyce practised instead of pawning my rifle, he would not have been so gun-shy.

Trench's pamphlet, *What Is the Use of Reviving Irish*, is written in the clear style of a Balliol man. 'Gaelic is a language of social genius; its use reveals the Irishman to himself and sets in motion the genial current of soul that has become frozen in an Anglicised atmosphere. It is the symbol of a native social culture which was dignified and attractive in lieu of being snobbish and imitative and for lack of which every man, woman and child in the country are denied their full expansion of personality.'

As an example of social culture, when Irish had become a 'political shibboleth' a high dignitary among the judges of the Supreme Court issued an invitation to a garden party, but instead of the script reading '... wishes the pleasure of your company at a garden party,' it read '... wishes the pleasure of your body in his potato patch.'

Trench, with an enthusiasm which is the mark of madness, or of genius, or of both, made himself into a fluent Gaelic speaker. When he went back to Oxford he fell into the hands of one of those poverty-stricken, designing fellows who farm Oxford, on the lookout for Trenches and for their sisters who may make rich wives. The fellow that got hold of Trench married a titled woman and lived on her happily, for him, ever afterwards. Trench himself blew his brains out for the hopeless love of Lady Mary Spring-Rice.

Just as Carlyle thought more of a bridge his father built at Ecclefechan than of any of his own books, Joyce thought more of the admirable tenor voice he had inherited from his father than of his literary works. When I was in England he wrote to me – the letter dated 1904 can be seen in the Public Library at Forty-second Street, in New York City – to tell me of a projected tour of English coastwise towns on which he would sing old English ballads and sea shanties. This was his idea forty years before such things were thought of, though they have since become the vogue. The tour fell through because for one thing Dolmetsch, the instrument maker, would not present the troubadour with a lute.

Another reason was a distracting SOS which Lady Gregory sent out from her Abbey Theatre. It had run out of geniuses. As everyone in Dublin was a genius, we all applied. I had little to offer so I did not seek the Presence; but Joyce called on Her Ladyship only to be instantly thrown out. He was not out of the top drawer: not out of any drawer for that matter. When he emerged, he addressed the Citizen, Vincent Cosgrove and me with the following impromptu limerick. He moved his fingers gravely as he recited:

'There was a kind Lady called "Gregory"
Said, "Come to me poets in beggary";
But found her imprudence
When thousands of students
Cried, "All we are in that category."'

Ignored and derided in Dublin, Joyce eloped with Nora Barnacle, who was a maid in Finn's Hotel, Lincoln Place. He sent me a postcard of himself dressed as Arthur Rimbaud, the French poet who tried to revolutionise the French language. Later, he sent two poems printed on galleys to his acquaintances – he would not admit a friend. These were *The Holy Office* and *Gas from a Burner*, a reference to the gas jet in the room where he found 'Maunsell's Manager's travelling bag', i.e., the suitcase with the twelve dozen undies which he removed and presented as has been recorded. He himself was the 'Burner'. That was in 1904.

Almost a year later I met the Citizen, who, with eyes dancing and his quizzical mouth smiling, asked, 'Did you hear the latest about the "artist"?'

'No.'

'He sent a telegram to his parents to announce the birth of his son.'

'Yes?'

'I always said he was an artist. This proves it. *Contra mundum* and no mistake!'

15 *Hospital Politics And Practice*

Flattery is all very well in its way; as the American said: if you don't inhale it. And to have a son can be flattering, if you don't subject the sentiment to analysis. I seldom analyse anything. I did not marry by analysis. And I was far from analysing myself or my son when he was born in Fairfield and placed in his perambulator in the garden daily under, but not directly under, the old mulberry tree. There was danger from a falling bough if the infant were to be put immediately under the tree.

A son can make you responsible. I became so responsible that I passed all the examinations which had begun to accumulate within a few weeks after marriage, and I became a qualified doctor. Examination passing is just the beginning. It is necessary to have practical knowledge of the craft; that meant a sojourn in Vienna.

Our infant son was left in Earlsfort Terrace, Dublin, with a competent nurse who had orders not to take the baby out of Earlsfort Terrace until our return. This was in order to prevent the child from being dumped in the dirty house of one of her cronies. A friendly doctor or two used to look in unexpectedly on nurse and child, so all was well except for the wrench it must have been for my wife to leave her infant son at home and follow a medico to Vienna.

It was no easy thing to get suitable rooms in that then great city. At last we rented the large chambers that had been the apartment of Krafft-Ebing, author of *Psychopathia Sexualis* and of course the instigator of that enemy of the human race, Freud.

What would you expect but sex in Vienna? It was protruding under my very nose. This was the way. After my wife had left, when I was settled, I gave up a large part of the apartment. One evening when my day at the hospital was done, I noticed the black and yellow uniform on a coachman and a footman who sat on the box seat of an ambling brougham but I paid little attention. On the stairs to my apartment stood a deeply veiled figure. I entered my room. I could hear the sounds of love-making intensely intimate coming from the other room! The lovers spoke English of all tongues – what a language to make love in! This obviously so as not to be understood if the landlady, who had rented the room as a rendezvous, overheard them.

> What they did, who may tell?
> But I do think 'twas nothing more
> Than you and I have done before
> With Bridget and with Nell.

Not wishing to be an eavesdropper, I went out, and slammed the other door as I went. Inadvertently I had locked the lovers in, for when I returned, darkling, from the Café Clinic at the end of the lane, I found a hole large enough to permit a person passing through cut in the great door. What would all the secrecy and precaution have availed a lady from the palace of K.K. Franz Joseph if a lady in waiting or whatever she was had stayed out all night? Obviously the officer had used his sabre.

What a city was Vienna in the last days of the Emperor! He was doddering. They used to tell the tale of how, when he opened the Donau Canal, all he had to do was to press an electric button to admit *Der Strom*. That is what they call the Danube there; but *Strom* is also the word used for the electric current. 'What?' asked the Emperor as he hesitated to admit *Der Strom*. 'Do you expect me to drown myself?'

The most civilised city in Europe; a city of music and the waltz, the city where even the girls in the kiosks are embalmed in love, city of the most ineffectual army in the world – not even excepting the Portuguese – and therefore all the more civilised. So civilisedly inefficient was its army that it was almost defeated by its only victory; for when it took Cordona's Italian army prisoner there were no regulations as to how to dispose of a captured force. The indiscretion has never been repeated.

In Vienna there were no trained nurses. Feudalism did not permit its daughters to do menial work unmarried, so nurses were recruited from retired streetwalkers. These administered the anaesthetics to a dozen women at a time in the gynaecological clinic; the doctor started when the patient snored. Surgery was savagery in the Vienna of 1907. There was a flag to be flown over that great hospital, the Krankenhaus, if one day passed without some inmate dying. I never saw it flown.

When I returned to Dublin I found it an easy town in which to obtain a livelihood. With my father and grandfather doctors before me, it was not hard to acquire a practice. I had had a thorough course in Vienna, where I studied under Bàràny and Alexander for ear work; under Chiari and Hajek for throat and nose. And I had something new in instruments – Bruning's bronchoscope. A bronchoscope is a tube with a bracketed handle in which there is a small electric bulb to illuminate the tube so that you can see directly into the lungs or gullet.

I was the first to bring the instrument to Ireland and, for that matter, England; but the code is strict in Dublin; medical etiquette there forbids advertisement. Since then I have noticed that certain surgeons in England and America have claimed the bronchoscope as their own so that a gullible public might think they had invented it.

The next thing was to acquire a house. Sir Thornley Stoker, whom I consulted, advised me to take the house in which Sir Thomas Dean, the architect of the National Library and Museum, lived. It was a Queen Anne house 'modernised' by Sir Thomas. It had a bronze Florentine knocker on the hall door and that decided me.

Sir Thornley himself lived in the great house in Ely Place which was built circa 1770 by the Marquis of Ely. It was nine windows wide; but three of them had been embodied in another house into which Sir Thomas placed Dr O'Dwyer Joyce. Sir Thornley wished to keep up the status of Ely Place and he did not hesitate to sacrifice his friends. Dr O'Dwyer Joyce made a large income by moving when he took a house in Merrion Square, the Harley Street of Dublin, which the wags called 'The Valley of the Shadow of Death'.

Sir Thomas Dean, according to Sir Thornley, was very hard up, so hard up that he would take eight hundred pounds, which in those days was worth far more than that, for 'A house built by an architect for an architect,' so Sir Thornley put it. Now it is not in me to take advantage of a man's property. I offered fifteen hundred for the place and so revived did Sir Thomas Dean become that it took my outraged man of business a week before he beat the unfortunate Dean down to twelve hundred and fifty. I never regretted taking Sir Thornley's advice. Though, of course, I would have made much more money had I followed O'Dwyer Joyce to the Valley of the Shadow of Death. I had enough to carry on; and what more does or should one want?

I stayed on in Ely Place. My house was at the end on the west side, for Ely Place ends in a cul-de-sac. The east side is longer, by five houses. In the fourth and second last of these dwelt George Moore. Moore used to say that Stoker lived in the eighteenth century because he had to live contemporaneously with the stucco of his home, called Ely House, which had the best stucco work of any of the Georgian houses in Dublin. All the good houses were Georgian because Dublin, the seventh city of Christendom, was built in the eighteenth century. It is the best thing that Orangemen ever built. Whether or not that be the cause, Sir Thornley – I was too young and too humble to call him Stoker, which was Moore's way of addressing the surgeon and of exalting himself and reminding Stoker that he was one of the landed gentry and owner of Moore Hall on lovely Lough Carra in County Mayo – did have stucco work of the best period. It was austere and graceful, not florid and over-flowery as the debased stucco of a later time.

Ely Place was closed by two gates which were the gates that protected the city at night before policemen took the place of the inadequate watchmen. These gates, if closed, would shut off the five houses in Upper Ely Place. These houses were built in 1800 and they were built of a different colour brick, which to me was a historical reminder of the ruin caused to Dublin by the Act of Union, passed by bribery and fraud in the very year those houses were built. The gates were rusty; they belonged to no one. I had them removed.

Life was very pleasant in 15 Ely Place. The teeming town was outside and unobtrusive. There was silence, and trees and a greensward in our cul-de-sac. George Moore kept the garden, and I gazed out on its greenery and composed verses while I waited for patients. Sir Thomas sent me the first. I was a 'specialist' on Nose, Throat and Ear; and if you specialise and are comparatively unknown, you have to wait until some colleague or other recommends patients to consult you. It was very kind of Sir T. and the faith he had in me was very touching. Then Sir Thornley Stoker, who had a rich and fashionable practice, saw to it that I remained solvent in Ely Place.

The next question was the matter of a hospital affiliation. Without a hospital after your name, practice in Dublin, and in any other city as far as I know, is greatly retarded. My luck came abruptly.

'The Board of the Richmond Hospital has the honour to invite Dr Oliver St. John Gogarty to meet Sir William Thompson in the Board Room on Wednesday morning, prox. at 9 a.m.' It was signed by all the members of the senior staff.

It should be understood that a student as a rule when he becomes a doctor does not hang around the hospital where he was trained. I did not. So what was the meaning of this epistle? We'll see.

Impatiently I waited until Wednesday dawned. I drove

over across the Liffey and up long and narrow Church Street, so called because of St. Michen's Church where they show visitors how the limy exudate preserves corpses, to the New Richmond with its bronze-capped towers. The members of the Board were formal and at the same time courteous. After some polite meaningless words, Sir William announced, 'You will perform for me a low tracheotomy on a patient whom you will find waiting in the auxiliary theatre. I will await your diagnosis.' So I was to operate in front of all the staff. What could that mean? It could mean that I was being tested, put through my paces; but for what?

A girl, about eighteen years of age, was waiting in the annexe to the large theatre. She was already anaesthetised, not too deeply. The anaesthetist told me that it required very little ether to put her asleep. I kept that in my mind. I took a stethoscope and examined heart and chest although there was a full report on her chart. I referred to the chart after I had made my own examination. I could see that the procedure registered favourably for me with the staff.

I did a low tracheotomy. 'When doing a tracheotomy never turn downwards the blade of the knife.' Well I remembered. Why low? Why was such an operation necessary? I could not go into that. I was obeying an invitation to operate. I had inserted the tube when by some awkwardness of a nurse it came out. When I tried to put it back, a dark object had moved up from the thorax and obstructed any approach to the trachea. It was the innominate vein, which had been pushed up from the thorax by multiple neoplasms, new growths. The poor girl suffered from lympho-sarcomata. That is why I found her chest semi-solid. That is why she went off at the first whiff of ether. I announced my finding to the staff. They had known all along this was a case of multiple sarcomata; but they liked to hear another opinion.

In a month I was invited to join the Richmond Hospital as Visiting Surgeon for cases of Nose, Throat and Ear in the place of Dr Robert Woods who had resigned. Why had he resigned? Sir Thornley and he were such close friends that Woods's eldest son was called Thornley. Woods, whose reputation was beginning to be international, was making too much money as a junior member of the staff. He had often, without knowing it, anticipated Sir Thornley in Naylor's Antique Shop and at many an auction of antiques. This, to a connoisseur, is an unforgivable fault.

It is all right to make money and flaunt it as you may; but to use it to thwart the man who considers that he has made you, no, oh, no! 'Sharper than a serpent's tooth,' etc. So life was made impossible for Dr Woods. He left the Richmond and I took his place. He was welcomed to Sir Patrick Dun's Hospital, which was quite close to his house, 39 Merrion Square. So I owed my election to hospital politics more than to any skill I possessed. I kept that in mind. I could not publicise the knowledge; but it prevented me from having a swelled head. I was the youngest surgeon on the staff. Shut up! You owe your job to a dispute and nothing else. Don't fool yourself. If you do, no one can lend you a hand. I remained a fast friend of Dr Woods until his death and that goes to show that he didn't resent my taking his job and that I did not fool myself into thinking that I had won it by any merit of my own.

I learned a great deal in the external department of the Richmond Hospital. But I was not out of hospital politics yet. One day an old friend of mine, the doctor who saved my little son's life when he had an undiagnosed appendicial abscess, called on my wife. They had had a long conversation before I appeared. Would I resign the Richmond and join the Meath Hospital, to which he belonged? There would be no entry fee in my case.

Let me explain. The doctors of the Meath, as in any other teaching hospital, except perhaps those religious hospitals where the money first goes to the Reverend Mother, cut up the students' fees among them. These fees, in prosperous times, came to many hundreds of pounds annually. Therefore, to get into the group of doctors, an entry fee of some fifteen hundred pounds or more is exacted. There would be no such fine in my case. I asked myself how much the Richmond Hospital means in private practice – nothing; but the Meath had the servants of all the rich people in the best parts of the city. It is also the County Dublin Infirmary and, as such, subject to some control or direction of the Dublin Corporation. Then he told me privately that the staff of the Meath were in a quandary because the Dublin Corporation wanted to nominate a certain Roman Catholic doctor to the staff. In my case the qualifications were higher; was I not an M.D. of Dublin University and a Fellow of the Royal College of Surgeons as well? My religion was right – not left – so, if I joined the staff of the Meath Hospital at once, the Dublin Corporation would be beaten to the draw; and they couldn't say a word against the election of a man with higher qualifications than their own nominee. The most important consideration was the selection of a staff member who would remain with the members of the staff, not with the Dublin Corporation.

I did as my friend advised. I sent in my resignation to the Richmond Hospital. It was not accepted, so for a long time I had two hospitals and double work. I was so busy that I often came home half anaesthetised myself by the ether fumes.

Now that you realise how hospital appointments are made and what is the deciding factor, you will forgive me if I do not take myself too seriously as a surgeon. Perhaps I was the exception that proves the rule. If so, I will grant you that I was exceptional.

There are some avocations which bring the representative in constant touch with the rich: architects, portrait painters, jewellers, antique dealers and picture dealers; but these people know only those who are rich whereas a doctor knows everyone, rich and poor; especially the poor because every morning he has to devote his hours to treating them. If he sticks to one part of the profession, that is, if he is a 'specialist' – a word hateful to Sir Thornley – his colleagues send him their patients and so he knows all the country. That explains how I, who was not born to the purple, got to know those who were.

16 *Dunsany*

The old road from Glendalough to Tara crossed the Liffey at the Hurdle Ford and thence, inclining to the northwest, passed between two strongholds, the castles of Killeen and Dunsany, about a mile apart, which straddled the road and took toll of travellers to and from Tara and Glendalough. I asked Mahaffy, who was an authority on everything, if the name 'Dunsany' was not derived from 'dun', a stronghold; and the river Skene which flows through the grounds? 'The most obvious derivations are usually incorrect.' So I gave up, having to satisfy myself with the derivation of Killeen, which means 'the little church'. Killeen Castle is held to the present day by the senior branch of the family of Plunkett, a name said to be derived from *blanche jenet*. There are two white jennets supporting the arms of Dunsany which are cut in stone over one of the gates. Both strongholds are in the territory of Fingall, or the Fair Strangers who occupied the eastern shelf of the fertile land which lies roughly between the rivers Boyne and Liffey and extends to Baldoyle, Baile dhu Gall, the land of the Dark Strangers of whom Tom Kettle was so proud.

The Fair Strangers were not only the Normans who subdued the Irish Pale which comprises the district but their ancestors too, who settled on the north coast of France three centuries earlier than the coming of the Plunketts to Fingall. The family of Plunkett traces its ancestry back to one Rollo, the Dane, who settled in Normandy in the year 800.

Killeen Castle, founded in 1181, was the larger of the two, as it is today. Castles of this kind were usually built on a *motte* or mound which was protected by a wooden stockade; but there is little reason to think that such was the origin of either Killeen or Dunsany. There is no trace of a mound on the actual site of either, though there are two large mounds in front of Dunsany.

Originally, such castles consisted of four square towers which formed a yard to hold horses, and cattle gathered from outlying herds in the event of a raid. These towers formed a definite pattern: the ground floors had the thickest walls and their roof consisted of an arch, not domed or groined but cylindrical. In the course of building, the cylinder was curved over bundles of brushwood which were set on fire to dry the mortar and fix the arch for the support of the floor above. In the east tower of Killeen the marks of the bundles of brushwood may still be seen on the mortar of the roof. At a much later period the connecting or curtain walls were raised almost to the height of the towers and pierced with windows to form the rooms of a patrician residence – all things being now at peace.

The entrance to Dunsany Castle is through a studded door under a four-centred, Gothicised arch in the western tower. On top of this tower, immune from noise, Dunsany dreams and composes. The only noise that could reach a resident less protected would be the not exotic sound of lowing herds or the crowing of a cock; but these might be mixed with the crunch of gravel under the tyres of unappreciative visitors. From such as these we find 'The Captain closit in his tower'.

Probably General Hammond, Dunsany's steward, when in Dublin at the sale of Sir Thornley Stoker's collection, was responsible for introducing me to Dunsany Castle. The general was sent to recover a prunus vase, one of a pair that used to be among the treasures in Dunsany. It was taken away by the curio-loving Sir Thornley when he went posthaste to attend the maimed butler whose arm had been blown off by a cannon. If I remember rightly it cost his present lordship eighty guineas to recover it.

The next incident was an invitation for my wife and me

to a ball at Dunsany. Now hunt balls are fashionable; and of these the Royal Meath Hunt, called 'royal' from Tara of the Kings, which lies in the heart of Meath, are the most fashionable even though they are subscription balls. A private ball is quite a higher thing.

This was a private ball. While it was in full swing I wandered through the castle searching for a place where I could sit in quiet and get the spirit of the ball without the action; for I am averse to group enjoyments of any kind. At last I found a settee in a corner of one end of which sat a tall young man biting a fingernail. His hair was fair, his forehead extraordinarily high, noble and unfurrowed. His mouth, which a slight moustache did not conceal, was imperious with a clear chin line under the cold beauty of eyes and brow. He looked as if he belonged to a race aloof from the pathos of the common concerns of mankind. It was my host, Lord Dunsany.

I took a seat beside him: there was none other to be had. I must have passed some remark about the ball. I am sure I did. I hope, that it matters little now, that it was not disparaging. Perhaps he would not have cared what I said, for he appeared to be avoiding the ball as much as I. He was tolerant for, before he left, I quoted all Herrick's *Hesperides* and I was about to start on his *Noble Numbers* when somebody drew my audience away.

That was the first of many times that I was his guest. He knew Herrick as well as I did. He knew Kipling. The first did not influence him as much as Herrick influenced me. Kipling, perhaps. But no poet likes to acknowledge that he is beholden to an older – or a contemporary one! You will look in vain for any of Kipling's jingoism in Dunsany's writings. Dunsany has travelled as much as Kipling, but he was not a commercial traveller by any means.

Dunsany's earlier poems tell of the wonders he saw when the hills of Africa looked like crumpled rose leaves in the setting sun. They tell of his thoughts by campfires and on the many journeys he made. They tell of the glamour of wild, unspoiled places in his *Mirage Water*. His is a

Vergilian regret that civilisation is the enemy of old simplicity:

> . . . a glamour lost to woodlands
> Which were old when Caesar came.

'Old when Caesar came': with such things he is familiar.

Horseman, soldier, sportsman, poet and playwright, Dunsany is the most representative man I know. His is a full life, a life I would choose were I not content with my own. It does me good to visit him; and the effect of those visits I have tried to record in the sonnet's 'narrow room'. As I say, I am a highbrow and as such I make no excuse for this my traffic with the Muse:

DUNSANY CASTLE

> The twin dunes rise before it and beneath
> Their tree-dark summits the Skene River flows;
> And old, divine, earth exaltation glows
> About it though no longer battles breathe;
> For Time puts all men's swords in his red sheath;
> And softlier now the air from Tara blows:
> Thus on the royalest ground that Ireland knows
> Stands your sheer house in immemorial Meath:
> It stands for actions done and days endured,
> Old causes God, in guiding Time, espoused
> Who never brooks the undeserving long.
> I found there pleasant places filled with song,
> (And never were the Muses better housed)
> Repose and dignity and fame assured.

17 *Sir Horace Plunkett*

When first I knew Sir Horace Plunkett he was one of those figures who are not only accepted as great but can be used to show how backward you are if you cannot see in what their greatness consists. In these days if Sir Horace is mentioned it is because he was Lord Dunsany's uncle. Then Dunsany was Sir Horace's nephew.

Sir Horace had secretaries, and to give them something to do, he wrote letters to *The Times* both in London and in New York, and he even gave gratuitous advice to the governor of South Africa. He became a member of Parliament. You are not to read into this an example of cause and effect.

The British Government made him Minister for Agriculture. Then his secretaries were in a turmoil of turnips, mangolds and brussels sprouts. Cattle, corn, cheeses and poultry, hackneys, mules, jennets and jackasses had to be treated by statistics. There was an abundance, if not of poultry, of things to be done. Sir Horace had no time. He couldn't take a holiday. Those who did not know him feared for his health. Little did I imagine that I would be a recipient of one of his letters. Yet I was. Here it is:

Royal Irish Automobile Club
Dublin

Dear Sir,

A complaint has been lodged with the Club and submitted to the Committee who in due course passed it on to me as President of the R.I.A.C.

It would appear that on Tuesday evening last at dusk you drove at an alarming speed through the village of Cabinteeley and ran over a duck just outside that village in the direction of Dublin. You failed to stop, and, to all accounts and appearances took no notice whatsoever of the accident.

The complainant is John Nolan of Merrion Cottage, Cabinteeley.

I hesitate to act as judge in this matter until I shall have heard both sides; but, as we motorists are a small group who depend on the goodwill of the public, it is but common sense not to arouse any ill feelings either by speeding or ignoring any accidents which may ensue.

It is to all our interests that satisfactory reparation should be made to John Nolan for the loss of his duck and that you or your chauffeur should drive at a reasonable pace in the future.

It is not without reluctance that I write this letter; but our interests as motorists are seriously involved and those interests are prevailing.

Yours faithfully,
Horace Plunkett, President.

'Sidney's sister, Pembroke's mother!' I don't know why I made that exclamation. I knew that Sir Horace would be president of any club which he could form or which would invite him. He is an unsuppressible President, Chairman, Controller, Consultant Unveiler and Director of his own or others' creations. I bet that the Royal Irish Automobile Club is his idea. The contradiction of 'Royal' and 'Irish' is obviously Horatian. It lies behind the ineffectuality of all his efforts for 'Ireland'. I learned that from Griffith. I had to assure him that I had nothing to do with the club when I showed him Sir Horace's letter.

But the letter, worse luck, requires an answer. I must write something that will be final and put a stop to Sir Horace and his secretaries tilting at ducks. Sir Horace is in his element when writing letters, especially those addressed to an editor. However, the only publicity he can get out of me is to make a mountain – forgive the mixture of the metaphor – out of John Nolan's duck.

I began 'Dear Sir'. Then I realised that 'Dear Mr President' would be more agreeable. He is not my President so I hope that he won't think 'Dear Mr President' is placatory. Here goes:

Dear Mr President,

Thanks for your letter. I have killed John Nolan's duck twice. On the third occasion when the opportunity was presented to me I refused to be an accessory before or after its death.

The first time was about a week ago. The duck crossed the road and flew with the greatest reluctance under my wheels. It was pulled by a string which, when I got out of the car to discuss the 'accident', had disappeared. I gave the aggrieved owner, a surly fellow, one pound which is about five times the price of a duck.

The second accident took place the following evening. This time I found the string. The duck was dead when I killed it. I pointed this out to the owner who refused to give me his address. I am glad that you have it and his name. Pulling a dead duck across the public highway at dusk may not be an offence in the eyes of the law; but it is surely a matter for the Society for the Prevention of Cruelty to Animals.

May I point out that, as you drive frequently on the Bray Road, you yourself are in imminent danger of killing John Nolan's duck in spite of the fact that by this time *rigor mortis* must have set in.

Yours faithfully

That touch about the Society for the Prevention of Cruelty to Animals comes well from 'yours faithfully' as you will see; but it will give Sir Horace a vent, so to speak. He will not write to me any more but bring the case of Nolan's duck to the notice of the committee, probably the same set of ladies that called on me, and eventually become Chairman of the S.P.C.A. now that a new source of cruelty to animals in the shape of the automobile is found.

Revising my letter, I liked 'imminent danger'; it is one of those clichés that are inseperable from the noun, like 'aching' void. It will alarm Sir Horace. Think of the President of the Royal Irish Automobile Club running over a duck. That may be all very fine for a doctor to do – after all, there is an association between quacks and ducks – but for *the* President!

It is very easy to make jokes but very hard not to promulgate them. That is why I did not send the letter about the duck and *rigor mortis* to Sir Horace. There was another reason: Who was I to set myself up as an equal to men of the stamp of Sir Horace? That is one way of getting yourself considered to be an upstart, so the letter I will send will not be impertinent but one of thanks for drawing my attention to the incident; and it will state that Nolan is exploiting the new form of transport, motoring. That will be enough. No mention of the S.P.C.A. and no such address as 'Mr President' – just 'Dear Sir Horace Plunkett'. I remembered how I resented the familiarity with which a shirtmaker wrote to me. He had taken advantage of an introduction in the United Services Club. As a doctor I can meet anyone but that's no reason for taking advantage.

Sir Horace is the brother of that Lord Dunsany who charged a cannon full of double cracks; and, when it would not go off, ordered his butler to see what was staying the explosion. The butler thrust his arm full length down the cannon's bore. There was a sudden burst. The butler's arm was blown off. Sir Thornley Stoker was summoned from Ely Place. What he did I do not know; but I do know that he took a prunus vase with him back to Dublin. Maybe he settled for the vase. Who knows? Maybe, when Lord Dunsany's man of business wrote to ask Sir Thornley what his honorarium was (Sir Thornley, who was of the old school, always spoke of his fees as his 'honorarium', for who can pay a doctor all he owes?), it was another matter.

I hope that I know enough to take a hint from Sir Thornley's effort at ingratiating himself with Lord Dunsany and not make a pup of myself.

No, the furthest I will go will be to show Sir Horace's letter at Moore's dinner next Saturday. Moore does not like Sir Horace. He blames him for sooting up his garden by smoke from the chimney of the Board of Works which lies between his garden and Stephen's Green. But if it isn't the smoke it will be something else, for Moore has to find fault with everyone since he is not happy with himself. He held the great Mahaffy up to ridicule when he compared him, with his side whiskers, to a butler; and, though he is a friend more or less of Diana, Dr Tyrrell's intelligent daughter, he is trying to find fault with her father, who is not only one of the greatest scholars living but one of the greatest wits. What a fool Moore will be if he tries to contend with Tyrrell in a battle of wits. Can it be that he who is a cause of wit in others resents their wit?

I have not forgiven Moore for his attempt at wit when my mother called on him to object to the use of my name in his novel, *The Lake*.

'Madame, if you can find me a name which is composed

of two dactyls, like the name of your son Oliver, I will substitute it for Oliver Gogarty.'

Perhaps it was some dim memory of this that brought the quotation about 'Sidney's sister, Pembroke's mother' into my head. *Pembroke* is a sound equivalent for *Plunkett*, and *Sidney* for *Horace.* It was not easy to live a dactylic life if you are born a spondee. – Geōrge Mōōre!

I was so right as occasion proved. Sir Horace later on consulted me as a doctor. Years later. He telephoned, it was a matter of the greatest secrecy, a 'top secret' in fact. He was going to the front. Had he not been at Eton with Haig? The only thing that had deterred him from going there long ago was the want of a 'national purpose'. He had found one: Irish girls, nurses of course, were to nurse American wounded. Irishmen would follow of course. All Ireland would join in the war. The idea for the moment must be kept a dead secret. And he was bringing me! I was weak enough not to refuse. Who could refuse Sir Horace when he wanted something. Meanwhile, I had to carry the secret: I couldn't open my heart to anyone. And I was getting more and more nervous. The fact that generals were never killed did little to comfort me. I thought of getting the soles of my boots painted white just in case!

He would let me know in a week. Meanwhile, mum was the word.

I saw the two of us seated in a railway carriage in Westland Row on our way to the front. I had solved somehow the problem of what to wear. Sir Horace would see to that. We were seated just waiting for the soft steam to enter the cylinders and to bear us off to the Front. The train started. We were off! Suddenly, Sir Horace leapt up. He had left the national purpose on the platform. 'Stop the train!' The station master rushed up to ask what was the matter. 'That suitcase there!' The station master looked at a solitary suitcase but one that was all important. It contained the 'national purpose'. I woke from the nightmare. It was not until a week later that Sir Horace accused me of letting out his secret. It seemed that some members of the Kildare Street Club had asked him in a railing manner, 'Horrie, where are your tabs?'

But I had had a narrow escape. Of course, I never revealed the secret. Quite possibly Sir Horace himself did.

18 *The White Lady*

On an evening in December I was walking home with Newburn, who lived on the south side of Stephen's Green. It was about 6 p.m. and quite dark. He asked me into his house. I waited in the hall while he searched for the light switch. He did not find it. Instead I heard him fumbling in a closet under the stairs. At last he emerged and lighted the hall. He looked perturbed. 'Say nothing about it to my wife,' he said. 'I saw the White Lady coming down the stairs when I came in. I thought she had hidden herself under it. There was no sign of her. I searched with my foot to where the stairs meet the floor. That's what delayed me.' The house is old enough to have a ghost, I thought.

Then I asked, 'Who is the White Lady?'

'I'll show you her miniature as soon as we go up. Don't worry about it now.'

When we reached the drawing room there was no sign of Mrs Newburn. Her husband went to the mantelpiece and took down a miniature, framed in pinchbeck, of a young woman, half length, dressed in white. 'For God's sake keep this and take it out of the house. It may put an end to her walking.'

Mrs Newburn, a quiet woman, appeared. We had some desultory talk, she glanced at the vacant place where the miniature had been but she made no remark. Soon I took my leave. When I got home, I put the miniature in a drawer and forgot about it for many years. When I found it, seeing that nothing had happened, I put it in the back drawing room over the mantel. Years later when I took it down – I must have been telling someone about it – the blue paper at the back had come loose and showed some writing in faded ink. 'Mary Medlicott drowned at sea when crossing from Barbados 1771.' So that was the name of the White Lady. I wondered if she or her people had been the owners of Newburn's house. The painting on ivory was the work of the eighteenth-century artist, Nathaniel Hone. It was a valuable gift that Newburn had given me.

Newburn was the greatest athlete I had ever known. He could always break evens for the hundred-yard dash *except in competition*. One fine evening I went out to Ballsbridge, where I had permission to train by courtesy of the Royal Dublin Society. Newburn was practising the broad jump. After a few tries by way of warming up, he told us to stand by and be ready to measure his next jump. He took what I considered to be a very long run. He rose high in the air with his legs pulled up under him and his hands forward. Out came the long legs. He had landed. He swayed; thrust his head forward and threw out his arms. Old Stevens was there, who represented the Amateur Athletic Association; 'old' Stevens the boys called him, and it was not used in his case as a term of endearment. He had a tall silk hat and a frock coat. He was a small red-nosed man who took himself very seriously. Why is it that we permit unathletic old fogies to get into responsible places in athletics?

I took the chain with, I think, Tom Cronin, one of the trainers. Newburn had jumped twenty-seven feet eleven inches. 'Mr Stevens, come and look at this.' It was no use. A world's record, and far more than a world's record, had been made; but Stevens was mulish. 'Can he not jump back too? The wind may have been in his favour.' I lit a match. It burned without a flicker in the calm air. 'Do you want me to break my ankles?' was all that Newburn said. Of course, there was no turf mould for a jump in the opposite direction. A few of the boys who were training came to look at the astounding jump. They spoke to Stevens, who tried to put on dignity; was he not the representative of the

A.A.A.? 'God blast you, anyway.' Newburn was not the only man to be spanceled by stupidity.

Newburn must have been six feet six. He was, as I said a wonderful man. He could pitch the fifty-six pound weight higher over the bar than anyone in Ireland. The fifty-six pound weight competition was discontinued as a result. Why he did not run in the 220 I could never make out. An athlete, a runner, is said to be at his fastest at 135 yards. Newburn should have done under twenty-one seconds for the 220 in practice. In competition he was useless. He must have had a faint heart. Maybe it was not in athletics. He seemed not to set much value on his jump and he cared not when the fifty-six pound weight was abolished.

For a year or so he was in the habit of going to London. Eventually, he became 'elocutionist' to Eton College, which meant that he taught stutterers and those with inhibited speech. He showed me a few of his cases: deaf mutes whom he had taught to speak. Infinite patience was required for this. Infinite patience he had. Perhaps it was this patience that accounted for the light way he treated Stevens, who had deprived him of a record, unofficial as it might have been. I remember that Stevens, among other objections, had said, 'He has not jumped in competition.' As for his treating deaf mutes: I put down the fact that I was invited to meet Dr Moure of Marseilles to examine Don Jaime, one of the sons of the Kip of Spain, to my friend Newburn. Perhaps someone in Eton had heard him speak of me. I did not go because I knew that no treatment could give hearing to one who was born deaf. To teach such a one to speak was another thing; and that was Newburn's business.

19 *The House Of The White Garden*

Man is the measure of all things. Where did I hear that? At school, when the teacher told us that Protagoras held that not universal humanity was the touchstone, but man as an individual. 'Nothing can appear to you as it appears to me.' And Protagoras was the most famous of the Sophists. We are in the age of sophists again. Karl Marx is the greatest scoundrel of them all.

We need not go into that just here; but when I say that man is the measure of all things, I don't mean what the wily Sophist meant about two thousand five hundred years ago, but man as the whole of humanity. I do not mean that a blind man cannot be proved wrong if you accept Protagoras, but I mean that to universal man a limitation must exist.

He has to be his own norm: to him the whale and the elephant are large, the fly and the streptococcus small. He talks of a normal climate. What is his norm but his own temperature of 98.6 degrees Fahrenheit? He cannot think of anything without a beginning; he can hear only within eight or nine octaves; he can see only the colours of the spectrum; and yet he prides himself on his health, his pedigree, his colour, his inheritance and his nationality, all of which are outside his control; all matter of what we call good luck.

I was priding myself on my children as I walked with a son on either shoulder down a tunnel of hawthorn, willow, ash and alder to the sea. One son was brown, the other fair. All the forethought in the world could not have influenced Nature's lucky bag when they were born sound and lively! And what am I doing now but congratulating myself on something I could not help? Even Julius Ceasar believed in the goddess Fortune, who favoured him more than most men.

In Connemara, Garranban House stands on a rounded hill with trees on either side, a lake to the south, a landlocked bay to the north. It was a good place for the holidays; and my hospitable sister-in-law invited us all.

I was teaching the boys to swim. In Ballynakill Bay the water was brimming, tide-full and clear. The water made no ripple on the gravel. It shone with an opalescence that recalled the colours of spilled oil. The children had been taught to put their faces in a basin of water and to blow bubbles. They loved the game and it taught them how to control their breathing when it came to teaching them how to swim. The water won't get into their mouths and cause a panic.

Out I was, waist-high. I pay in a son until he is merged. I tell him that the lower he goes the more buoyant he will be. He floats along until he is stranded. The next step is to let him strike out; but not too fast. 'Turn your face sideways when you want a breath.' My dark son was conscientious: he put no leg on the bottom while he stroked with his arms; he did not keep time; that will come later. The fair son swam well. Then I noticed that he had one leg on the bottom. Well, well; don't let them get chilled. Home we go.

Looking back, I realise that those were the happiest days of my life. Did I realise it then? From what I know of myself I must have done so, but not as much as I do in retrospect.

This retrospectful look is what makes a Golden Age. That age was mine and it was contemporary. I had attained the greatest happiness that man can reach. I had dwelt in the Golden Age. Who can realise it fully until he leaves it, or it leaves him?

Who was I to be so blest? This is an enigma that I must refer to my Lord Mayor of Dublin, Larry O'Neill, who will, playing for safety as is his wont, answer with 'There I leave you.' As you cannot answer it yourself and as the chief citizen evades the subject, you can only fall back on the cliché, 'The ways of God are inscrutable.' They have little to do with desert.

As I let the boys run homewards a strange sight met my eyes. A man stood upside down in a field; at least so it appeared at a distance. On coming closer, I found Snodgrass, the artist from Birmingham to whom, with his wife, my generous sister-in-law had lent a house by the beach of the bay Rossdhu. His head was bent down between his legs; his backside towards me. A breech presentation! Odd! He was not studying astronomy with his hinder part, as the merry bard suggested that another 'artist' was doing long ago. No, he was getting a fresh view of the scenery with a different and unused part, so he said, of his retina! Odder still; but then you must be prepared for anything from an artist. They have different ways of looking at things from the more common folk.

Snodgrass had been recommended to me by my friend McElroy, one of the most generous and enthusiastic men I ever met; this is out of the character attributed to Scotsmen by those who seek to denigrate whole nations to distract attention from themselves. He sent Snodgrass to Ireland during the war. Snodgrass was rejected by the recruiting station to which he had to present himself because of chronic mastoiditis and a large polypus in his left ear. No subject for hardship and the trenches, but an eligible visitor from Birmingham. he was now with us in the Many Coloured Land.

So this morning I find him upside down studying Diamond Mountain, that glistens when the rain lights its quartz. The painting which he exhibited in Dublin proved that he had seen it with a fresh eye. I wish I had bought that landscape, seen by a foreign artist; but I was intent on having the children painted, and so they were. The painting, sadly mutilated by the louts whom an alien loosed on the country when he plunged it into civil war, still exists, patched up by some expert in Chelsea. So do three magnificent water colours of the children.

What a refreshing sight the Twelve Bens – or Benna Buela as the Gaelic has it – at whose head stands Diamond Mountain, must have been to a youth born in Birmingham and raised beside its underground canals. The Twelve Bens form a massif with twelve peaks which lies between Kylemore Lakes on the north and the lakes round Ballinahinch on the south. To the east it is bounded by the long stretch of Lough Inagh; to the west is the town of Clifden and the plateau which falls down to Garranban.

To the east beyond the Twelve Bens runs the only fjord in Ireland's coast. It is called Killary Harbour. It is said that a whole squadron of the British fleet could anchor in it; the only objection to that is the fact that one submarine at its mouth could hold the squadron.

It is not the long drive by the side of the Killary that enticed me out but the restlessness of a holiday on which you want to 'go places' regardless of whether they are interesting or not. But nobody can say that Leenane at the head of Killary Harbour is not interesting. It is full of interest, or of that feeling that you are missing something.

That is a delusion from which I suffer: I want to get the sentiment of a place whether it is there or not. To the denizens the village must be the hell of a bore when tourists are not about. They have nothing unusual to look for but the village idiot, and he has become a part of the local scene.

A word must be said about the village idiot and about village idiots in general. There is one, or there should be one, to every village in Ireland. In cases where villages have become overgrown and turned into towns, the village idiot is not so recognisable. He may have been elected to Parliament; anyway, he is not as easily found as in the more countrified hamlets where he is spoken of as 'a natural' and has been accepted as a part of the community, just as the odd thorn tree is accepted on the top of the fairy rath.

The Leenane 'natural' crossed the road as the car was coming to a stop. He had a sack, worn capelike across his shoulders though, for a wonder, it was not raining.

'Gar, come in outa that!' a voice called. He turned his head. So his name was Gar. Most of the naturals have no name or, if they have, a fellow such as I will go a long time before he finds it out.

The Leenane fool was spoiled by the tourists, who seized the chance of proving to themselves their own superiority by talking to him. But now after lunch there were few tourists about. I had a talk with the man who serviced cars in the garage across the road over from the hotel. After the usual exchange of compliments Jim told me that Gar had been abandoned by some tinkers, when he was about two or three years old, and widow Feeney insisted on taking care of him, which was better than letting him go to the workhouse. His name was Gar because it was the only sound he could make. The last census people wanted to know exactly how to register him. Naturally, they could get nowhere, so his surname was entered as blank on the files. He was called 'files' after that. His name was given to the recruiting sergeant as Gar Files and he would have been taken away to fight for 'freedom' – when is a fight not for freedom? – and to see the world, as the posters announced. He had a good chance of seeing the other world as well. But the widow Feeney tapped her forehead significantly and the sergeant nodded; and Gar Files was left to brood on ambition unfulfilled. So they thought; but the ways of a loony are wily. So were the sergeant's. They met in the adjoining village and Gar became a private in His Majesty's Expeditionary Force. Later, during the retreat from Mons, when the exhausted British soldiers fell asleep, cemented by their blood to the floor of some church, Gar woke up to find the beribboned uniform which had just been cut off a general beside him. Delighted, he put it on. The Germans came and took him prisoner. He was treated as a general while imprisoned and he received a general's pension from the British War Office. For all I know to the contrary, he has it still. Such is war.

I found Snodgrass admiring the weaver at his loom in a shed beside the tavern. He should have been admiring the scenery, I, in my ignorance, imagined.

It is hard to acknowledge that your ideas about art and artists are wrong. I was under the impression that a true artist would stand gaping at the wonderful colours among the mountains of the west. The only one who stood agape was Gar Files, and he was gaping not at the mountains, which he had seen to distraction, but at an automobile.

Don't think that idiots are amazed at anything new. Remember the story of the Congo natives who dismissed a hydroplane that landed on the river with 'White Man's juju'. As soon as Gar found out that it was not an army lorry to take him to the battlefield his gaping ceased.

Yes, Snodgrass would have a drink. That was understandable. What I could not understand was his meek-and-mildness. It took me some time to realise that the man was in a strange country and his only armour was distrust. He would not trust even the army doctor who certified him as unfit. Our idiot wanted to join up; the artist did not. It takes a 'private person', as the Greek calls the idiot, to make a private soldier.

The waterfall of the river was flowing white. There was plenty of water in its winding stream. Off to the south the road rose, and the long drive through the Joyce Country began. Paudraic O'Malley's house was in the valley. Paudraic was the first man 'on the run'. The Black and Tans, irregular troops whom Lloyd George loosed on Ireland, riddled his house from a Lancia lorry on the road. You could see the bullets gleaming in the mortar. But Paudraic was never taken.

Somehow I did not want to take the artist any farther. He was not interested in the scenery, in spite of his looking at it between his legs! No, in spite of his fresh eye his painting of the Diamond lacks true atmosphere, which goes to show that you can be an artist without atmosphere. Could it be that that upside-down view was put on to fool me? I used to favour an upright outlook until I met this subterranean Birmingham boy.

Why is it that I don't want to drive through the Joyce Country? I used to love to dawdle on through scenery that defies definition and possesses, as no other scenery in the world does, a magic that is almost tangible. Instead I feel as if I were visiting the reptile house in some zoo. I must cure this sensitivity. Who would be a slave to sensation?

Things were silent at Garranban. Something had happened. The children had to be put to bed. What is wrong? Are they ill?

The information came with the reluctance of indignation: the children had been invited to the artist's cottage on the beach. They had come back drunk – my children. And not for the first time or I would not have mentioned it. Again that feeling of malaise.

20 *The Society For The Prevention Of Cruelty To Animals*

One afternoon while I was waiting for patients four of them were announced. At first I thought that there was but one who needed advice or treatment and that the others had come just to look on and feel superior to their friend. I was wrong. None of them was in need of my services as a doctor but they asked if I would preside at a meeting for the prevention of cruelty to animals. It seemed that they were the committee. It took me a long time to satisfy them, if satisfy them I did, that my engagements prevented me from presiding at a meeting for a purpose that was so near to my heart. They left in silence. And left me guessing.

At that moment I looked out on the garden and there was a black cat stalking George Moore's blackbird. As keeper of the bird during the day, I have a bow with half a dozen arrows all ready: the bow has only to be strung, the arrow fitted and through the open window . . . the cat was about fifty yards away or less. Often have I shot at that cat but never hit it. Sometimes my arrows deflect the cat from its quarry; sometimes I have to take the more undignified measure of shouting. This time, fortunately for the bird's sake and very unfortunately for mine, my arrow found its mark. The old ladies from the Committee of the Society for the Prevention, etc., must have guided the missile to punish me for refusing to preside at their meeting. In consternation I ran downstairs. As I did so I looked out through the little windows of the staircase. The cat had jumped the wall and was making off down the street after the committee with my accusing arrow, initials and all, stuck in his rump.

At that moment when despair was about to numb my faculties, a small boy knocked at the hall door. He was the boy with the evening papers. I opened the door and thrust a half crown into his palm. 'Drop the papers and get the arrow that is sticking into that cat.' For a wonder he comprehended. He turned and rushed after the animal, who was rapidly catching up with the committee. His bare foot pinned down the arrow just in time. He bore it back in triumph.

I restored the papers he had dropped and I was about to show my relief in another tip when I remembered that if I were too lavish it might arouse curiosity. He grinned with a conspirator's cunning. 'The cat got off,' he said. 'Next time shoot it in the head.'

Strange, this business about Cruelty to Animals and anti-vivisection societies. Old ladies all. In Latin countries there is unnecessary cruelty to horses. In England up to the time of Dickens there was cruelty to human beings. Even now the jails are sadistic, so is capital punishment although its theory is not an eye for an eye but that the criminal, having rendered himself anti-social, cannot justly be made a charge on the community, and must be killed. Was I to watch the blackbird being stalked and killed? Arrows a few inches off did not stop the cat, the only one that did was that attended by unfortunate circumstances. Had the old ladies rescued the cat and read my initials, which are unusual and unmistakable, on the arrow it would not have helped my career. I would have been branded as a monster. What is there for it but to offer to all such old ladies a compensatory poem?

God made the rat
And then above
The rat he placed
The playful cat
for GOD IS LOVE.

All of which touches the origin of Evil; and goes to show that there are exigencies; that Nature has tears: '*sunt lacrymae rerum*,' and so on.

21 *McGeehan*

One day as I was going out by the Front Gate, through which I had entered Trinity College ten years ago, the porters touched the peaks of their black velvet huntsman's hats. I returned the salute. Had I driven out in my automobile, then one of the half dozen in all Ireland, they might not have had as much respect for me, though the salutes would have shown little difference. College porters are opinion makers; they also make reputations which, once they are made, stick to a man for life. I am not 'a most superior person', I wish to be unassuming and to remain so.

College Green was in front of me with Grattan on a pedestal. His bronze figure addressed the college. His right hand was upraised. There was no mistaking his statue for that of an orator. I wondered if it were to be removed secretly by night how many citizens would miss it by day. A statue has come to be a subconscious landmark that no one notices; but don't remove the pedestal.

The half-circle of a Palladian masterpiece, the Bank of Ireland, which was Grattan's parliament house in the eighteenth century, was on my right with a gap in the middle of the curve, gaping for clients. Opposite, on the other side of the street, were three or four more banks. Traffic passed in a medley in front of the college. I felt like a bather taken by surprise, for doctors do not walk in the street.

That is a custom born of necessity, because a doctor is at the mercy of any of his acquaintances if he is caught in a public place; and, if he is caught, free advice can make hypochondriacs of us all. So the unwritten law is for doctors not to walk in the street; and I hope that I have explained the reason why. Take, for instance, the case of a gynaecologist ... now you see what I mean? It is not that doctors wish to pretend that they are busy; but they don't want to be consulted; accosted is the better word.

There is an exception I must admit. That exception is Dr Kegley, 'Surgeon' as he calls himself. At five o'clock every afternoon he may be seen – you can't miss him – walking up Grafton Street with his umbrella tightly reefed. He carries it with its muzzle pointing to the ground, its stock under his arm. He is coming from Jervis Street Hospital. Everyone knows that operations are all over in Dublin by noon. Kegley, who can operate only on hernias, wears a bowler hat; well, if that doesn't suggest a hernia; but you can't very well consult a man about a hernia in the open street, so Kegley is safe to stroll along the sidewalk with his umbrella tightened up. It may be a symbol of the tightened tendons of a corrected hernia; but 'there I leave you,' as Larry O'Neill said; Larry, the chronic Lord Mayor of Dublin. They tell me that I am too prone to look for symbols.

My misfortune was Hamish McGeehan. He stood with his shoulder pointed towards the college. He had seen me saluted by the porters; he was in wait. His greasy little eyes brightened as his podgy body turned. He, like Kegley, had an umbrella; but it was not tightly wrapped. His mouth was. Over his silver hair was a soft black hat which associated him with the Church, of which he was a blameless though insinuating son.

'I saw you coming out of Trinity College,' he said leaving me to defend myself for having belonged to such a black organisation. I looked at my watch.

'You'll have time to hear what your friend, George Moore's secretary, is supposed to have done.'

'Which one?' I asked, for I knew that George had two or three a year.

I knew that one of them had gone off to hide her pregnancy and to have her child in peace without the knowledge of the omniscient novelist. I also knew that pregnancy was not one of McGeehan's subjects nor was it one of his wife's for she led the fat and sexless life of a Chinese eunuch. He emphasised the 'friend' when he mentioned George Moore so that I would be sure to be in the wrong. If he were a man at all, I thought he would find something to laugh at in the supposedly omniscient – as far as women were concerned – Moore missing his secretary's condition, which was under his eyes. No; it must be something that is more discussable than sex and, if possible, worse.

'She has been stealing his manuscripts and selling them.'

I saw it all in a flash. I am afraid that my conscience is easy-going. The poor little woman wanted money badly to pay for her confinement, which had to be in the country to ensure privacy. Her morale was not helped by Moore's dictation. She took a bundle of his manuscript and 'went to see her mother', only to come back one.

'She hasn't stolen any of yours?' I asked.

The professor smiled as a man armed with a stiletto might smile.

'No,' he said. 'And I don't suppose that she'll bother to steal yours though you live in Ely Place.'

So it was a sin to live in Ely Place, contaminated as it was by the presence of George Moore!

'Miss Jago has been delivered of a fine boy: mother and child both doing well.'

'It has an official sound but for the "Miss". Who is Miss Jago?' I asked Hamish.

He smiled that smile of his which made you uneasy: it suggested that you either knew and were pretending you didn't, or that, if you didn't know, you were exposing your ignorance. The kind of smile that is called quizzical and it's not a bad name for it. I repeated the question snappily enough to stop that irritating smile.

'George Moore's secretary, of course. His present one. She told me that she had to go away to be with her mother.

Instead of that she went away to become a mother – all this, and he prides himself on his knowledge of women.'

I remembered Moore telling us that his secretary was away.

'What will he do when he finds out?'

'Why should he find out? Of course if fellows like you go about sneering he cannot help but find out,' I said.

'It's already all over the place.'

This is the kind of thing that would amuse Yeats, I thought. I shall have to wait until he hears it if it is 'all over the place'. I have secrets enough without adding an open secret to them. Yeats will take a different view from anyone. He will imagine Moore himself 'lying in', doing a kind of *couvade* as the primitive tribes do and receiving presents because his secretary has had a child. The more illegitimate the better for Moore. That will be Yeat's theory. But I cannot see Moore tolerating any scandals that affect himself; scandals are all very well for other people. They supply copy for Moore's books; but in his own household, NO!

You have to be careful how you part from Hamish. He is touchy. If you look at your watch and say that you must be off, he will be offended. If you linger he will become quarrelsome. I jumped into a tram. This Hamish is not the same as another Hamish, Joyce's friend. This man is some sort of professor in arts in the law. That's why he has that superior grin on his face. It was a long time before I could get the taste of him and his ilk out of my mouth.

There is in Ireland a kind of third person which, though married, is sexless. The male of the species is more a churchman than a layman; and the female of the species is more churchman than the male. These McGeehans like to 'keep in touch'. After a lengthy trial when there is not a kick left in them they get a job with more patronage than any bought slave has to endure.

Once in his job, he stays put for the rest of his life, which is filled with envy and hatred for all free and indifferent spirits. He strives to get them into his Holy Office and to exhibit them as a proof of his rectitude and his zeal. He has been so accustomed to prove his devotion that he can't stop.

The Church as a rule doesn't want to be bothered by its McGeehans. It considers that they are busybodies. If left to itself, the Church wouldn't care a damn. I hope you get the gist of what I am trying to show. Instead of selling smutty postcards at the doors of the great cathedrals, instead of carving the seats of the confessionals as did the monks of old, the McGeehans wear miraculous medals and burn your character at the stake.

It is pleasant at any time, except when it is raining, to cross from the Front to the Back Gate of Trinity. After you pass the great dark grey library and the New Square, the College Park opens on your right. It is smooth and green and, in the hottest summer, hardly ever burned. I was walking along under the young trees when I met Joe Ridgeway. He had a stutter but he was quite understandable. It was worth while to be patient with him because he always had a new subject, and one removed from the expected, to discuss.

'Did you hear that Lady Dudley got acute appendicitis and had to be carried into the nearest hospital, which was the Mater?' he broke out.

'You don't say?'

'I'm wondering who will operate on her. I don't know much about the doctors in the Mater; that's why I'm asking you.'

'Well,' I said, 'there's Blaney, Chance and Lentaigne. Chance is about the best of them; but as Blaney's leading by half a dozen masses and two benedictions, he'll be sure to get the job.'

'It means a knighthood for whomever gets it.'

'A knighthood! Then they'll remove her to a Protestant hospital, for they don't want to give knighthoods to Roman Catholics, except for politics, at least not until they've exhausted the privileged list.'

Ridgeway eyed me thoughtfully. He was pondering

something I had said. Ridgeway does not take a joke or a slight sarcasm readily.

'What do you mean "leading by half a dozen masses"? Leading what?' he asked.

'I meant it as a joke. Blaney is the most docile of the Mater staff, and the most devout. He kowtows to the nuns more regularly than Chance or Lentaigne. And, as the nuns have the apportioning of operations, Blaney has the best chance of operating on Lady Dudley's appendix.'

Ridgeway could not see it at all.

'What does a nun know about surgery? I'm afraid I don't understand.'

It was too late to hand him over to McGeehan at the Front Gate. I would have given a lot to see Mac's face as Ridgeway's difficulty, and my villainy, dawned.

I heard afterwards that they did remove Lady Dudley from the Mater Hospital. It would never do to have Catholic hands palpating a Protestant abdomen.

When I left Ridgeway he was beside the Pavilion. When I looked back he was gone. It was a way he had of disappearing. Maybe he went into the Pavilion. There was nothing mystical about Ridgeway. And yet I was not disappointed because what endeared Ridgeway to us was his faculty of disappearing. He was such a void, he had no room for an ache. That's why, if we didn't all like him. No one objected to him.

22 *'Who Is Stella, What Is She?'*

My wife ran the house in Ely Place so smoothly that everthing seemed to go by itself. We had the same cook for years until she became so blind that she sent up potatoes instead of apples for dessert one night.

On Friday evenings George Russell, a constant friend,

would come in from Rathgar; Yeats from nearby Merrion Square; Griffith very occasionally, for he was not a visiting man; Tom Kettle and George Moore and many others. Everyone could 'affirm his own philosophy' except George Moore, for he had only opinions, shocking ones, on gentle occasions; he could be Senior Wrangler for all his lack of philosophy. This I was presently to experience.

I had bought a picture from Jack Yeats without first consulting Moore, who considered his taste in artistic matters infallible. I had acted on the advice of Æ, who had said that there were only two artists whose paintings were worth buying in Dublin – Jack Yeats and Nathaniel Hone. In his own medium Jack Yeats expressed the spirit of Ireland as well as his better-known brother, William, did in his. The poems of William Butler Yeats are more famous than the paintings of his brother, for the living word when winged with music can travel farther than the still life of any pigment, oil, tempera or water colour.

When Moore saw the picture on the wall and remembered that he had not been consulted, he began, 'Oh, where did you get that? It's all a mess of green and brown.'

I mumbled.

'By whom did you say?' he continued.

'Jack Yeats.'

He shook his head. 'Well, if you are prepared to throw your money away without asking the advice which I am always prepared to give, it is your own doing. I cannot help you.'

'I bought it not because of the artist but because of its message to me. That green is the green of the eternal hills, the colour of Eternity . . . '

'Now, my dear fellow, what colour is Eternity?'

I proceeded unperturbed. ' . . . and the sea that makes immortal motion is filling up the bay. Soon the brown seaweed will be covered over and the long effulgence will brim Clifden Bay with water and with light.'

Moore listened to his own trick of turning one medium into another; painting into words. He went across to inspect the picture at close range. 'Well, yes; but the next time you buy a picture ask me to come with you. You might have done worse. You have had a narrow escape. Good-bye!'

'Pernickety' was the name that described Moore.

He was walking in the garden one day with a lady as tall, if not taller, than himself. She stooped a little, but not from the neck. 'Back she had of bended yew.' Her complexion was as pink and white as Dresden china. She had high cheekbones and no chin: English, obviously. I recalled a love poem of my early period:

> The girl by whom I am beguiled
> Must have high cheek bones and a child.

There was no way of knowing whether or not she had had a child. But her cheekbones tallied with the invoice. She did not appear to be full-bosomed. Don't let that deceive you. You'd be surprised!

As Moore walked beside her he was gesticulating with both hands. At times his walking stick would rise heavenward as he raised his arms up in the air. The lady only murmured, her voice was soft and low. What can the argument be about? After his habit, Moore is carrying war into the enemy's camp: he is putting the poor lady in the wrong. But what is he doing in his garden at this hour? It is about three o'clock. He should be arguing with his secretary, 'composing,' as he calls the daily wrangle. Well, I wouldn't have to wait long to hear about it; not if I knew George Moore.

'Some men kiss and tell; Moore tells but does not kiss,' Susan Mitchell, Æ's secretary, said of him; quite untruly, I learned after. Lady Cunard was my informant and she ought to know. Yes, Moore would tell me, of that there was no doubt. And I would tell it, if it had a hint of scandal, to Yeats, who loved to hear a bit of scandal about Moore. It could wait. But could I? I was devoured with curiosity. His house is only sixty yards diagonally from my hall door. I could not well call before teatime.

When I rang and was admitted, I found Moore in the drawing room on the first floor. The folding doors were open, so the two rooms were thrown into one which went from window to window, the depth of the house. The mantelpiece was covered by little water colours of warm interiors with bright armchairs, and windows with curtains of bright chintz; obviously the work of a woman. Moore was putting on an air of fatigue.

'Those are by Stella,' he said languidly. 'I forgot – you do not know her. She followed me over from London. She has taken a house at Templeogue so as to be near me. Ah! Perhaps you saw us in the garden this afternoon. That was she.'

'Yes,' I said. 'I saw you in the garden. You did not seem exactly to be burning "with a hard gemlike flame".'

This reference to Walter Pater brought out one of his hissing laughs, which left you uncertain whether he was amused by your quotation or laughing at you for being so ostentatious with it.

'Stella is a charming . . . or rather she can be a charming woman when she likes. But like all women she is unreasonable. She makes me angry at times.'

That must have been one of the times, I thought to myself. It accounts for his stick going up in the air in an ecstasy of expostulation.

'She has plenty of money and she ought to have more sense.'

I would soon hear what it was all about, provided I betrayed no curiosity.

'It is not your fault if people admire your writings, especially women,' I said, and realised at once that I had said the wrong thing. I should have said, in a grave voice, 'Oh?' or something as non-committal as that. But to imply that his writings were admired 'especially by women' was a *gaffe*. Conversation with Moore was always a *gaffe* and this was no exception. I would not now hear what the argument was about.

In a changed voice, as if the only thing I understood was

some sort of refreshment, he asked, 'Won't you have some tea?'

He was about to ring the bell when the maid came in with the tea tray. During tea I was cross-examined: 'I hope that you have not been indulging in art purchases without consulting me?'

I did not dare to say that I had fourteen Hones hanging in the room that looked out on his garden, the best room in the house with a southern aspect.

'Do you know Hone?' I asked, knowing that he did not, and was unlikely to be received by that very independent and particular old gentleman.

'I haven't time for that kind of thing.' He shrugged. Then, brightening, 'There's a picture for you.' He pointed to the large oil which hung over the mantelpiece, a picture of a flooded river, willow trees half submerged.

'The Seine?' I said.

'Of course; but the subject of a painting is the last thing you should think about. Look how the paint is put on. It is like cream. You see?'

I let my face fall into repose, because when it is in repose they tell me that I look quite idiotic.

'What are you staring at? *Claude* Monet was a friend of mine.' He put great emphasis on the 'Cluade'. 'We had many a long evening in the Nouvelle Athène. Those were my Parisian days.'

'It must be pleasant to have artistic friends?' I said.

'Oh, don't let me hear you use that word "artistic". It is a word that Stoker is always using. He knows nothing about art. Secondhand furniture, yes, but not Art. Oh no.'

The teapot was Sèvres. The spout had been broken and repaired. He caught me examining it. 'Oh, some foolish maid broke it. I had quite a row. The cook left because I held her responsible. If you can't hold someone responsible for the behaviour of those under them, you might despair of running a house, particularly in this country. Don't forget that you are to dine here on Saturday, Kuno Meyer is expected. Æ, of course, and Douglas Hyde.'

It was the first time that I had heard of it. I took the

invitation to dinner as a dismissal from tea. I left the author to renew his war with Stella, and found my way out.

At home I found a woman waiting, in a downstairs room, to be transilluminated; that is, examined for sinusitis by a lighted electric lamp placed in the patient's mouth in a dark room. (If there be a denture or upper plate, it must be first removed.) When it is being transilluminated, the face looks like 'a face carved out of a turnip', as Yeats described the face of Moore. Don't get the impression that Yeats was vindictive. He would never have made that remark had not Moore first described him as looking like an umbrella forgotten at a picnic. This is an aside.

While the eight-volt lamp was in the seated patient's mouth, I had the misfortune to touch a hand-basin full of water. Instantly I was flung down and spread-eagled upon the floor. I had grounded the electric wire and sent the town's interrupted current of more than two hundred volts into my chest. There was no sensation of pins and needles, but a tornado that went raging through my chest. I was all but electrocuted. I remember thinking of the agony of electrocuted persons. At last the flex broke: I was saved. Oh, the relief! A voice from the chair inquired anxiously, 'Oh, Doctor, am I as bad as that?'

Dinner at George Moore's would be an experience. You could trust George to provide entertainment for his guests, whimsical as well as culinary.

Kuno Meyer, the German scholar who was studying early Irish – that is, pre-Christian – literature, was the last to arrive. I came in the middle so as to avoid a tête-à-tête – had I arrived first – and to avoid expostulations and sarcasm – had I come last. It was Kuno Meyer who came last. Evidently he was forgiven. He was a very scholarly man on a subject of which none of us knew anything, except Douglas Hyde. And Meyer was crippled with rheumatism, so Moore had every excuse to make allowances for his last guest.

When we were all assembled, Moore said, with an air of

diffidence, 'Gentlemen, dinner tonight will be at best an experiment. I have engaged a new cook. She was well recommended. We shall soon see what her capabilities are.'

He sat at the head of an oval table with his back to the garden and the street. In the quiet cul-de-sac nothing stirred; neither vehicles nor foot passengers entered Ely Place after sundown. The soup passed scrutiny. Moore was acting as a gourmet of the most exquisite taste before his guests. He had been in France and we were paying for it.

'It is impossible to convince a cook that she should heat the tureen before pouring in the soup. In these old houses the stairs to the kitchen are enough to cool the soup. The real test of a cook, however, is the omelette. Now we shall see.'

If his attitudinising had not been so characteristic it would have been boring. But Moore managed to make affectation an effective part of himself.

He lifted the lid of the chafing dish. He replaced it with an exclamation. He went hurriedly into his hall, opened the hall door and blew a police whistle. He returned with a young constable whose helmet was held respectfully under his arm. Moore again raised the lid of the dish and, pointing to the omelette, said, 'Look at that!' While the lid was coming off, the constable's helmet was being put on. The constable gazed at the omelette, looked at us all, and then at the omelette. Moore said, 'I want you to arrest the perpetrator of that atrocity.' The young policeman stood bewildered.

Douglas Hyde said, 'Oh, serve us some before it gets chilled. How can you tell whether it is good or bad until you have tasted it?' Kuno Meyer looked as if he would have preferred to be back in Berlin with a stein of beer and sauerkraut. On Æ's bearded face there was an impatient expression. He wanted dinner to be dispatched with all possible speed so that the talk could begin, unimpaired by mastication.

I wondered if Moore had not gone too far by bringing in the police. It might be a *cause célèbre* for a week if it got into the newspaper. Stoker would hear of it and be duly impressed by the importance Moore attached to good cooking.

The constable at last spoke: 'On what charge, sir?'

For a moment Moore was nonplussed. Then he rallied and, lifting the lid, pointed with it. 'That is no omelette. Go down and arrest her for obtaining money under false pretences.'

I was about to say, 'We have had drama enough, now let us have dinner,' when I remembered that I was younger than any of the guests, and my host too.

Douglas Hyde said, 'If you give the constable a drink, we will forgive the omelette.' After expostulating and complaining that he was not supported in his fight for good food, Moore waved the constable and the maid out of the room. I could hear them whispering in the hall.

When the maid appeared with the next course, Moore, now an authority on wines, raised his decanter and announced: 'I get this from an old Frenchman who visits his clients in Dublin once a year. He sends it to me in a barrel directly from Marseilles. It is called St. Pierre de Mou. I have it bottled by an expert. Gogarty can tell you how excellent it is. I sent my dealer over to see him. Hyde, whiskey? The decanter is in front of you.'

Neither Hyde nor Meyer cared for wine. Æ was abstemious to the point of teetotalism. Hyde drank John Jameson, and as for Meyer, he drank whatever his German doctor ordered, or what the doctor in some spa in Hungary permitted. Hungary was the only place in which Meyer got relief from pain, and I am sure that it was not wine that was prescribed for him.

Suddenly Hyde spluttered, 'Moore, this isn't whiskey. What is it?'

'But I ordered it from Sedley especially for you.'

'It may be Sedley, but it certainly is not whiskey.' And in a quieter voice, 'Who ever heard of a man ordering his whiskey from a grocer?'

Trying to divert him from Hyde, I said, turning to

Moore: 'Anything will do for me.' I had released all his frustration: 'Never say, "Anything will do for me." You cannot go through life disregarding what you eat or drink. "Anything will do for me" is what a pig or some omnivorous animal might say to his keeper. For animals, food is merely nourishment, for men, it is a subject for art. Don't you agree with me, Æ?'

Æ hesitated a moment, until he had swallowed something, then, pushing his knife and fork past his plate, threw back his head and announced, 'Art means an imaginative control over your medium.'

'Precisely,' said Moore, interrupting the sage. 'Or changing the medium, as in a translation,' he added.

'No, no,' Meyer grunted. 'You do not change the medium, which is language, when you translate.'

Moore looked bewildered. It seemed that he was not on firm ground; that art, his favourite subject, was about to betray him. Hyde, who had become reconciled to his beverage, said: 'Take Meyer's translation of *The Tryst after Death*, where a warrior appears to his love with, "Hush, woman, do not speak to me. My bloody corpse lies by the side of the Slope of the two Brinks": that is more than slipping from one language into another. If you do not know the original, how can it be held that a translation is more or less than it?'

There was the danger into which Moore felt he might have slipped. He knew nothing about Irish, Old, Middle or Modern.

'I can give *The Tryst after Death* word by word from Meyer's translation,' Æ announced.

Moore said, 'Oh, if we are to have recitals, let us have them with the coffee upstairs.'

Upstairs in the drawing room, under the Monet and over the Aubusson carpet, coffee was served. Meyer was not allowed coffee, Hyde did not take it; Æ sat in a corner and accepted automatically anything that was handed to him. Whether he noticed it or not was another matter. He was longing for an opportunity to expound Plotinus or recite something.

'I wish that Hyde would tell us what he considers the best poem in his *Love Songs of Connaught*?'

'*The Red Man's Wife*,' Hyde answered without hesitation.

Moore pricked up his ears at the mention of that poem. 'What a title for a novel, *The Red Man's Wife*.' He threw up his hands.

'I have Hyde's book here.'

'We don't want it. I can recite it word for word. I don't want a book,' Æ announced. And he could, because he had the most prodigious memory for verse or prose of any man alive. Verily, Memory is Mother of the Muses, which saying was well borne out in Æ, who was a considerable poet himself in days when poets were rife.

'The singer of this is in prison. He is the rejected lover of the Red Man's Wife. Probably he committed some outrage. He is working himself up as he lies fast bound with "bolts on my smalls", that is, on every isthmus of the body, ankles, wrists, waist and neck.'

'Give us it without the surface anatomy, as Gogarty here might say.'

This was a reference to my being Honourable Anatomist to the Royal Hibernian Academy, an art school. Thus hurried by Moore, Æ began:

> ''Tis what they say,
>   Your little heel fits in a shoe,
> 'Tis what they say,
>   Your little mouth kisses well too,
> 'Tis what they say,
>   Thousand loves that you made me to rue,
> That the tailor went the way
>   That the wife of the Red man knew.
>
> 'Nine months did I spend
>   In prison closed tightly and bound
> Bolts on my smalls
>   And a thousand locks frowning around;
> But o'er the tide
>   I would leap with the leap of a swan

Could I once set my side
  By the bride of the Red-haired man.

'I thought, O my life,
  That one house love, between us, would be;
And I thought I would find
  You coaxing my child on your knee;
But now the curse of the High One,
  On him let it be,
And on all the liars
  Who put silence between you and me.

'There grows a tree in the garden
  With blossoms that tremble and shake
I lay my hand on its bark
  And I feel that my heart must break:
On one wish alone
  My soul through the long months ran:
One little kiss
  From the wife of the Red-haired man.

'But the day of Doom shall come,
  And the hills and the harbours be rent;
A mist shall fall from the sun
  From the dark clouds heavily sent;
The sea shall be dry
  And earth under mourning and ban,
Then shall I cry
  For the wife of the Red-haired man.'

When he had concluded, the air seemed drained. Silence fell on the assembly. Moore got up from his chair to poke the fire, for though it was June the weather in Dublin calls for fires in the evening, even if the homeliness they bring would not be a justification in itself.

When Moore had finished attending to the fire, he stood up with his back to the mantelpiece and announced: 'I was walking in my garden on, was it Tuesday or Wednesday? Gogarty can tell you, for nothing that goes on in that garden escapes him. Stella – you all know her name – had followed me from London and had taken the moated grange in Templeogue. I had, it seems, neglected her for three weeks. That is what made her come in from the country and call on me in the middle of my work, and it was all the more annoying now that my usual secretary is gone to see her mother – oh, she is dying – and have to work by myself. Stella called. And I took her into the garden. Well, the upshot of it was that I had to go out to see her next day.

'As I pushed the gate open, she came to meet me halfway down the drive. I felt that soon there would be an explosion, so I said, "I don't care what your gardener has done to the herbaceous border, nor do I care what you have done to the house. There is a frightful tension in the atmosphere worse than thunder. Tell me, tell me, what is it all about?" At long last, after question upon question, she still sulked and would not speak. I turned to go when she said in a whisper, "George, you do not make love to me often enough." At that, I took her by the arm: "Let us go into the house." She shook herself free. "How dare you?" she said. Now what are you to do with a woman like that? She accuses you of balking and, when you show her your preparedness, she brushes you off. Next day, I left for Dublin, a little dazed, a little shaken. I assure you it is propinquity that breaks up more homes than divorce!'

The discussion in the garden was explained. I might have guessed it. And I had guessed aright when I thought that Moore could not fail to announce it sooner or later.

'That's all very fine, Moore,' Hyde said, 'but this business of bringing women over from London and giving them a house in the country will soon be all over the place. This is a talkative town and you are the last person it will spare.'

Moore raised his eyebrows in feigned surprise. He was as pleased as a child to be the centre of interest. I knew that it would be useless to call him a cad for giving a woman away. It would give him an opportunity to use his old answer: 'Of course I am. My brother, the colonel is the gentleman of our family.' Susan Mitchell is right – Moore tells and does not kiss, not enough anyway. Has he not divulged the fact by his account of his interview with Stella?

When I look back on my tolerance at the time and my lack, all our lack, of indignation, I can account for them only by the incredulity with which Moore's 'affairs' were regarded. They were so advertised that no one believed them. He was a novelist: his amours, and his characters, were fictitious.

Kuno Meyer, like Queen Victoria, was 'not amused'. Æ was about to philosophise when Moore went on in answer to Douglas Hyde. 'But, my dear Hyde, I brought no woman over from London. She brought herself. It was not I who took the house in Templeogue. Stella has money of her own. If an English lady cannot rent a house in Ireland to do a little landscape painting without being made the subject of gossip, Ireland is full of Calvinism still.'

Who has made her 'the subject of gossip'? I thought. The others, I felt sure, did too; but we all let it pass. Douglas Hyde had made his protest. It was Æ's turn.

'In India,' said the sage, 'there are temple prostitutes; women's virtue is subordinated to communion with the divine.' Æ had never been in India, but let that not prevent an Irishman from being an authority *in absentia.* This is probably one of the results of Irishmen being tenants of absentee landlords for so long.

Moore's face assumed a beatific look. 'I see a solution to the whole problem. Meyer, listen to this. Temple prostitutes; one for every priest and two for every bishop. Then there would not be all this rancour about sex: making salvation depend on atrophy of an organ.'

Æ said, 'You have been too hasty, Moore. You have misunderstood me. Good conduct is man's chiefest contribution to the deity. Temple prostitutes are used in India to remove any carnal distractions that may arise when a man is about to seek communion with the Divine. They come from the highest caste. I have not heard that they had any traffic with the priests. They give themselves only to members of the congregation. The idea is to dissolve sex, the entangler; to achieve *samadhi.*'

'They first decant the worshipper and then leave him to

his prayers, if he has any energy left with which to pray,' I added to help Æ out.

Æ, heartened, as I thought, began again, 'Now take Ramakrishna ... '

'I will not take Rama ... whatever you call him. I won't have you diverting me from my idea of having temple prostitutes for Ireland. It is in Ireland, not India, we have to live.' He hissed behind his moustache as was his habit when he laughed. He was ridden by his idea; he wanted us all to develop it for him.

Meyer announced that it was time for him to go. He got out of his chair stiffly, and changed his stick to his right hand. Moore went with him down the stairs. We could hear his stick tapping against the floor of the hall. The hall door closed.

Æ asked, 'How far is it justifiable for an artist to sacrifice the proprieties to his art?'

'Moore sacrifices himself,' said I.

'I don't quite follow you,' Hyde remarked.

'Take, for instance, the lady of the house in Templeogue. By hinting that he was more or less impotent, he gave himself away.'

'He gave both of them away,' said Æ.

'That is what I mean by sacrificing the proprieties. That is the only sacrifice to which he ever attains.'

'He loves to shock people,' I interjected, for I hoped to be asked for an example: their silence invited me. 'He was on the same boat as Thomas Cook during his journey to the Holy Land when he was writing *Brook Kerith* which, only for me – I may be flattering myself; I am, of course, for he must have consulted others – would have been called *By Kidron's Stream*. For three weeks or whatever time it takes to make the journey from London to Palestine, he deliberately snubbed Thomas Cook, who he well knew was the great travel agent. But when they arrived at Joppa and Moore saw the horizon stippled with the humps of Cook's camels, he was impressed. Cook, noticing this, took his courage in his hands and addressed him, "You are the great novelist, George Moore?" "And are you *the* Thomas Cook? Why did you not reveal yourself to me?"

'Conveniently overlooking the snubbings through the voyage, Cook fell for Moore's expostulations: "I have heard that you are going to the Holy Land to gather local colour for your book. If I can be of the least assistance, I will gladly detail some of my men to show you the places of interest. For instance in the morning I will send round a guide to conduct you to the Holy Sepulchre . . . "

'"Oh, for goodness' sake, nothing so hackneyed, Cook!" "Where would you like to go?" "Well, if you would ask your man to bring me to where the woman was taken in adultery . . . " Cook was greatly shocked; so Moore had his joke.'

Hyde did not laugh. I began to fear that I was too shocking when I heard Moore on the stairs. When he came back to the room, it was evident that he was still full of his idea.

'What does Gogarty think of it?' he asked. 'I know that Æ thinks that my plan of introducing temple prostitutes in Ireland is an outrage on his favourite India. Hyde, you on principle cannot approve; but I have Gogarty to back me. He is not like Yeats, afraid to make up his mind.'

'It would narrow the basis of meditation,' I remarked, hoping that I would not be put to the question any further. Then I added, knowing that it would be provocative, 'I do not think that for Holy Ireland the word "prostitute" should be connected with the Church.'

'No; I agree,' said Moore, 'we must find some other word.' Then striking his forehead and leaning backwards, he asked as if inspired, 'What about calling them "Divine Decanters"?'

'Have it any way you like; but don't father it on me,' Æ said and he bade us good night.

I went with him, for I knew that Moore went early to bed. On the landing he exclaimed, to Æ's dismay, 'Divine Decanters! I am very grateful indeed. Divine Decanters!'

Leaving Moore to dream of ritual prostitutions, I

walked with Æ to where he could catch the tram to Rathgar. It was a mellow night, as so few in Dublin are. I remarked how pleasant it was; but Æ was still annoyed at the way Moore had treated his favourite philosophy or else he was wrapped in some meditation. He did not answer. I said that I was delighted with his remembering *The Red Man's Wife*. Still he said nothing. I went on to say that Kuno Meyer was almost morose: he had contributed very little to the conversation. He could have recited his wonderful translation of *The Tryst after Death*, where the ghost of the warrior speaks to his mistress: 'It is blindness for anyone making a tryst to set aside the tryst with death.' And then, ''Tis not I alone who in the fullness of desire have gone astray to meet a woman.'

'Moore didn't,' said Æ.

When his tram came he muttered something as he got into it. He seemed to raise his hand in a farewell gesture. He may only have been grasping the rail.

There was light in the third storey of Moore's house. He was going to bed still hugging his idea and wondering how he would fit it into his next book. So I thought. I hoped that it would save him from the dreadful nightmares of which he complained to me.

Why does he confide in me? And then why does he take it for granted that I am an atheist, that all doctors are atheists? Is it because we are supposed to regard all human beings as merely bundles of reflexes? Can he not give us credit for asking ourselves, 'Whence did the reflexes come?' It should be as simple as for the child who, when she was being instructed in evolution and taught that all life came from the sea, asked simply, 'Where did the sea come from?'

Yes; whence did life proceed? Even if we have to think of everything in terms of cause and effect, even if our intellect is that far limited, why are we aware of that limitation? What told us? Oh, quit philosophising, I said to myself, and come down to the consideration of George Moore. Well you know that for him you, Hyde, Meyer and Æ will be but puppets or marionettes in his next creation. I comforted myself with the thought that it is better to have God for a creator than to depend for existence on George Moore. Nightmares, eh?

23 *Walking Home*

On a day as I walked up Merrion Square, I saw on my left the beautiful fountain, called after Lord Rutland, which conceals the lodge of the attendant of the Square. On my right, in front of the National Portrait Gallery, stood the statue of Dargan, who led into Dublin the soft water from Wicklow's granite hills and made fountains for the town. A little farther, apropos of nothing but the White Man's Burden, the British Empire, was a statue to the man who discovered Mr Livingstone, the Bible reader from Scotland who got lost in Africa.

Imagine a statue to a man who discovered a Bible reader! Why, I could discover one or two every Sunday; and on Saturday the whole Salvation Army singing by Portobello Bridge! Had it been one of the pygmies who got lost in darkest London while trying to convert its citizens to the hunting of elephants and a simpler life, I could understand a statue to that misguided man. But to erect a statue to a fellow who dug out Dave Livingstone while he was trying to pervert the simple pygmies and dose them with an oriental anthology which contained forms of ideation alien to their thought would have made me laugh had I not seen the cynical message behind the statue.

We, the Irish, were being gradually proselytised into the British Empire, which contains trends of thought certainly alien to the Gael. This is subtler than the system of Intermediate Examinations. Will Arthur Griffith, who lives on 17/6 a week, be able to tackle it at all?

The red tiles of my roof were about a hundred yards

away when I crossed Merrion Row. On my right were three or four houses which in the afternoon never caught the sun. On the ground floor, and for all I knew the rest of the floors, were the offices of Mr McDonald, architect. He built the house for Mr Wilcox in Connemara and drove the salmon out of the adjoining lakes for years after dynamiting the rock for the foundations. Out he came and I ran into him.

What did I say about doctors avoiding the street? He weighed at least four hundred pounds, as became a cousin of Larkey Waldron. His collar was twenty inches around: his mouth was open, and his whole face turned upwards, for, even though your neck has taken over, you must breathe. He was gasping when I met him. To give him time to catch his breath, I stood and waited. Was he leaving his office or entering it? What did it matter? He was breathing easier now.

'How is Larkey?' I asked.

After a moment he gargled in his deep bass, 'Splendid. You should see him since his cure. A child can speak to him. I don't believe in this slimming. Tell me, do you?'

'Which side is he slimming?' I asked.

'I must hurry,' he said, as if to explain his breathlessness, and stepped into his office.

Hume Street enters Ely Place in its middle, like the shaft of a cross. At the near corner the rounded house of Mrs Foule, the Belgian wife of a colonel of remounts, opened its hospitable door on Hume Street. Ely House, once the town house of the Marquis of Ely (now Sir Thornley Stoker's), looks down Hume Street and takes the dust from it whenever the west wind blows.

The sun was setting beyond Stephen's Green, behind the College of Surgeons. If I were a novelist it should have reminded me of Goya, El Greco, Monet or Manet, Constable, Turner or Fantin-latour. It only gave me an increased respect for the man to whom 'a primrose by the river's brim' etc. I saw myself talking to him at evening in his village inn over a pint of the best. I would wait until the psychological moment. 'And did that primrose remind you of nothing?' I would ask casually. 'Sure it did. It reminded me of a trouser button which was missing from my fly.' 'Was that because of its association with water?' No, I couldn't ask that. If it were beyond him, he would think that I was frivolous and maybe fooling him. But how happy I would be in his company, while he drew on his pipe and sipped his pint and I sipped mine. He must have been as addicted to clear thinking as Larkey Waldron.

'Who is Larkey?' you will rightly ask. He is a brother of General Waldron but he lives in his own right. Don't mind George Moore when he writes of 'the obscene bulk of Larkey Waldron'. I admit that Larkey is a substantial man; he weighs four hundred pounds and over, but then he is a stockbroker to the Catholic Church; and St Thomas Aquinas was no lightweight and yet he wrote the *Summa* and fixed the school. Larkey has to do sums for the bishops and archbishops and invest money for the Little Sisters of the Poor. He lives sumptuously in a beautiful house on Killiney Hill.

Yes: Larkey is a great fellow in every sense. He sits in his office in Anglesea Street with two telephones and four mantelpieces by Bossi in the room. He wears a skullcap of black silk topped by a large pink rhododendron. He hasn't seen his feet for years.

He kept me on my own feet by refusing to invest £500 for me in the Dundalk Meat Packing Company when even Solomons, another stockbroker, lost money in that very promising speculation. 'Did you pick up this cash in the gutter?' Larkey asked. 'No,' I said. 'Then home you go with it.' Weeks later the whole thing burst. I remember leaving his office trying to console myself with the thought that I wouldn't like a layman to tell me my business so why should I try to tell Larkey Waldron his? Stocks and shares were his business; leave him to it. Luckily I did.

You won't be surprised now to hear that Larkey's hobby is clear thinking; and Dr Johnson. He lingers among the secondhand bookshops on the quays on his way from

Westland Row to Anglesea Street. He puts Murray the bookseller in his place, because he pays good prices.

Perhaps the sunset should have reminded me of a painter instead of Larkey Waldron. A good novelist should always be reminded of something artistic. George Moore, when he and I were crossing the railway viaduct at Donabate, was reminded by the sunset of Nathaniel Hone, the landscape painter who lived nearby. He said, 'I would give ten pounds to see how that sunset will imitate Hone.' I tried to save him five by pulling the communication cord, because the fine is only five pounds if you pull it wantonly. I knew that you could never explain to a railway guard that art is more important than an accident. He must have had artistic sympathies though, because he 'forgot' the incident for ten shillings! Instead of being grateful to me as I was to Larkey for moneysaving, Moore expostulated and told me that I was impossible. I bore that in silence. I could have retorted that he was a plagiarist, for years ago Oscar Wilde had said that Nature was always trying to imitate Art. Do not look for gratitude from novelists.

On the way home I took care not to pass close to Sir Thornley Stoker's house. If he came out I would be put to the question: what was I doing on the street? Sir Thornley is the arbiter of Ely Place, and of the behaviour of those members of the profession who are immediately associated with him. I crossed Hume Street hurriedly and, as I passed the letter box at the corner, I heard the staccato yelps of Lady Stoker's black Pom. Betty Webb, the secretary, was taking it for a walk. Had she met me, I might have met Sir Thornley.

Oh, what a relief to get behind my hall door! What etiquettical, nonsensical precautions is all this unwritten rule about doctors not being supposed to walk on the street; with the exception, of course, of Kegley, and Gibson the gynaecologist, both safe from open consultation.

Gibson has or had a bad stutter so he collects Waterford glass – explanation later, if I don't forget it. Now you cure a stutter by instructing the patient to imitate someone else, any character he may choose, always provided that it is an edifying character. You never hear an actor stutter; nor a singer. Gibson selected some person so highfalutin that unsympathetic students nicknamed him 'Bardelys'.

I went into my library to read before dinner. Now I have not got a library in my house; there are bookcases here and there in passages and in a few rooms; but there is no 'library' for the simple reason that I think that, wherever a book is, a reading man can make a library.

This reminds me – when Lord Kingston and I, after driving up from Castleforbes, which owes its restoration to Lady Forbes, an American, were having tea here, Kingston exclaimed, 'Now I know what was wrong with Castleforbes, there were no books around.' 'No,' I said. 'They were all in the library.'

Books are all over the house in Ely Place; that is why I maintain that books and not a room can make a library.

> And after him a finicking lass
> Did shine like the glistering gold.

That's what I was reading. To find such a picture you must read the *Gestes of Robin Hood* and, before that, you must be attuned to poetry. Otherwise, all is vain.

If you have no affinity for verse, better skip this, or you'll be bored stiff and to bore anybody is beyond me. I got such a boring in my schooldays that I have had enough for the rest of my life and I am resolved not to inflict boredom on even the most deserving.

As I read of Robin Hood, that hero of England, I began to think many things, because a well-known book becomes a kind of crystal for me into which I gaze and think of something else, as a crystal-gazer professes to do. I thought that I was quite wrong to blame or to poke fun at novelists because sunsets remind them of paintings. I could not expect sunsets to remind them of the back of Thesus, for instance, for that is sculpture; and has not to do with colour. Colour reminds some novelists of music. They used to be reminded of Beethoven, but latterly Villa-Lobos gives a more up-to-date touch to their memories.

I couldn't expect novelists, especially George Moore, who is almost illiterate, to be reminded of a chorus-ending of Euripides or something out of *Prometheus Bound*. Thinking of illiteracy reminds me of Dr Yelverton Tyrrell's reply when he was told that George Moore was about to pillory him in a trilogy which he was calling *Ave atque Vale*. 'Moore, of course, thinks that *atque* was a Roman centurion.' On this being repeated to George, he changed the title to the rather redundant *Ave, Salve, Vale*.

And yet illiterates can be stylists.

This bids well to be a great book because it is becoming boring. I cannot help it.

No; art must refer to art, for art represents the world of the imagination, and it is imagination that makes artists, not reason. Imagination is truer than reason is or ever can be. To those who think differently belong the Kinseys of this world. Yes; the artist must speak his own language.

I was thinking, probably at the same time, about the word 'finicking'. I know that it means 'fastidious' – so much the dictionary tells you – but it means, to me at least, far more. First of all it is like a present particle and suggests walking along with mincing steps; and there is the suggestion of 'fine' in it and of something fresh, inexperienced and young. 'Glistering,' too, is a better word for the lass's hair than 'glittering'. Dictionaries, which suffer from the rigor mortis of words, will tell you that 'glistering' and 'glittering' are the same.

Back of my mind was Robin Hood and the thought that the green wood is the backdrop of all the forests of England, in prose or rhyme. Merry Sherwood waves its branches in the Forest of Arden and in all the woodland scenes of the poets of England. And how England loves the greenwood and all that it contains:

> The wood wele sang and would not cease
> Sitting upon a spray.

That's what poets can do; they can summon up a vision of peace.

> And evening full of the linnets' wings.

They should never be rivals, or be jealous of the hierophants of another mystery. They have a religion of their own which is their own 'exceeding great reward', and it extends its salvation to them. Never should they feel 'The Necessity of Atheism'.

I laid down the ballads of Robin Hood and hunted out a copy of Yeats's letter to Moore. I am so bad at keeping, much less arranging, manuscripts that it is a wonder how I found it. Don't ask me how I got it. I came by it innocently. It was only a draft but it explained the bad feeling between Yeats and Moore.

Here it is – Moore tried to hide it in vain. It has to do with their collaboration for the two years it took to produce the rather trivial play, *Diarmuid and Grania*, two years of wrangling and, for Yeats at least, frustration after frustration:

> My dear Moore,
>
> You say both should make concessions. I think so too but I so far have made them all. I have acknowledged that you have a knowledge of the stage, a power of construction, a power of inventing a dramatic climax far beyond me, and I have given way again and again. I have continually given up motives and ideas that I preferred to yours because I admitted your authority to be greater than mine. On the question of style however I will make no concessions. Here you need give way to me ...

There is more of the letter, but I read no further because I saw the impossibility of any writer sacrificing his style to another.

What has any author got but his style? It is the man; and his manhood goes with his style. To sacrifice it is to obliterate himself, to ask to be devoured. So that was it.

That was the cause of the lifelong enmity between Yeats and Moore; and the abusive terms they threw at each other.

The fact that Moore revealed himself to be what modern psychiatrists would call a 'paranoid' was the cause of the quarrel and the subsequent abuse, and Yeats's mischievous delight at Moore's discomfitures. And was not Yeats right? His standing up to the older and the then more famous man, and his belief in himself, shows a grit that no one guessed was in him at the time; and the time was 1901.

Tonight is Friday night. I expect him after dinner and Æ and a few more. We have an embryo salon on Friday nights. My wife loves them. Now what will I talk about? Yeats likes men who ride upon horses. His poem on the Galway Races shows that. William the Conqueror died from a fall from his horse. William III of England also died as the result of a fall from his horse. George V fell from his horse in World War I. Yeats, the old Irish Republican Brotherhood man, will like that. Perhaps he won't like the 'William' part of it. Maybe I had better avoid the subject. I have it! I know what I will say, or rather bring out nonchalantly in the course of conversation. I will quote those lines by an unknown poet which I came across in the Bodleian. It will convey at the same time that I was at Oxford – even at the risk of Yeats's going to live at Oxford, I will say that I found them in the Bodleian. And what an effect they will have on Yeats! Why, they even affect me:

> Cupid abroad was lated in the night;
> His wings were wet from ranging in the rain.

After that I will keep my mouth shut.

Why talk on any subject when the best talkers of their time, Yeats and Æ, are coming? It will do me good to listen for a change.

If I had only listened, what a Boswell I would have been! Instead of listening, I keep on interrupting. I am as bad – well, almost as bad – as Stephens's wife, who prefers to chatter when her husband, the lightest lyrist of them all, should be talking or singing to us, swaying to the rhythm as he sings.

Lovely and airy the view from the hill
That looks down Ballylee;
But no good look is good until
By great good luck you see
The Blossom of the Branches coming towards you
Airily.

That is how Stephens recaptured the lines that Blind Raftery wrote in Gaelic, a hundred years ago, about Mary Hynes, 'The Blossom of the Branches,' who was one of those beauties who appear, in court or cottage, but one in a century, or less.

But no good look is good until
By great good luck you see.

The sooner I go to dinner the sooner I will get it over, and then for the feast!

24 *The Divine Doctor*

Jan was on the telephone. Jan was an engineering student in Trinity College. He was a close friend. He had worked hard on me on the morning of my wedding. He was my best man. We had been at that English school together; like the companions of Ulysses, we had suffered much. But we had also enjoyed much. One of Jan's enjoyments was the company of the Divine Doctor. Of him he was speaking now. Jan had an halt in his speech which grew worse when he was excited. He was excited and no mistake.

'The Divine Doctor is in a spot. He doesn't realise all its implications. I have him here at lunch. When can you come along?'

'What's happened?'

'I can't tell you on the telephone. I will meet you in his rooms in an hour's time.'

It is not easy for me to get out in the afternoon. I am in my office all the afternoon; but this was an emergency and had to be treated as such. What could have happened to the doctor? That he had a little diabetes, I knew. He couldn't have had an attack of coma? 'Doesn't realise all its implications.'

The Divine Doctor was Jan's name for Dr Yelverton Tyrrell, our preceptor, a perfect Greek. It was Dr Tyrrell who first 'hailed my light' (such as it was) in college. He was a Senior Fellow; and so could not be a tutor to college men; but his company tutored us. To him I owe all of the little acquaintance I have of the classics and all my love of the plangent word or unalterable line. Though he was thirty years or so older than us, he tolerated our company, sometimes he appeared to enjoy it; we were body servants promoted to boon companions. Now what could have happened to him? Jan's voice, allowing for lunch, was anxious. It did not suggest that anything sudden such as a stroke had happened to the doctor. I felt that it was something that had turned up while they talked at lunch.

It had nothing to do with pecuniary matters: the doctor's income was ample. It could not be a matter of health – I had dismissed that, though I knew that Old Tobin, a retired army surgeon who was the doctor's medical adviser, had said that the doctor had a little diabetes; a little diabetes does not put you suddenly 'in a spot'. It seemed more probable to me that the doctor had fallen asleep at some important public function or had made one of his bons mots about some self-important personage who had resented it and even had gone so far as reporting the doctor to the Board. There was little good to be got from conjectures: soon I would know what had happened to our benevolent friend. And yet as I drove along in a rickety cab I could not help wondering what has happened.

Maybe he has had a row with the Archbishop of Dublin, Dr Bernard, whose sharp nose he dislikes. It was bad enough when Bernard got the committee of the University Club to put all drinking out of bounds except on the top floor. Tyrrell's remark when he met his lordship on the stairs must have rankled; the irreverance of it! 'They shall be afraid of that which is high.' The first instance of acrophobia in literature. And when I thought of the doctor telling me how he had reacted to an invitation to dinner at the archbishop's palace. 'I wouldn't give it to that old curmudgeon to say that I got drunk in his house. I took the obvious precaution of coming drunk.'

In his rooms on the first floor at the northern corner of the West Front, the doctor was explaining to Jan, 'I was looking for a book when I came across thirteen bottles of Bass's ale. Now why were there thirteen and not twelve? I pondered on this – some messenger by mistake has left a baker's dozen or I have drunk eleven and forgot all about it? Anyway the thirteen bottles looked so forlorn that I did not wish them to think that they were ignored. Oh, here's Gogarty!' Then to me, after he had me seated, he said 'McCabe and I have just come from Jammet's where we had an excellent lunch. I think he will agree . . .'

'What did you have, sir?' I inquired.

'Well, let me see. I think we had a few lobsters and of course we had a few whiskeys and sodas to wash them down.'

'Lobsters and whiskey!' I could not help exclaiming.

'Oh well,' said the doctor, smiling, 'I recognise your medical conscience; but I make it a rule to let my stomach fight it out.'

Then he said, 'What was I saying? Oh yes. After the thirteen bottles of Bass, I was beginning to grow depressed when, what did I find? Just behind the shutter I found two bottles of marsala. I had an hour to kill before the time came to yield myself up to the bosom of my family. Marsala as you know comes from the southwest corner of Sicily where the grape is so abundant that the natives never think of fortifying it with the cheap and trashy brandy that is put into so many light wines to help them in their journey overseas. It has a somewhat sulphurous aroma; but on the whole it is not unpalatable.'

There is not the slightest sign of trouble. Why did Jan call me?

As I was asking myself that, the doctor remarked, smiling: 'You know I would rather discuss two bottles of marsala than any other subject with Tom Thompson Gray.'

'Ah yes, ah, ah!' Jan stuttered. 'Tom Thompson Gray has been chivvying the doctor since the last meeting of the Board.'

'Let us be fair to Gray. I was appointed secretary and at the first meeting I must confess that I fell asleep. I was awakened by the roaring of the Provost, "What! No minutes? The whole meeting had gone to waste." Gray added, "Tyrrell, if you cannot keep awake at a Board meeting, you should resign. I do not intend to let this dereliction of duty pass. I will frame a motion to that effect for the next meeting of the Board." The next meeting is in ten days,' the doctor added.

Gloom was beginning to usurp mirth. No use going into it now. Gray is a bluenose. He hates the doctor and all that he stands for. How well the name gives the man: Tom Thompson Gray. How appropriate it is that Gray's portrait by Orpen hangs in the dining room of the only club in Dublin that drinks in secret, and in secret transports its members home. Gray's portrait is an excellent camouflage. Who would think, to see it in the dining room of the Friendly Brothers, that alcohol could possibly be about?

The internal fight was beginning to influence the field of battle. The doctor was growing despondent. Maybe it was at the thought of Gray. To cheer him I said briskly:

'We have ten days. A lot may happen in ten days. The Sultan himself may die.'

'If I have to resign,' the doctor said, 'you know what that would mean to my family and to me.'

'There will be no question of resigning. It will not come to that,' Jan said. 'Let's see, You have Mahaffy, and the

Professor of Moral Philosophy, and Smithers is a gentleman. How will Wilkins vote?' Jan muttered as he counted on his fingers.

'Oh, for God's sake, Jan, don't ford your rivers till you come to them.' Then to the doctor: 'What did you say when the Provost complained?'

'"I don't like listening to scandal," I remarked; but instead of placating him it only made him worse. "You call a plenary meeting, a disciplinary meeting of the Board, scandal?" he asked, infuriated. I should tell you that the Board was meeting to consider a letter of complaint and the case of a Greek student who was found with two women in his rooms in college. It seems that the parent of some lady student wrote a letter complaining angrily about the way the Professor of Romance Languages illustrated the performance in the Provençal Courts of Love.'

'Why did she take Romance Languages if she couldn't take the romance?' I simply couldn't resist.

But uninterrupted the doctor continued: 'The Greek student I hear, was astonished. He explained to the Provost that it was not unusual in his country to have one if not two girls in one's rooms for comfort before such an emotional experience as an examination.'

The doctor could not forbear to smile.

'If that was the same student who, when asked sardonically by Mahaffy during a Greek examination, "Where did you get that accent?" answered "In Athens sir," it will go hard with him.' I suggested.

Privately I took heart: there never has been a case of expulsion of a don during the centuries of Trinity College's life. I forgot at the time that this was not a case of expulsion but of resignation, and so of the curtailment of an income. Universities have to avoid scandal: it will be forgiveness for the doctor; a stiff reprimand for the student from Greece.

'I hear that they have put an organ in his rooms,' said Jan.

'To exorcise his rooms, no doubt,' I suggested.

'To me it seems a homoeopathic remedy invented to

drive out the effect of the smaller by the larger.'

The doctor groaned as he came out of a reverie.

'Talking of Mahaffy, let us be fair to him. Though there is no love lost between us, he stood up for me when he saw that Gray was determined on victimisation.

'"Gray would murder sleep," he said.

'"But he has left us without minutes," Gray insisted.

'"We have reached decisions without them before this. We do not want every peccadillo that occurs in college recorded in black and white. He who makes an occasional mistake does far more for truth than the pedant who spends all his life trying to appear infallible."

'If that wasn't a slap in Gray's face, I would like to know for whom "trying to appear infallible" was intended. Nevertheless, if Gray perseveres with his motion against me and the Board supports him, I shall have to resign.' So said the divine one with a sigh.

Again Jan counted on his fingers:

'But you have Mahaffy, and the Professor of Moral Philosophy, and Smithers is a gentleman. How will Wilkins vote?' he repeated.

'Oh, for goodness' sake, Jan, don't let us take it for granted that it will ever come to a vote,' I said.

I wanted to keep our friend's mind from revolving on things to come. We had a long way to go before the next Board; and there were many wires still to be pulled. Before you can pull a wire you must first locate it.

25 *The Opinion Of A Moralist*

In spite of the fact that I had corrected Jan for anticipating the voting of the Board, I resolved to ask my friend, the Professor of Moral Philosophy, what he thought of Dr Tyrrell's predicament. I went to see him early, before he should have gone out.

The Professor of Moral Philosophy received me blandly.

'Sauterne,' he said, 'is more suited to the morning than Guinness's stout.'

When the bottle was finished, I broached, not another bottle as you in your haste might think, but the subject. He knew more about it than I.

'I am afraid that the venerably dull members of the Board have agreed to support their fellow, Tom Thompson, in this matter. Very much afraid. I do not wish to dispirit you, my dear chap; but I can hold out no hope, no hope at all. It is the culmination of much resentment.'

Despondency fell upon me. I was more concerned about my friend than I could possibly be about myself and I am by no means an altruist. Strange that I could be sorrier for a friend than for myself. Was it because I could not believe that circumstances could possibly affect me? Perhaps it was that I felt a little elation at my friend's discomfort and at the chance it gave me of helping him. But why should I examine my motives when the question is, what can be done for the doctor, and it is urgent at that?

I remember gazing stupidly in front of me at the wall of the philosopher's room. A coloured print of a Norwegian marriage feast, and a newly presented plaque of him who philosophises without effeminacy, Mahaffy, of course. Mahaffy, who could be sarcastic in a genial way when the spirit moved him. I recalled his crushing question to a man who was claiming respect for Swift McNeill – 'You know, he is descended from Dean Swift.' 'By whom? Stella or Vanessa?' Mahaffy inquired with a smile.

Mahaffy was superior to the chances and changes of this mortal state; not so Dr Tyrrell.

'Who did that?' I asked, pointing to the plaque on the wall.

'Some little *émigré* sculptor called Brissac, who lives in Harcourt Place. We gave him the order because he was recommended to us as a promising artist. He is, as you can see for yourself, still in his promissory stage . . . '

The professor smiled his sad and gentle smile. As I went

down the stairs I could hear him singing the rhythmic sentences of some old Moorish refrain:

> Allah, remember me;
> I have lived in Granada
> At the house of the falconer;
> And a woman taught me love
> In the evening before sunset.

Jan had a long face which shaded a smile when I met him again. He made me think of the Frenchman who said, 'There is something not altogether unpleasing in the misfortunes of our friends.' But Jan was, in spite of his intermittent way of speaking, sincerely concerned. We exchanged notes. It was evident that there was but little hope for our friend.

What goes on in the mind; and what has time got to say to it? Is it because it is immortal that it takes its time? Why should there be such a thing as a doorstep witticism: *esprit d'escalier?* That is, something that you think of when the opportunity has passed?

The opportunity for putting my plan for saving Dr Tyrrell into immediate execution was almost lost. Suddenly it came to me: not too late, thank goodness!

'The problem is as good as solved,' I said.

'Oh, is it?' Jan answered incredulously.

'Listen, will you. You know that plaque which his friends presented to Mahaffy on his birthday? Very well. If we can get one like it done of the doctor and get a splurge into the daily papers and build him up in such a way before the Board meets that it will think twice before putting a petty domestic, splenetic quarrel ahead of world-wide publicity, the thing is done. Any Board would be disgraced, and so would the college that persevered in calling for the resignation of such a distinguished scholar. Why, man, he is Honorary Doctor of Literature in Cambridge University; Doctor of Common Law in Oxford; LL.D. of Edinburgh; Doctor of Lit., Queen's University, and Fellow of the Royal Academy of Letters and something else in the University of Durham.'

Jan was not carried off his feet; but for an engineering student he was quite flexible. He said that he would be round later to see me. I told him to fix the commission up with Brissac while he was on his way. No time to spare. This was Wednesday, and the Board would meet on Tuesday. Yes; yes, I would take care of the publicity. But we would have to keep well out of it. Consent? Of course we would get the doctor's consent. It was tantamount to consenting to be saved.

Jan was quite right. I am thoughtless. He pointed out that we could not present the case to the doctor as I had presented it to him, Jan. We would not expect the doctor to enter into what was more or less a conspiracy, without loss of self-respect. No. We would have to proceed as if the idea had cropped up in the ordinary course of events. We would have to get a few names to preside over the unveiling, including the editors of the dailies and the London correspondents of the same. Sir Horace, of course, would do the unveiling and use the opportunity to discuss catch-cropping. I was to see the doctor as early as possible in the morning. Jan would drop in during our talk.

When an idea impinges on me, I am at first exalted, then the impact of the idea causes me to pass into shock. As a result of this I felt listless and despondent when I called on the doctor. I found him in a state, if not of despondency, of dejection, and in an irritable mood which with him took on a sarcastic tinge.

He was reading some comments that Mahaffy had sent to the daily paper about some poor old woman whom superstitious villagers had buried alive because they thought that she was a witch. Little did I know, though I might have guessed it, that the village in question was the vilage in which the doctor's father had had his parish.

'After all,' he said quietly as he laid down the paper, 'it is only a question of premature burial, which is not such an obnoxious thing as delayed burial, which Mahaffy so obtrusively represents.'

'Well, you cannot say with Shakespeare that she is one of those inhabitants of earth who "yet are on't". Perhaps it was she who "set the minister of hell at work". I am thinking of the obsession of Tom Thompson ... '

But the doctor was more interested in the source of the quotation than in its application. I told him that it was from Rowe's *Jane Shore*. I thought of Jowett's definition of a scholar as one who could point to his references. That is why the doctor had to get my quotation right.

'By the way,' I went on carelessly, 'there are certain friends of yours who want you to sit for a portrait bust. Later it can be cast in bronze.'

Then I added, and I thought that this was the height of diplomacy – it was as far as I have ever risen, almost to Talleyrand form: 'Sir, if I may make a suggestion, don't be too hard on Mahaffy. At any rate not until you have had a better plaque than his cast in bronze.'

The doctor took thought for a minute or two. At last he asked: 'You don't mean to tell me that Mahaffy approves of this?'

Now I was in a real quandary. What would Talleyrand have done, or rather Machiavelli?

Fortunately Jan appeared at the door.

'May I come in?'

'Come in, come in!' says the doctor.

I caught what sounded like a note of enthusiasm, not for Jan, of course, but for my suggestion. He wanted to tell it all to Jan. I rushed to anticipate him, for Jan could not yet know what we had been saying or how far the project had developed.

'Jan,' I said, 'you know the quotation at the base of Mahaffy's bust, *"Philosophoumen aneu malakias"*? What would you suggest for a bust of the doctor here?'

Jan hummed and hawed and spoke intermittently. But as it turned out eloquence would not have got him half as far as his halting suggestion, for it made the doctor take the bust for granted and jump to the consideration of the quotation that was to go on the plaque.

What Jan said was this:

'Isn't there? It seems to me that there is . . . I can't recall it accurately though . . . some remark of Dido when her city was being built . . . It could be used to refer to the walls of the Classical School which the doctor has founded in college . . . if you see what I mean. *"Meos muros vidi."* Those may not be the exact words. They don't scan. My Latin is rather rusty . . . '

The doctor groaned. Then he softened, out of his affection for Jan.

'"*Muros*" means a partition wall like the wall of a water closet; the word you want is "*moenia*". And the quotation which you quite rightly attribute to Dido is "*Meo moenia vidi*": "I have seen my walls rising."'

'I cannot imagine a more suitable legend for a plaque of the doctor,' I added hastily.

So it was arranged!

Before the doctor had time to ask himself why this should be left to his most irresponsible friends we must rush the sittings through. I saw Brissac at once. He was delighted. He would do it for nothing. That was out of the question. What we wanted was a plaque the same as the one he did of Mahaffy; and we wanted it completed in two days so that it could be photographed for the daily papers. The deadline would be Friday. Saturday for the ceremony.

While Brissac was seeing himself elected as official sculptor to the university, Jan was entertaining the doctor to what was a 'holding lunch'. Jan was to engage the doctor while I instructed Brissac. When we got the doctor back to his rooms Brissac was to begin.

The floor had already been covered with tarpaulin, the dais in place and the clay prepared. Brissac was instructed not to insist on the dais but to start on the head whether the doctor posed deliberately or not.

Very few would be interested in a description of a sculptor in action and of a sitter in inaction. It is enough to say that all went well.

We had a scratch audience for the well-chosen words that we got Sir Horace to say at the unveiling. The photographers from the various dailies were enthusiastic; they imagined that they had made a scoop. 'Publicity' had been foreseen; and printed matter, explaining the occasion of the presentation to Dr Tyrrell, had been made available, for obviously neither Jan nor I could pose as the 'onlie begetter' of the plaque idea. So let us pass over the unveiling. Suffice it to say neither the plot nor its purpose was unveiled.

It was at the beginning of the week after the meeting of the Board that Jan got a word with the doctor. He did not allude to the Board meeting. He refused to dine with Jan and me. He was dining elsewhere.

Jan looked at me. I looked at Jan.

'It must have gone well,' we said together.

It deserved a celebration to itself. What a pity that the doctor could not be let in on this.

When I did see the doctor, in his rooms, I thought that his manner was somewhat distant or rather lofty, as if he had turned himself into an examiner again and I was 'up'. He sat at his table under the window, and he was writing. The table was crowded with letters. The wastepaper basket was full of envelopes.

'You must excuse me. I have a considerable amount of correspondence to deal with. I am trying to explain to the Master of Balliol why I did not give him timely notice about the presentation of my plaque.'

I felt superfluous. On tiptoe I withdrew. I regret to say that I was not missed.

Anyway, I knew where to find Jan. His hours were his own. He had drunk himself into the Local Government Board and was a treasured fixture, for he had not been found wanting during the prolonged initiation. Old history; ours was new. He gave the order, and I took my seat.

'I saw the doctor,' I began. 'He was answering letters of which there was a pile on his desk. He was so busy that he did not ask me to stay. He was rather short with me. Not a word about the Board. Not even a hint of a drink; not a "won't you be seated for a while until I get this letter off my chest." Not a thing. I slipped out.'

Jan hawed a little. 'When I saw him, he was rushing off to dine with the Provost.'

I could see that Jan was trying to read a real excuse into that, rather than admit to himself that he too had been brushed off.

We sat silent. How long I could not say, but it must have been for at least a few minutes; and that is a very long time if you follow it on your watch; but it was at least five minutes because, when I did speak, the outlook had changed completely. I am a slow thinker. That is why, when I say five minutes, I am not exaggerating.

'Do you know what has happened?' I asked.

Jan made one of his inarticulate sounds which was meant to show that he was surveying the situation in all its aspects.

'Nemesis has interposed. When we undertook to draw a red herring, no, a red gurnet, across the track of the Board, we little thought of the factors which were out of our control ... '

'Such as?' Jan asked in a hushed way.

'The stature of the man for one thing. How were we to know what an inundation would follow the publicity? Then how were we to know that we would have to keep out of the whole business for the obvious reason that, if our scheme were found out, it would stultify its object and render the doctor suspect as an accessory to a trick. I did not realise, but you did, that we could never tell the doctor that the only thing we could think of to save him was this publicity. When you remember the abject state he was in before the Board meeting and compare it with his present state, when the Provost asks him to dinner, you will realise how successful our scheme was. You will also recognise that the greater the success the greater the need for the preservation of our secret.'

'We have started an avalanche,' said Jan.

'If we could only get him out of the way. To take a holiday, for instance,' I suggested.

‘We may have to get ourselves out of the way before very long.’

When I met Jan next day he had an air of reserve about him, something withheld, aloof. It was not until I told him that I had a letter by the morning’s post asking me to call on the doctor that his good cheer returned.

‘What hour did he happen to mention?’ Jan asked.

‘Four-thirty,’ I said briskly, though I was far from feeling comfortable.

‘Same here.’

‘Rather formal this letter writing – disconcerting, what?’

‘You know he never uses the telephone,’ said Jan.

‘Oh, so we’re both up before the Board so to speak, only it is a one-man Board consisting of the doctor?’

I interpreted Jan’s grunts to be equivalent to a more eloquent person’s ‘Well I’ll be damned!’

‘Well, young men,’ said Dr Tyrrell, ‘when I consented to sit for that plaque I was surprised by the haste and the suddenness of your arrangements. I have still to see the reasons for such a stampede: and many of my friends also have been taken by surprise; and they have written in no uncertain terms to complain to me about their treatment, as if I were responsible. Why was it so rushed?

‘As for the artist: no one has ever heard of him, and, though far be it from me to suggest it, there are those who state that I was his most important subject.’

Jan looked at me. I know that he wanted to ask, ‘What about Mahaffy?’ I wanted to ask that question myself; but how could we?

‘Nevertheless,’ the doctor proceeded, ‘he modelled me with my eyes half shut or altogether shut. One might think that was asleep. Then there was the publicity for which there was no discernible reason. It was little short of indecent; my picture, or rather reproductions, in Monday morning’s paper of that fellow’s (what do you call him?) bust that purports to be me. Then there is all the huggermugger about the donors. At first when they congratulated me I thought that the portrait was being presented to me by some members of the Board; but when I thanked Mahaffy he was astounded, genuinely so, I will admit. "My dear Tyrrell," he said, "is it not enough to immolate myself to a wretched artist to please Macran without adding you to the sacrifice? I am thanking my stars that the artist is not another Pygmalion and that my statue is not likely to come alive." His attitude left me feeling that I had become the victim of a practical joke ... '

'Sir!' we expostulated in unison.

'I won't go as far as to say that; but I cannot rid myself of the suspicion that the invitations to dinner that have been pouring in on me are not free from a touch of condolence; that they are intended to comfort me. Tonight I am dining with the Archbishop of Dublin, no very intimate friend of mine. It is the only way I can account for it. Who can tell how deserving an object of pity I may appear to such as he?

'On the other hand, you have always seemed to be good friends of mine. You have been indiscreet in this matter, though I have little doubt but that you both meant well.'

The doctor rose.

'Well I'll be damned,' said Jan when we got outside.

'You are already damned, so am I – in his opinion at any rate. Let me tell you this. It is the last time that I will try to save anybody. There are too many saviours in this world. Saviours always come to a bad end. The world is filled with people who are trying to do good and force others to do likewise. It is the cause of half the trouble on the planet.'

'I wish you would speak for yourself and leave me out of it.'

'You, Jan?'

'Yes. It was your idea, don't forget.'

'*Et tu, Brute*!' was all I said.

Jan looked at me. 'You need not take it so seriously. He is out of it this time but it won't be long before he is in the soup again.'

'Then it will be your turn,' I said; and led the way into Fanning's.

As if to comfort both of us Jan stuttered, 'After all we

were not as badly snubbed as was the fellow who broke in on the doctor's conversation with the rude inquiry, "Where's the urinal?"

'"Oh, go along that passage until you come to a door marked GENTLEMEN but don't let that deter you."'

26 *A Sea-Grey House*

I saw a model-T Ford trembling outside a shop in Nassau Street. I hastened home and asked for a compass and a map of Ireland. 'What new folly possesses you now?' my wife asked as I bent over the map. 'I am looking for the largest house farthest from the railhead in Ireland, something that may be even two days away, because this afternoon I saw an automobile that will bring that house within half a day's reach in – allowing for the lag in human thinking – a few years at most. I want to get it while it is almost unsaleable, while it is still cheap.' But she was not as enthusiastic as I; few people are.

I remember when I collected old mills, no one took any interest in my suggestions; and now what do you see? Temple Mills on the Liffey with its own power from the river. The owner has merely to pull a wire like a bellpull and he gets boiling water for his bath; his house is warmed and lighted and cleaned by electricity.

The mill at Swords could be adapted just as well. It had the advantage of a millpond on which water lilies lie, and a little brook to feed the pond. The rectory, 'a haunt of ancient peace,' stands beside the millpond, which is probably overgrown with weeds by now; but when I tried to collect it, the owner, a shopkeeper who dwelt beside it, became suspicious because I was too honest and I told him all the possibilities I saw. As far as I know, it is still a half-ruined store.

Then I tried to collect lakes, depending on the fact that sooner or later their beauty would be recognised by town-stifled citizens. Meanwhile, I could have them for a song and dwell by them in the summer. Before I had time to go into the title deeds, a sale came on in Connemara: Renvyle House with sixty or more rooms. It was less than nine miles from Garranban where the boys had learned to swim; Garranban; the open house! It was fifteen miles from the nearest town and the nearest town was seven or eight hours from Dublin; two days if the connection between trains was off. With automobiles running in my head and full of hope, I bought the place. An extra hundred pounds accelerated the sale. I had a house in the heart of Connemara on the edge of the sea on the last shelf of Europe in the next parish to New York!

Geologically it was a wonder: a storm beach enclosed a little lake which was fed by a brook that fell from a rocky rise on the south side. The lake was forty yards from the house, the house was less than a hundred yards from the sea. In the lake was a little peninsula, wooded still with the last specimens of the old Irish fir trees. It was called Roisindhu, the Little Dark Wood, and it gave its name to the lake. Above it rose Letter Hill, a mountain that, as the mists of morning lifted, could be seen, plum-blue, reflected in the lake.

It was Mahaffy who said 'plum-blue' when I found him early one morning seated outside the house watching the mist rise from the water and the mountain upside down in the lake. Letter Hill can turn to purple from blue-black as the light grows. On a fine evening the sun sinks double, a golden ball far out on the ocean, and a ball reflected in the lake, with only a thin green strip of land separating the real from its reflection. Far to the west and ending the view, the ruined castle of Renvyle stands. It was built, some said, by the O'Hurleys; and stone cannon balls were found embedded in its walls at the time of the auction of the house. Some said that these were thrown by the guns of Granuaile, Grace O'Malley, because she claimed the land on which the castle stood; but no galleys of those days could throw such cannon balls.

It was split in two on the orders from Cromwell to leave no fortress standing in Connaught. He had garrisoned the outlying island of Inisbofin, the Isle of the White Cow, with coast guards to prevent smuggling from friendly Spain. When he died these guards were abandoned and left to their own devices. They were not slaughtered, for the names of Heather, Hazel and King point to intermarriage with the people on the mainland.

There was an old library in the house. In it I found a first edition of More's *Utopia* printed at Basle; and what I should have appreciated, for it was unique, a first edition of Chaucer's lesson on the astrolabe to his son. It began, 'Little Lewis.' I should have presented it to the Library of Trinity College as I did the *Utopia*. But perhaps I only learned the value of the *Utopia* from Mahaffy when he came to visit me again some years after I had Renvyle House. The library went up in flames during the civil war; and with it the priceless book on the astrolabe, together with other irreplaceable things.

Touching the origin of Renvyle House, the story ran that a ship laden with a cargo of precious timber was wrecked on the beach hard by. Blake, the owner of the lands, was informed because all that went ashore between two points on the beach came under the 'manorial rights' which went with the property. Blake hastened from London – it must have taken him weeks, for model-Ts were far from being invented then. He saw the site on which stood a cottage owned by one O'Flaherty. He built between lake and sea. He pannelled the house with foreign wood and made his own glass, thick and uncouth but homemade. The roof he covered with great slabs from a slate quarry near by. In order to withstand the thrust of the Atlantic gales the roof was low, and the walls of the house were six feet thick in order to bear the pressure of the unmansarded roof. It was to report on the quarry of slates that I brought two Welshmen, of a Sunday, from a famous quarry of rustic slates in Wales and saw them back to the boat on the same day. About four hundred miles of a journey, nothing now, but quite an achievement then.

Some of the indoor walls were six feet thick, and where they were pierced, the doors were double. Sometimes the doors would open and shut by themselves. We took no notice of this, for we thought that it was the effect of draught in the corridors, or that the children were playing at hide-and-seek. It was otherwise when the Yeatses came to stay with us on their honeymoon; but thereby hangs a tale.

In the days when Renvyle House was built the inhabitants of the country dwelt either in castles or in cottages. Important people had to live behind battlements; it mattered little where the humble lived. It was strange, then, to find Renvyle unprotected by battlements or even window bars. The explanation was that its remoteness was its protection. There were no iron rails on the windows, which were less than breast-high from the ground; but a window of an upstairs room, the only room in the house with a northern aspect, was heavily guarded. Why was this?

I should tell you that the house was built like the letter H, with the crosspiece nearer one end. The house was built round three sides of a courtyard, the fourth side enclosed by a wrought iron gate. Galleries connected the two sides of the house, and off the upstairs gallery was the room with the barred windows. No servant maid would sleep in that room. There was a 'presence' there which could be felt, they said.

One day a heavy linen chest that stood immediately inside the door of this room somehow moved so as to prevent the door being opened. A man had to remove the window bars to get into the room to release the door. Was the house haunted? None of the country people would give a straight answer. Such a question caused silence, and sometimes made the person who was asked walk away.

One windy night I was sleeping alone in the west wing in a great four-poster bed, with old gilt on the posts which turned out to be made of tilting spears, rare enough, when I heard or thought I heard a person walking along the corridor. Whoever it was halted as if he had a wooden leg. Nearer and nearer the limping thing approached. The sound was plain in spite of the storm outside. I could endure the tension no longer. I jumped out of bed. Nothing was to be gained by cowering. I lit a candle. I pulled open the door suddenly.

The candle was blown out. I was alone in the dark with the thing in the passage. I tried to strike out. It was no use crying for help; any servants there were slept in the other wing where my shouts could not be heard or, if they were, would be put down to the howling wind or the waves on the beach.

I could not strike out; my arms felt weighted, as if I were exercising with rubber ropes. But there was no need to strike out or to shout for help because nothing happened. There was a silence of sorts, after a kind of sobbing. It took some time to find the matches.

So I have a haunted house. Splendid when I have company. I don't want to be there alone again. Wait till Yeats hears this. He will be interested. Interested, yes, provided that I do not attempt to rationalise it and to explain the affair away. No mention of the possibility of a nightmare. I am very much inclined to put it all down to a nightmare, with its muscle-bound sensation and the fact that nothing happened when I was sufficiently awake to open the door.

Why did nothing happen? You had better ask Yeats. Æ would be impatient and preoccupied with something he wished to say. He would waive the whole business aside as an infringement on what he saw in a vision: 'Immortal, mild, proud shadows.' Mine was anything but mild. Why? I never saw it. A nightmare could account for it all; but who can account for a nightmare?

Ash and sycamore trees sheltered the old place from the north and west, the points of the prevailing winds. Sycamore trees can thrive at the sea's edge; so can the ash. There was an ash grove to the northeast of the house. It looked lovely in the early morning when the level sun lit the clean boles and the bright grass growing up to the very roots. Later, in spite of a special stipulation and a promise to preserve the ash wood, some local oaf cut down all when Sir Something-or-other – Patrick, I think – Doran, head of the Land Commission deprived me compulsorily of half of the two hundred acres I had bought, when the estate was divided among the tenants. They were Blake's tenants, a scion of him who built the place. I have no tenants. And yet fellows like Larry Ginnell think that there should be more 'locals' than cattle in a land already over-populated.

To impress on farmers the value of a tree should be a matter for the schools. Instead of confusing their sons and daughters with *ersatz* Gaelic, it would be more practical, and better for the country, to impress on children the value of a tree. Shelter for cattle would appeal to them. For what cow could yield a proper quota of milk when exposed to the wind? If they could not recognise the importance of a tree as a drainer, that is, a dryer of land and a preserver of the country's soil, let it be hinted that it is just as unlucky to cut down a tree as a white thornbush. Thornbushes are exempt because they are preserved by superstition. It seems that the whole country was once run by superstition. If superstition works yet, let it save the trees. Except Iceland, Ireland has the lowest percentage of trees of any country in Europe, thanks to the ignorance of the farmer and the apathy of Anglicised commissioners.

A month earlier than the market, daffodils broke out under the trees; snowdrops came before them, closer to the earth and hidden in the grass for protection. Protection against the winds of February, not against frost; for winds, not frost, were the enemies on that western shelf of an arctic island made semi-tropical by the Gulf Stream from the United States. Flowers white and yellow beside the grey sea, and the aberrations of the Irish character alike are due to the beneficent current from America!

Dawns, sunsets, winds, trees and flowers can be found in any place that is cherished, and even in those places, if there be any, where no one has been.

There was something else, something indescribable but as real as dim colour or soft sound. It was the spirit of the place: the countryside was faintly magical even in the rain. Half tones told of it; and the soft atmosphere made you feel that you were in a region that was your proper home, a home where there was neither time, nor tide, nor any change at all, something friendly and akin and full of all that might be needed, if need were to arise; but it never did, for you felt that nothing was lacking. And you did not want to speak.

27 *The Coming Of Augustus*

If man were perfect, life, as we know it, would not be worth living. Think of it: there would be no need for religion with its sacraments; no need for Baptism, Confirmation, Communion; no need for Redemption even. More than this; if man were perfect there would be no movement in his world: everything would be static; there would be no poetry and no thought. The reasoning that leads to this conclusion should be less abrupt. Jumping to conclusions is not permissible even among philosophers. I am no philosopher, so I will stop here ... and introduce Francis Macnamara through whom I met Augustus John, a man of deep shadows and dazzling light.

Francis Macnamara was tall, golden-haired and blue-eyed. His nose was straight but it ended in a triangle that at times was red. He was a gangling young man. His father was squire of Doolin House, County Clare. It was said that he had taken advantage of the prerogative of all country gentlemen in the west of Ireland and married his cook. It was only a rumour of course, marriage and all, so let us leave it at that and concentrate on Francis. He went to Magdalen College, Oxford, where he learned to be introspective and to be aware of Art. How he met Augustus I do not know.

Francis had a pretty wife and a prettier sister-in-law. They were both French. The word went round – since everything in Ireland that is not in the newspapers, which are by no means general, goes by rumour – that Francis slept with his sister-in-law and his wife in the same bed to save hotel expenses. Correct enough, for his sister-in-law could not have had a better chaperone. In spite of these rumours, or because of them, I liked Francis, perhaps because of an additional rumour that he told his dentist, when asked his profession, 'I am a poet; and I teach poetry.' Now in an age when the common man reigns, that is refreshing. After all, why should a man be ashamed of his predilection? An artist is not; nor a musician and as for a tenor . . . Must a poet subscribe to the lowbrows and hide his head? Francis did not. Though I never met one of his pupils, except his sister-in-law, I got a paper-covered booklet of his poems. I forget all – a bad sign – but a part of one; it was addressed to an aviator in the days when flying was a dangerous novelty:

> The lofty mountains pointing at you stand.

That, I thought, is a fine image, giving as it does both altitude and speed. I can see the aeroplane speeding over the established mountains, high over their tops.

He was influenced by that fine forgotten poet, George Meredith. There were schools of poetry in ancient Ireland where the pupil had to study for fourteen years before he was considered proficient. Francis studied all his days. I cannot be sure that the adjective was 'lofty' in his line about the aviator and I cannot recover it now, for the little book is long ago out of print. It was probably one of those books of verse which Blackwell publishes for earnest youths and maidens at Oxford, and makes them pay for through their Muses. The last I saw of Francis was in a white-washed cottage in the Dublin mountains where he was reading Bunyan's *Pilgrim's Progress*. He tried to get me to read that book in vain. I much preferred to read of Lancelot and how love constrained him, than Bunyan mouthing morality from jail.

But long before Francis took to Bunyan and whitewash, he invited over from London Augustus John. And Augustus arrived in Dublin like a lion, or some sea king with golden moustache and beard. John is a Welshman; and a fair-haired Welshman is rare. So it is conjectured that the ancestors of Augustus were men who fought with Harold against the invader under William the Bastard from Normandy, and, after that disastrous day at Hastings, took refuge in the mountain fastnesses of Wales. It seems improbable, for the Welshmen so scorned the Saxons that they refused to extend to them the blessings of Christianity in the third century; so why shelter them in the eleventh? Augustus assuredly is descended from the Vikings who founded Haverford where he was born.

There must be more Welsh than Saxon in Augustus in spite of his colouring because imagination is the gift of the Gaels and Welshmen are Cymric Gaels, and you have only to look at his paintings to see what imagination Augustus has. Now he is the only man painting in England that matters at all. And that is why the English Government honoured him with the Order of Merit. The Order of Merit is the closest club in existence: it is limited to nine members. In the old days it suggested gout more than merit; but I give it credit for honouring the man whose imagination enabled him to see beauty in truth and who has more colour in his retina than any man I have met.

When I saw him for the first time I noticed that he had a magnificent body. He could have posed for the Nordic Man, whoever he is. He was tall, broad-shouldered and narrow-hipped. His limbs were not heavy, his hands and feet were long. When I told Æ of John's long hands, he at once began a theosophical dissertation on Lu, the Long-Handed god of all the arts, the Irish equivalent of Apollo. 'For, you see, there is a similarity and a relationship between all the gods of every religion.'

What to do with Augustus? No one talks art to an artist. Augustus was – and still is – a moody man. Francis had offered Augustus the freedom of the island, but such freedom is not free. You have to pay for it. Therefore, the first thing to do was to get suitable lodgings for Augustus. The Royal Hotel, Dalkey, would have answered, but it had no rooms vacant. But the house next door had.

Augustus was duly installed on the second floor; and his face looked out of the window when I called to show him what Dalkey had to offer. It had the Cosy Kitchen with a nice room behind the bar, which occupied the front room. The Cosy Kitchen was backed against a granite wall on the top of which tufts of pink valerian grew. It stood by itself and was full only on Sundays and other days of obligation. We sat for hours saying nothing in the little back room. Suddenly from his corner Augustus broke into song:

> 'In Jurytown where I was born;
> In Newgate jail I lie with scorn.'

It was a song about a highwayman and seemed appropriate when John put his vigour into it. But a strange thing: as he sang his body seemed to grow small. It was as if it all went into his voice. He dwindled.

> 'At seventeen I took a wife;
> I loved her as I loved my life.'

If he threw himself into a song it was a promise that he would throw himself into a portrait. Now there are artists whose selves I would not like to have painting me. One is Billy Orpen, high-shouldered, short-bodied, long-legged – he will be 'Sir' William later, wait and see! And there are others who are mean men. With Augustus it is different. His would be a personality to have in your portrait.

I know you will sense the fact that I look upon portraits as stamping grounds whereupon the painter may dance. The fact is that no one who is up in things artistic ever speaks of So-and-so's portrait but 'Did you see the John of Lady Ottoline?' I know that much about art and very little more. Augustus John has magnificent eyes so there the sitter is safe. I have already remarked on his perfect frame so what more do you want? Shannon had not fine eyes, but he had a good mouth, so his portraits all show people whose mouths are comely. As for Leonardo da Vinci, that enigmatical smile of his looks out on life from every portrait he has painted. After this you will say that I have been impressed by someone's statement to the effect that artists, like children, paint themselves. And you will be right.

But what about the savage portraits he paints, such as those of Lady Ottoline Morrell and David Lloyd George? Exactly. He knew the rascality of Lloyd George, the schemer, the double-crosser and the rogue that he was. It is all there in that unscrupulous face. Lady Ottoline, in his opinion, stood for false values and they are in the humps on her breast and back.

Dalkey is a lovely place. It looks out over Shanagolden Bay that sweeps in a curve to the south, so like the Bay of Naples that the pretentious owners of the villas around, who have probably never been to Naples, have given their villas Italian names. The whole terrace, in the second last house of which Macran lives, is called Sorrento Terrace. There must have been a regular wave of Italianism, for you can see it beginning at Blackrock, where there is a house called *Qui si Sano* and so on. Energetic Browning's time.

The visit of Augustus was a great excuse to take a day off now and then. I called for him one morning and he was all set to go. We would pick up Joe Hone, who lived at Killiney, and go to Glendalough, the Glen of the Lakes, in Wicklow. Joe, for all his quiet ways and his delicate health, which assured old age, knew all the artists and he was acceptable to Augustus. On through the lovely country we went. Augustus, who was sitting in the back, could not be distracted by scenery, for beside him sat Vera Hone.

I decided against going into Pluck's at Kilmacanoge. It might be hours before I could get the artist out. The drive to Glendalough takes two hours. We could have drinks at the hotel that has a clear river at the back. We bowled along the Rocky Valley. Suddenly I heard the word 'Stop.' As it evidently was not meant for me, I didn't stop. Joe Hone did not turn his head, so why should I? High to the left rose the peak of the Golden Spear, called latterly the Sugarloaf. The past was more romantic than the present, though the present was romantic enough just now.

Glendalough is set in a deep valley, between mountains which are near on either side. It is famous for an early monkish town which was walled, and for its round tower and the Seven Churches. In the upper lake, about thirty feet up in the cliff, is an excavation, about eleven feet long and less than four feet high, for it is impossible to stand up in it. This is St Kevin's Bed. St Kevin was a pre-Patrician 'saint' whose chief act was to repulse the female in the person of Kathleen. He threw her into the lake below, and she sank. Was that why they called him an anchorite? Apparently he expected the human race to be propagated by fission. This and the graveyard prevent it from being a place of enjoyment for me. Yet we arrived; so it provided a destination, for the road could go no farther and the Austrian who ran the hotel was a friend of mine.

The Austrian stood a drink 'on the house' when he saw Augustus John. Austrians are sensitive and highly cultivated, and the proprietor immediately recognised an outstanding human being when he beheld the Master. I for my poor part stood on the wooden bridge behind the hotel and gazed so long at the water that I felt I had a thirst, and so in and ordered a drink. John was toying with his whisky. His pipe lay on the table, unlit. Would it be the right time to tell him about Gendalough? He might not like the story about St Kevin. He might be short with me. Well, it's a nice state of affairs not to dare to speak to an artist about scenery. I might tell him what Sir Edwin Lutyens told me about the churches when I took him to Glendalough. Why tell him anything? He is entertaining Vera Hone with his silences. I think that I'll take a stroll with Joe along by the lake where you can see the water through the pines. Joe will know all about Glendalough and early Christianity and St Kevin.

28 *Mr Short*

Donnycarney is on the way to Santry, famous for the Lord Santry who was 'reduced' to a baronetcy in the eighteenth century for running a footman through. I mention Donnycarney because Joyce loved the name and wove it into one of his exquisite lyrics. Donnycarney would be in the sequence of the alphabet if it were Carneydonny; but it would not sound so well. It would not be so magical, and the magic of words was dear to Joyce. What is the alphabet anyway? It was the first attempt to reduce language to its radicals: 'You have the letters Cadmus gave.'

There is another way out of Dublin, which has roads out of it as the Statue of Liberty has rays out of her head. This road goes out from the capital through Drumcondra. Somewhere about Drumcondra was a lunatic asylum, set in the fields far from the road. It was about to be condemned, because it was in private hands and the doctor who owned it was recently dead. I knew another private asylum owned by a friend of mine who lived round the corner from Ely Place in Hume Street. His name was Dr Swan. He had a beautiful eighteenth-century house out near Templeogue. The dining room had three windows in the end walls, which were curved. I dined there one evening with him and the matron of his mental home, which was built as an annexe to the old house with the curved walls.

Why am I writing about private asylums near Dublin? Because from one of them, the one deep in the fields out Drumcondra way, I got the idea of kidnapping the Chief Secretary for Ireland, who had the temerity to visit the country. His name was Mr Short. He looked like a horse coper. He was Mr Short at the time, 1918, though doubtless he was later lost in an alias of the peerage. He went round with an armed guard, a symbol of the love the Irish People bore to those who rule their country. To capture the Chief Secretary and to conscript him among the patients in the Drumcondra Asylum was an original idea and one that would evoke the laughter of the British masses who are ever fair-minded. They would laugh at anything awkward that befell a member of their government.

I passed on the idea to those who could work it out. It was accepted with enthusiasm. First the guard would have to be bought off. This was found to be impossible. That meant that he was a member of the Royal Irish Constabulary. If he were an Englishman, he would have seen the light; and few things are lighter than Bank of England notes. No: he would have to be bumped off. I have scruples about assassination, increased no doubt by an attempt on my own life.

England was ruling through the Chief Secretary. If he were to be driven up in a van to the lonely house near Drumcondra and registered as an Englishman whose relatives wanted his mental derangement to be kept as secret as possible, all would be plausible. Any assertions that he was the Chief Secretary and that it was an outrage to confine him would only confirm the wisdom of his family in having him confined in another country. He would be diagnosed by the hardy attendants as another case of delusions of grandeur.

Very sad: we all know what that means. Delusions of grandeur is the form of insanity that should be expected in an Englishman, Is not the British Empire based on delusions of grandeur? Grandeur for its officials: durbars and delusions for its subjects.

He would be well fed and well treated. The asylum, if he were discovered in it, would become famous and perhaps would not be closed after all. All his statements while he was a patient would be subsequently published. We would see to that. The reports would make good reading, even though they were made in the days before the mouthings of lunatics became literature.

All this was a good idea, an excellent idea; but there was the obstacle of the armed guard. He too might be accommodated, but first it would be necessary to disarm him, and, alas, alas, as I have said, he would have to be killed. That would more than counteract the farce of the whole thing, for the English masses would never tolerate murder. So it was that the hardheadedness of Northern policemen prevented the tables from being dissolved amid laughter, and saved the routine of Mr Short.

Now that we are on the subject, let us discuss the traits of a good lunatic. Augustine Birrell, another Chief Secretary whom later I met, would have been unsatisfactory for our purpose. His face would be against him for one thing. It was square and logical. And then he seemed to have been born with glasses. You could not imagine him decently with them off. He would have looked naked. Lunatics seldom wear spectacles. At any rate, they remove them from the dangerous ones. They are held to be superfluous in the padded cell.

Mr Birrell's forehead was not that of a lunatic. It was not made for a fine frenzy. It was flat on top – plenty of knowledge, no imagination. That must have been what George Moore sensed when he met Birrell – no imagination. Moore resented Birrell's using his position in the Cabinet to add authority to authorship. Moore had the instincts of a woman: he was always right. There was a time when Birrell was right too. That was when he was twitted about the insurrection which broke out during his term as Chief Secretary: 'I haven't the money to buy them all.' That was true so far as the officials of Dublin Castle were concerned, not one of whom resigned; but to the nation at large it had no application. Money could not have paid for centuries of British despoliation or have bought off a nation's desire to be free. All of which only points to that satrap's ignorance, and ignorance alone is not a qualification for lunacy.

Field Marshal Montgomery would make a typical lunatic because of his phobias and his beret. He hates smoking (aminophobia) and drinking (oinophobia) and coughing – 'There must be no coughing in my presence.' The warders could not clear their throats even on a Monday morning. He would issue orders (stratego-mania). His razor would be removed until he looked like a 'naval person'; and then he would grow worse. Now Winston is beyond a joke: – a subject for 'psychiatry'.

Once you are locked up in a bughouse, everything you say is used against you. The very natural wish to get out is used as a proof that you should be kept in. It is like a tea party with an old maid where every word you say is at cross-purposes and you cannot put yourself right in her eyes. Only it is much worse: you are licked before you start.

The only people who would get along quite nicely in a lunatic asylum are a king and queen, to whom boredom is first, not second, nature. They would never know that they were confined, but they'd be dazed if set at large. If by any mischance they grew restless, they could have shock treatment, that is, a series of electric shocks sent through the frontal lobe of the brain to ensure concussion. Everyone knows that concussion of the brain makes for conservatism and continuance and what more do you want in a monarch? If King George III had been confined all the time, America might not have been lost. From this you will see that there is much to be said for a lunatic asylum.

What about me? I would make an excellent lunatic. Already I know most of the ropes. Is it not a tradition that the heads of all lunatic asylums become affected in the end? Would it not be subtle flattery to persuade the doctors, warders, nurses and floor cleaners that they were qualifying for directorship? The more eccentric they got the less would they trouble about me. There may be something in it. Have I not lived in the rooms once occupied by Krafft-Ebing in Vienna? I am a harmless lunatic and I do not need to be locked up. Confine, rather, those Irishmen, the Royal Irish Constabulary, for instance, who would die before letting their disciplinarians down.

Here is the psychiatrists' imaginary report shorn of nine-tenths of its verbiage: 'Winston Churchill was born in the ladies' cloakroom in Blenheim on St Andrew's day. He was born prematurely – a seven months child. To the place of his birth may be traced his wish to pose as 'a naval person'; and the cloak and dagger acts that have characterised his life. His mental precocity is due to his premature birth.'

It was not called 'The Ladies' Cloak Room' in the days in which Winston was born; but psychiatrists cannot be expected to know everything.

29 *The City Of Dreadful Knights*

'Lunacy,' said Connolly Norman, 'is a condition where dreams overflow into life.' Bad enough, you will say; but what about dreams (and those of a pompous bully) overflowing into other people's lives?

'England's difficulty is Ireland's opportunity'; that is a wrong quotation. The correct one is, 'England's extremity is Ireland's opportunity,' etc. Now there is a play of words when you use 'extremity' that might suggest to some minds a kick in the rump.

Extremity, or difficulty, hardly accounts for Arthur Griffith shouldering a rifle. Yet I saw his sturdy figure clad in a dark green uniform marching in company with other men in uniform. No; this conduct does not agree with his constitutional methods. Bloodlessly by these he was to bring about separation from England in the very same way that Kossuth freed Hungary. Those who read Griffith's *Resurrection of Hungary* must have wondered, when they saw him marching in Dublin. What had happened? Did he at last come to realise what all who went before him to the gibbet or the pitch cap, in fruitless rebellion after rebellion, had realised and that is that England never opens anything but a trembling hand? The few hundred who marched with Griffith were unlikely to make 'England shake'. Rather she will dispense bland and lavish promises all redeemable, mark you, *after* the war.

Thus was John Redmond fooled and Tom Kettle, who went recruiting for his chief, John Redmond; but forbore to ask men to go to a battle he himself would refuse to join. He was not like Sir James Percy, owner of the *Irish Wheelman*, or Sir Simon Maddock, curator of Mount Jerome Cemetery. Both were knighted, one for keeping peace in the cemetery, no doubt, and Sir James for his enigmatical smile. Tom Kettle fell at Ginchy. Sir James, who stayed at home, was presented with a cutlass of Honour because of his efforts at recruiting for the Navy. Sir William Thompson was knighted for chaperoning Lady Aberdeen. Hugh Lane, the picture dealer, was knighted for admiring Manet, as Sickert, the artist, said.

The situation is becoming serious – what about my voluntary work in war hospitals and consultant to them all? That is sure to be awarded. The only thing to do is to write to Lloyd's and take out an insurance policy against knighthood. It is not as amusing or as farcical as might at first appear. It is quite serious. Apart altogether from the association with me of characters that have been knighted in Dublin, I will lose the bulk of my practice – such as is left of it – because the bulk of it is among Irishmen who are Nationalists. They are no longer filled with awe at knighthoods, not after the last accolades. And if I refuse a knighthood it will be said that I am one of the disgruntled Irish and I shall lose all the moneyed garrison and the Church of Ireland as well. A bit of a quandary; but there is one hope: Percy, Maddock and the rest *sought* knighthoods and only God knows what they paid for it. And what about the fellow who was made a peer for pretending to be a Prime Minister's bastard? Yes, but that's the peerage. We are talking about knighthood.

John Robert O'Connell was knighted for putting trust funds at the disposal of Lady Aberdeen. He was the smallest attorney in Dublin as far as stature went. It is told that when the accolade was over and Lord Aberdeen pronounced the words, 'Arise, Sir John,' the onlookers did not know whether he had risen or was still kneeling. Later he became a Benedictine monk. The abbot sent for him one day to explain that spats did not accord with the habit he wore. He was sent to the belfry where, if you can believe anyone, he went up with the rope and was never seen again. Thus the accolade was followed by an assumption. He had risen. Spats in the belfry!

I do not want honours either on the King's Birthday or the New Year. The insurance will compensate me and the premium cannot be great, seeing that the request is, if not unprecedented, unusual. Of course, no insurance will compensate me if Arthur uses his gun. That is a contingency that need not be considered; but coolness or the loss outright of his friendship must be. He whom Griffith thinks unworthy is unworthy indeed.

I could have hobnobbed with those in power, always excluding Lloyd George, who is a reflection on power and even on politics; but I did not take the trouble. I suppose a sense of what was befitting saved me. The cobbler should stick to his last, and the doctor to his patients and avoid the society of knights who could not sit on a horse. All this may be part of some divine event; but to me it is not yet revealed. Jimmy Percy, now Sir James, got a Napoleonic complex: the walls of the stairway of his house were furnished with pictures of Napoleon in many attitudes and after many glorious victories. He was depicted in the days of his glory, but there was no picture of him on the deck of the *Bellerophon.* Simon Maddock, not satisfied with his British knighthood, spent quite a lot of money trying to become a senator, after the Irish Free State was created. He died trying to save a parrot, whose only cry was 'God Save the King,' from a fire which broke out in his house in the cemetery. I am too prone to see symbols where there are none; so I desist.

Before I take credit to myself for having discovered that the less intelligent a general be, the more successful, I must submit my discovery to the test of the converse; that is, whether the opposite holds good. Can I show that intelligence makes for bad soldiers? I have only two examples, but then my acquaintance with military men is limited. I was walking in Hyde Park one morning when I met Shane Leslie, now Sir Shane, with General Sir Ian Hamilton, who conducted the disembarkation after the gross and stupid insistence on the Gallipoli landing. It was said that he paid the most scrupulous attention to the prose of his dispatches, which never mentioned the two millions in gold which, according to rumour in London, was the price that Atatürk set for the escape of Irish and Australian troops from that deadly peninsula. Sir Ian talked about another general. He said, 'He could get a hundred thousand troops into Hyde Park; but he could never get them out.' This was for me an insight into military problems. I knew that London policemen could handle one hundred and thirty thousand spectators at a football final, and get them in as well as out!

30 *Stupidity Is The Only Wear*

When celebrating the Charge of the Light Brigade at Balaclava, the Poet Laureate, Tennyson, wrote, 'Someone had blundered.' Blundering or 'muddling through' would appear to be the *modus vivendi* of England. It is a great country that can make its empties pay for its full ones!

Tom Kettle, who saw the incident, told me that the appropriately named Kitchener, who could feed an army but not lead it, was carried out 'blind to the world' from 10, Downing Street by two flunkies and put into a taxicab. He was blind to the world physically when he had to be carried; and figuratively when he ignored and thereby discouraged the first – and last – outburst of Irish enthusiasm for a war ostensibly to free small nations. Ireland was ready to cross the seas and fight, when England was unwilling to submit to conscription, that, is to be drafted to fight for itself. Perhaps it was the belief, prevalent in Ireland, that 'a good fight justifies any cause'.

There were thin, half-hearted Kitchener Armies but no general enlistment at a time when England was up against a foe of its own weight and colour. It was no longer a battle against fuzzy-wuzzys but against a mighty enemy with modern equipment. English armies were on the run – 'delaying action' – from Mons and Le Cateau, and they delayed no one. The blundering became contagious. The French armies under Joffre attacked through Lorraine in the south and were bloodily repulsed when they should have stemmed the German onrush through Belgium. The result of the combined effort of France and England was to abandon all Belgium to Germany, a large part of France, and eighty per cent. of its coal. Then came Tannenberg, at which Hindenberg and Ludendorff slaughtered three hundred thousand wretchedly armed Russians or drove them into the marshes to drown. This was on August 30, 1914, when the war had been a little over three weeks begun.

To give Russia arms; that was the paramount need. The Baltic was closed. It would be necessary to force the Dardanelles. That portion of the Royal Navy to which this task had been assigned did its work so well that it left but one fort standing. This fort had but two long-range guns left and these had only thirty-five shells. Liman von Saunders had not yet arrived with his infantry to help the Turks. The road to Constantinople was wide open. Ah, but the Royal Navy had lost three battleships and at least five hundred men in opening it. Naval intelligence was unaware of the victory! There was a council of war on board the *Suffern*. The captains could not make out what had sunk their ships. They decided to break off action. It cost two extra years of fighting and the lives of millions of men, and it brought about the fall of the Asquith government.

Set a thief to catch a thief. Lloyd George, a Welshman, was made Prime Minister instead of Asquith. His job was to win the war. First he had to create two peerages and make one of his conspirators Viceroy of India, before his financial scandals could be hushed sufficiently. He began organising for victory by kicking the Commander in Chief, Lord French, upstairs to the viceroyalty of Ireland. Haig (of Haig and Haig), a Scotsman and a cavalry officer, was appointed in the place of Lord French. Lloyd George, with a rogue's nature, became suspicious of the most straightforward of men, Haig. He suspected that Haig's propensity to attack might cost so many lives that his own popularity as Prime Minister would be affected. Before he could blunder, America entered the war.

Here is a tale that will try your credulity. Haig's sister had married the great Irish whiskey distiller, John Jameson. Through the offices of Lady Fingall I was invited in the last year of the war to lunch at St. Marnock's, a delightful place where the Jamesons lived by the Portmarnock beach north-west of Howth Head and about seven miles from Dublin. After the lunch, I was taken into the study, or library, and asked with great seriousness if I could organise another rebellion so that the attention of Lloyd George might be diverted from her brother, the Commander in Chief, whom she had reasons to know Lloyd George intended to sack!

I explained as well as I could that it was not in my power to arrange rebellions. The implication did not dawn on me at the time. I was not sufficiently alive to what people like the Jamesons must think of me. Obviously, they must have thought that I was deep in the councils of the provisional government of Ireland. But this is a retrospective view of the situation. It goes to show, too, what the sister of the field marshal must have thought of Lloyd George. It is not the first time that a warrior has been fired for trying to win a war.

31 *Easter Week*

I took a few days off in Connemara before Easter, 1916. I was returning by train from Galway when the first rumours of the insurrection were heard. Rumour upon rumour as the train went along. It was delayed at Athlone, which is about the centre of Ireland, to allow artillery from the barracks there to go ahead to Dublin. Then I knew that there was something serious in the air. At Mullingar, fifty miles west of Dublin, the train came to a halt. It could go no further because the lines were cut. This evidently was to prevent the passage of guns to Dublin. It convinced me that the country must have risen, as it had; in spite of the efforts of Professor MacNeill to call the rebellion off at the last moment.

Dublin was 'up'. All the old ballads surged through my mind: 'The debt so long unpaid.' Every century had seen a rising against the oppressor and now we were in another rebellion. I felt that I was a lucky man.

There was but one car that could be hired at Mullingar. Needless to say, it was not a good one. Its owner charged enough to buy it; but what did I care? I had to get to Dublin, not to see patients on Tuesday morning but to see what was happening on Easter Monday, now. Just as I was about to start, a middle-sized, middle-aged man with a grey beard and a tall silk hat came hurrying. Would I be so kind as to let him share the car? He could not get one for love or money in Mullingar and he had to be in London to attend an emergency meeting on Tuesday morning. Love? Here was the well-known Larry Ginnell, member of Parliament for

Westmeath and instigator of the 'hazel-wand' treatment of the graziers.

Cattle-driving was then the vogue. Cattle instead of men were supposed to be the enemies of the country and those who owned cattle were to be punished by having their herds driven by the hazel wand. My own opinion was exactly the opposite. I regarded his membership in John Redmond's Parliamentary Party with disapproval, but it did not prevent me from giving him a lift.

I wondered what was the Emergency Session of the House of Commons which he had to attend? He did not tell me. It was one of those sessions so secret that a voter could not be confided in by an elected man. This is the habit of those on governments; once elected, they turn against those who elected them and form a commando of their own. Needless, to say I did not ask Larry what the secret session might be. I was hoping that the rebellion would put an end to all those who carried their complaints into the spider's parlour. Even though there might be more to complain of, let us have a parlour of our own.

We drove more or less in silence for an hour and a half. Then the member of Parliament woke out of his trance. We were going down Cabra Road – a detour of some sort was necessary – when a bullet struck the windscreen and a few others whined over our heads. This was most unparliamentary. I did not like it any more than the M.P.

At once the driver put out the headlights, Cautiously we came to the railway bridge at Cabra, which had been turned into a barricade. A boy with a rifle stood beside it. He said his name was John Fogarty. His name, of which mine is a corruption or a derivative, took some of the force out of my expostulations that a bullet had been fired through our windscreen. He explained that we were mistaken for 'military' because we drove with lights undimmed. And the Republic could not afford to take chances. Hence we were given the benefit of the doubt. Benefit? The shots over our heads were the beneficial ones. I told him of the artillery train on its way. He said that it did not mean anything because there were no shells. He seemed full of hope for the rising. I left him so. He could not have been more than sixteen.

If symbols were prophetic, I might have seen in the first shots of the Easter Week revolution, fired against friendly Irishmen, civil war. I did not forsee anything of the kind. I thought only of the generations of the brave who in every century had risen in dark and evil days to right their native land and had been met with the pitch cap, the rack and the gibbet. Lord Edward Fitzgerald, Robert Emmet, Wolfe Tone, all done to death, and a divided Ireland left.

Don't imagine that this has been accidental through the centuries. It is the result of a policy which is very old; secret and deliberate. Here is what Sir John Mason wrote to the Privy Council as long ago as 1550 concerning the government of Ireland: 'These wild beasts should be hunted aforce, and at the beginning should be so bearded, before the whole herd run together, as might know with whom they had to do; wherein *the old and necessary* policy hath been to keep them by all means possible at war betwen themselves.'

The leopard does not change his spots. The John Masons are in council in London; and they will find means to keep the Irish 'by all means possible' at war between themselves. Who planned and prophesied the civil war?

When I had dismissed the car and with it Larry Ginnell, M.P., I took a stroll about the city. Dublin seemed normal. The street lights were brilliant. But there were crowds about, and this was unusual, for the streets of Dublin are rarely crowded.

The air was full of rumours. Engagements had already taken place. Victory for the insurgents. Engagements with whom? I asked myself. Key points were 'occupied'. There was much military textbook talk going about. Enthusiasm too.

I grew melancholy. And this feeling of oppression was, if anything, aggravated by what I read on a poster that had just been pasted on a pillar of the General Post Office.

POBLACHT NA H-EIREANN

THE PROVISIONAL GOVERNMENT OF THE IRISH REPUBLIC TO THE PEOPLE OF IRELAND

Irishmen and Irish Women: In the name of God and of the dead generations from which she receives her old tradition of nationhood, Ireland through us summons her children to her flag and strikes for her freedom.

Having organised and trained her manhood through her secret revolutionary organisation, the Irish Republican Brotherhood, and through her open military organisations, the Irish Volunteers and the Irish Citizen Army; having patiently perfected her discipline, having resolutely waited for the right moment to reveal herself, she now seizes that moment, and, supported by her exiled children in America and by gallant allies in Europe, but relying first on her own strength, she strikes in full confidence of victory.

We declare the right of the people of Ireland to the ownership of Ireland and to the unfettered control of Irish destinies to be sovereign and indefeasible. The long usurpation of that right by a foreign people and government has not extinguished the right, nor can it ever be extinguished except by the destruction of the Irish people. In every generation the Irish people have asserted their right to national freedom and sovereignty: six times during the past three hundred years they have asserted it in arms. Standing on that fundamental right and again asserting it in arms in the face of the world, we hereby proclaim the Irish Republic as a sovereign Independent State, and we pledge our lives and the lives of our comrades in arms to the cause of its freedom, of its welfare and of its exaltation among the nations.

The Irish Republic is entitled to, and hereby claims, the allegiance of every Irishman and every woman. The Republic guarantees religious and civil liberty, equal rights and equal opportunities to all its citizens, and declares its resolve to pursue the happiness and prosperity of the whole nation and of all its parts, cherishing all the children of the nation, equally and oblivious of the difference carefully fostered by an alien government, which had divided a minority from a majority in the past.

Until our arms have brought the opportune moment for the

establishment of a permanent National Government, representative of the whole people of Ireland and elected by the suffrage of all her men and women, the Provisional Government hereby constituted will administer the civil and military affairs of the Republic in trust for the people.

We place the cause of the Irish Republic under the protection of the Most High God, whose blessing we invoke upon our arms, and we pray that no one who serve that cause will dishonour it by cowardice, inhumanity or rapine. In this supreme hour the Irish Nation must, by its valour and discipline and by the readiness of its children to sacrifice themselves for the common good, prove worthy of the august destiny to which it is called.

Signed on behalf of the Provisional Government
Thomas Clarke

Sean MacDiarmada	Thomas MacDonagh
P. H. Pearse	Eamon Ceannt
James Connolly	Joseph Plunkett

Yes. She has 'seized the moment'. Ireland's opportunity! It is taken!

I got one of these proclamations and brought it home. It was printed on poor paper and there were at least two founts of type used. It was badly punctuated: things which witnessed the secrecy and haste of its printing.

I examined the names of the signatories first. Not one was known to me, except in one case and that was by reading of the exploits of James Connolly whose patriotism seemed to be the patriotism of a labour agitator. I had met not one of those who had proposed themselves as the Provisional Government.

The words were brave and true. However, I did not like that clause about cowardice, inhumanity or rapine. Did he who wrote that sentence know the potentialities of some of the 'Irish People'? Rapine we had and inhumanity. Absurdity, yes; but no cowardice. Not unless you count pretending that you are a citizen loyal to Great Britain when, on your way to join its army, your good intentions are frustrated by your arrest as a suspect!

As I said, I was studying the names of the signatories of the brave proclamation. I suspected that there was not a Protestant among the signatories. I would have liked it better if there had been. I must ask someone about the men who issued it.

I went round on the morrow to see Hicks, the furniture master-craftsman in Lower Pembroke Street. He snuffled and was bent on ignoring both the question and myself at first. It was a mannerism he had, instead of manners. I knew Hicks. After some desultory visitors had left the shop Hicks opened up. 'Tom Clarke is all right, an old Fenian. There's nothing wrong with Tom Clarke. Patrick Pearse? His father is a tombstone cutter over in England. Sean MacDiarmada has a bit of a limp. Eamon Ceannt is Edward Kent, born in England. Tom MacDonagh, I don't think he is a Dublin man. Jospeh Plunkett? Isn't he one of the sons of auld Count Plunkett by one of his marriages, the old fellow with the beard? He had one son anyway who was riddled with tuberculosis . . . But what the hell is all this about?' Don't alarm yourself. It was only Hicks's way of repudiating any information he conveyed.

His detached summing up of the leaders of the rebellion was typical. Hicks stood to lose everything; and yet, like many wealthier men, he kept dabbling in revolution. How can that be explained? You see it among the wealthy actors of Hollywood. Is it in their case a sense of guilt, of undeserving, that inclines them to placate the remorseless enemy of non-political wealth, Communism? I am afraid I shall have to act the Lord Mayor once more with, 'There I leave you.'

War is not altogether grim, at least not in Ireland. The cheap book on military tactics that the Command of the Irish Republican Army seemed to rely on must have directed that sentries be posted at key positions in 'occupied territory'. That probably accounted for the stationing of young Dan Crowley (sixteen years of age but soldier of the Republic) with his rifle at the top of Grafton Street where it runs into Stephen's Green. At the hour of tavern-closing which was about 11 p.m. he was on duty, He took himself and his duties seriously. It certainly was a serious matter to be caught with a rifle by the British Government; but that thought was not what was uppermost in his mind. He was thinking of the position he had to hold, to let no one pass. No one offered to pass because most of the citizens were indoors wondering what would become of them. Suddenly sentry Crowley heard singing round the corner in the direction of the Gaiety Theatre and of Mother Mason's and of many a 'pub'. The voice got closer and louder. You could hear the words now . . .

'I robbed no man; I took no life,
  Yet they sent me to jail
Because I am O'Donovan Rosse,
  A son of Grainn Ualie.'

An enormous coal porter swung into view, cap with button on the top; leather bands beneath each knee.

'I robbed no man . . .'

'Halt!' the sentry challenged meekly. But the song was not interrupted. It roared more defiantly than ever. The son of Grainn Ualie was in fine voice.

'Halt!' the sentry repeated. This time the song it was that halted for a moment. The singer swung down the street. When he had passed the sentry by a yard or two, he looked back at his interrupter.

'Be careful now, young fellah, with the rifle, or you might get hurt.' And what was learned in sorrow he continued to teach in song.

I left Dublin after first notifying the public through the newspapers that I would be out of town. After all, if the country was to revolt, my place was with my family and not with the 'leaders' who had not consulted me. There were no Edward Fitzgeralds among them; no Wolfe Tone nor a Robert Emmet. I noticed that. No doubt there will be cases of cowardice and rapine. Give them time and all will follow the pattern of revolutionary history. Little did I guess that I myself would be the subject of rapine and arson and that an alien born in Lexington Avenue, New York, would plunge our country into civil war.

From none of those who signed 'On behalf of the Provisional Government' was I inclined to take orders. What did they know about government? Yet, to be fair, what could they know? In them, and only in such as they, did the national being reside, and the dream of freedom. Ireland was decapitated and deprived of its gentry so long ago, and even of its middle classes.

Look at myself. Here I am depending on the good will of a class that considers a fight for freedom mere obstreperousness. A doctor has to be all things to all men. These men have staked their lives on a throw. They have everything to lose; and they will lose all. England will send over just enough troops to arrest the insurgents and to execute the ringleaders. They have 'become obstreperous'; they have asked for it, and they will get it, for all their bravery. Meanwhile, when law is in abeyance what will happen to my family? Patriotism covers a multitude of sins. Kidnapping may be one of them. Before I am confined to the city, in the name of Liberty, let me get out.

I turned my face to the west.

Trains were still running. The Dublin-Galway train went nearly as far as Oranmore, about six miles east of Galway. It could go no farther because the line was cut. I got out, cursing the upset. I fear that my enthusiasm for freedom did not cover being marooned. I saw a railway truck, or sled, with wheels that fitted the line. With the help of some of the passengers we put the women, such as would go, and a child or two on it and ran it as far as Oranmore. Then I walked about half a mile looking for help.

Oranmore was deserted, at least the house at which I called was. I went back. There was no sign of the truck. Exasperated at having my journey interrupted, I cast about for a way to proceed. To remain on the deserted track was useless. But wait. It would be more direct than the road.

Against this was the advantage of the road, which might have an automobile on it going in the direction of Galway.

Perhaps the owner of the substantial house at which I had called might be back by this time. I went to see. I found him in. Yes; he would drive me to the Citie of the Tribes. He was the manager of the model farm at Athenry. He would not hear of remuneration. As he drove me I found out that he was a Britisher; that, is a Scotsman employed by the English Government to show the Irish natives how to farm. The fact that the natives took no notice was none of his business. Obviously he never thought that, upset as I was, my sympathies could be with the rebels. We did not discuss the rebellion. He was glad to drive me. A strange figure; but only strange because he was sitting between two stools: the secure stool of an established government and the provisional stool.

The nights were clear in the part of Connemara where we were. Sometimes, strange whistles sounded in the starlight. Snodgrass, the artist in the cottage by the beach, was full of nerves. Well, what does he expect? Artistic temperaments have to be full of nerves.

There was no sign of the rebellion down in Connemara. Evidently it had not spread to the small farmers, without whom no rebellion can be a success.

The newspapers came through. As I thought: the principals were held in prison in Dublin's infamous Kilmainham jail. There they awaited execution. General Maxwell was appointed to hold the city under military discipline. His idea of discipline was to shoot the rebels by twos, and extend the shootings over a number of weeks. This will go well in America where, in spite of all that is spent yearly in propaganda favourable to the British, the Irish have a voice. They can be 'obstreperous'. And this even though their patriotism has been made synonymous with Roman Catholicism, a religion that can never give a President to the United States any more than it can give a monarch to Great Britain. And the identification of the Irish cause with religion, called Transmontanism, is emphasised by British propaganda. Yet for all that, there are other critics of England, fair-minded folk, in America who may ask why a war to free small nations should begin by oppressing the one nearest to England. And General Maxwell is extending the killings in Dublin Town.

Over forty prisons in England were used to hold the rebels. Scotland and Wales were requisitioned. But ninety per cent of the prisoners were held in English jails – Portland, Dartmoor, Parkhurst, Lincoln, Wormwood Scrubs, Wandsworth, Pentonville, Reading, Winchester, Birmingham, Lewes, Stafford, Manchester, etc.

So the Ireland that seized the moment, supported by her exiled children in America and by gallant allies in Europe, and struck in full confidence of victory, ends in every available jail in the three kingdoms.

That fair-minded historian, H. G. Wells, commented on the farce provided by the spectacle of Galloper Smith on the woolsack as Lord Birkenhead, Lord Chancellor of England, sentencing Sir Roger Casement to death for doing the very same thing that he himself, a Liverpool man, had done in Ulster when with Edward Carson – a briefless barrister from Dublin – he threatened to bring in the Kaiser if Ulster were to be included in the Home Rule Bill.

What, you will ask, were two such characters doing in Ulster? Ulster is the principal springboard where bigotry can be played upon by outsiders who adopt the Great and Glorious cause. Thus it came about that a man from Dublin and a man from Liverpool got themselves preferment in England at the expense of Ulster. Carson became Lord Carson, and Galloper Smith because Chancellor of England, with the title of Lord Birkenhead. He sat on the woolsack; Casement stood on the trap door. Such is the hatred and fear of Roman Catholicism in Ulster and England.

The support of 'her exiled children in America' – that was quite another thing. It was not the time to notice it, when English propaganda was endeavouring to bring America to Europe's aid. Better leave the Irish alone. The figures will never be known, but English propaganda in the United States before America came to Europe's (and Britain's) aid must have far exceeded the $800,000 which is now spent annually by England on pro-British propaganda in America.

So Ireland's manhood, as represented by the secret revolutionary organisation, the Irish Republican Brotherhood and her 'open military organisations', the 'Irish Volunteers and the Irish Citizen Army' were distributed among the prisons of England, Scotland and Wales. Arthur Griffith was in prison; his policy became all the stronger because of that. The first by-election in April, 1917, was won on the principle laid down by Griffith: boycott Westminster.

It was decided to put Count Plunkett up as a candidate because his son had died before a firing squad the year before in Kilmainham jail. The count was a count of the Holy Roman Empire, a slow-going man above middle size with a fine forehead and a long forked beard. There must not have been much behind the fine forehead because, after he had won his seat, it took all his backers could do to explain that he won it only because he was pledged not to go over to the Parliament in London. It took a lot to keep the count out of the limelight. Joe McGuinness won the second election; and the abstention policy of Sinn Fein was growing stronger. Not all 'Ireland's manhood' was in prison. It is difficult to put a whole nation in jail.

Griffith, Collins and Barton with the amiable Duggan were over in Hans Place, in London, fighting for fiscal control of their country. Nothing mattered so much. Economics rule the roost. Freedom and Liberty could come afterwards; they were political shibboleths used to fool Indians and such. What was 'freedom' compared with economic control of the country's wealth? Griffith and Collins were plenipotentiaries. Mark that. De Valera stayed behind. He was too important to go into the breach. He left that to 'plenipotentiaries'. Erskine Childers, whose typewriter never ceased night and day, was watchdog; and his job was to report everything. It was the one mistake of his life when Griffith yielded the leadership to De Valera. In fact it cost him his life, and the life of Collins went with it.

On the opposite side of the table sat Galloper Smith (Lord Birkenhead now), Churchill and Lloyd George: 'Could Satan send for such an end worthier tools than they?' Lloyd George bluffed – his bluff had carried him on through life. He spoke in Welsh to his secretary, Jones; politeness itself when you think of it. Winston scowled, as far as his face was capable of scowling; and Birkenhead, an admirer of Collins, sat pale. No word spoken at the table could be altered; but in Lady Lavery's house, 5, Cromwell Place, the talks could go on and not be recorded.

At last the 'Treaty' was signed by Griffith, Collins and Barton. Barton afterwards repudiated his signature; but then he was a cousin of Erskine Childers – Irishmen both!

The Treaty was brought back and passed by the Dail, by a majority of six. De Valera stormed – it was easy to storm; but where was he when Lloyd George and his trickery were being faced? De Valera did not go to the country. Oh no! The country had first to be roused.

32 *You Carry Caesar*

It is all very well to talk of wearing a revolver. Instead of you wearing it, it wears you. If you carry it in a hip pocket, your trousers sag on that side; one leg becomes longer than the other and you are inclined to trip. If it will fit in a coat pocket, the sight is liable to stick, and, as for the holster, leave that to detective stories. Now you will wonder what this is all about. I will try to explain.

On some occasions when I had finished gossiping in the Staff Room of the Richmond Hospital, I used to stop my car outside Tommy Costello's oculist's shop and go in to pick up the gossip of that part of the town which was known to me only as the external department of the hospital. He assured me that it was good for trade to have a well-known car seen outside his shop.

It did me good to call on Tommy. He had been a racing cyclist and, if he was not in the first flight, he was useful in increasing the field for others to beat. He used to complain of shooting pains down his right leg and tell me that he was being slowly poisoned with arsenic. I sent him to an X-ray man who reported that he could find nothing the matter, so I put him down as a hypochondriac. Soon he would forget his ailment and tell me about his dogs, which he kept behind the shop.

But one morning – it must have been late in December – he was full of mysterious whisperings. He waited until a customer had departed and then drew me into a little dark room behind the shop. Mystery and more mystery. At last he began: 'Last Sunday I was taking a stroll along the central road in the park. There was a group of four men in front of me. I heard them say distinctly, "We'll get Gogarty first."'

'What does that mean?' I asked.

Tommy went on, 'Two of them had belted coats like trench coats. The other two were taller. They looked back and saw me, and shut up. I stooped down and patted one of the dogs.'

Tommy knew things I did not know. He knew that mystery was in the air and, though he did not tell me directly, his manner was meant to warn me. It was enough for me to get his message and the warning implied. 'Remember what I told you and don't forget that you are a senator,' he said.

I met Desmond Fitzgerald, the Minister for Foreign Affairs, a few days later. To my surprise he took the message seriously. I did not mention my informant's name, though I will say this for Tommy, he had not bound me to secrecy though he was exposed to reprisals if it leaked out that he had warned one of the government. Now I was really astonished when Desmond said, 'You must go armed.'

'Oh hell!' said I.

'You are not leaving this office until I hand you a revolver.' He gave me a Colt with a long handle that did not suit my grip. Just to please him I took it. 'You must promise me to wear it,' he said.

The captain of the government guard saw it as I was leaving. 'Let me tell you one thing: you should never put that under your pillow. Wear it between your knees and shoot through the bedclothes if you are surprised in bed.'

What had I let myself in for? First I had called on Tommy and he had told me what he overheard in the Phoenix Park. Then I report this to Desmond and he makes me promise to carry a revolver! In fact, he gives me one. And now the captain of the guard, obviously an expert, tells me how to wear it in bed!

For a few days I tried carrying it. I forgot it in the toilet of the Shelbourne Hotel and a nervous fellow came shrieking out, 'There's a revolver on the seat!' I had to get it back from the manager.

I could not sit down with any comfort in a chair. The boys in Kit Marlowe's day wore daggers in their belts and they had to push them behind them and out over the edge of the bench when they sat down. I tried to feel warlike; but it soon passed. The spectacle of an armed doctor was too much of a contradiction for me. At last I threw Desmond's revolver in the drawer of my dressing table among ties and odds and ends. For that I was very sorry as it later will appear.

All the members of the government had themselves locked up in what was known as the Government Building, a building which was intended for a college of science under the British regime. The regiment guarding it was drawn mostly from the North.

Civil war brought treachery with it. Evidently the government did not trust the troops immediately about them. From that alone I saw how serious the situation was. John MacNeill, the dreamer who nearly wrecked the rebellion of Easter Week, J. J. Walsh, Minister of Posts and Telegraphs, Desmont Fitzgerald, William Cosgrove, and some others were in residence, which was little more than protective arrest.

I was free and accessible because it was easy to get into my house: a doctor is always accessible, or should be. That's what added to my anger when the raiders raided mine, a doctor's house.

It also helped me to be contemptuous of the kind of riffraff that had taken advantage of the civil war under the guise of patriotism. Had not the selfish and vain – I mean some of them – done so? It was under a pretence of impersonal devotion to a country in which they were not born, and to which they belonged not with the closest bonds, that they raised the civil war. Really their concern for their own ends and their vanity egged them on. Of course the watchdog, Erskine Childers – 'that damned Englishman,' as Griffith called him – was not far off to 'advise'. It was remarkable that between them they did not bring back the English. Never could the English have found a better excuse: 'Look at the Irish now. They cannot govern themselves.'

How far the British were behind Childers will never be known. If he were a member of their secret service, the one thing is certain is that it would remain a secret. Suffice to say that Childers spent his youth and manhood in the English service. Gerald Balfour said of his book, *The Riddle of the Sands,* 'If it is a novel, it is one of the best ever written. If it is a true account, it is the creator of the Baltic Fleet.'

One evening about eight o'clock on January 12, 1923, if I remember rightly, I was lolling in my bath. The bathroom was next to my dressing room. I was alone in the house but for a few servants. My family had gone to the country for the Christmas holidays. I lay in the bath and steam filled the room. I was trying to turn off a tap with my toes when I felt something cold on the back of my neck. I looked around. There was a gunman in a belted trench coat of dark blue material.

'Out! And be quick!' He waved the gun.

'If this is murder, may I scribble a few lines to my wife?'

Pale and agitated, he again threatened me with the gun.

'For a housebreaker, you seem very nervous,' I said.

Through the door of the bathroom I could see two gunmen on the stairs. I put a towel about me and cursed myself for leaving the gun in the drawer of the mock Chippendale table in the dressing room. To open that drawer it was necessary to place a foot against either leg of the table; even then the drawer was jammed.

Oh, how I regretted that gun now! I could have blown the head off the unsuspecting gunman and then rushed at the two guarding the stairs. Who expects a naked man to be armed? Slowly I drew on the trousers of my dinner suit and put on the comfortable old shoes which were down at heel. The other two gunmen were now in the room with me, while I dressed.

I looked in the mirror. My face was almost white. That does not come from thought. Maybe it does: what about 'sicklied o'er'? But the pupils were dilated. However, my thinking was unimpaired.

I was thinking that even if I could get my gun out, and find the trigger guard unobstructed by a tie or two, I could never beat the gunman who had his gun in my kidney to the draw. Geometry was against it. He had to move his finger only half an inch and my spine would be shot through. Besides, if I opened the drawer, it would reveal the fact that I had a pistol and 'justify' the already worked-up gunman in putting an end to me. He could discharge my revolver after I was dead. No, I had better leave the drawer alone.

Over by the fireplace I saw a pair of riding boots with trees in them. If I could get the tree out, I would have a weapon. But the brain, which was beginning to get hysterical with fear and excitement, thought absurdly of Fergus McRoy and his wooden sword. Amusing if the situation were in accord.

'Put those bloody pumps in your pocket and put on these.' I was handed a pair of skiing boots and an old coat of buffalo leather with the furry side in. They must have found these on the back stairs. So there was probably a gunman there and I was counting on those back stairs to make a dash for it. Hopeless now.

Clad in a pair of trousers, a white shirt, a great coat and heavy shoes, I was led down. A hunchbacked woman was waiting in the hall. I noticed that the telephone wire had been dragged out. A large sedan stood at the door with a big fellow at the wheel. The little crippled woman got in beside him. Evidently she was used for the purpose of making it look like a social visit if they were interrupted by the guards.

A gunman sat on either side of me; I could feel the pressure of a gun on each kidney. Another sat in my lap and lay back. I was crushed into the cushions and completely out of sight. We started.

'If you shout when we are passing any of your bloody soldiers, you will be blown to smithereens.'

Well, Julius Caesar was in a like position when he was taken by pirates in the Adriatic, and he promised them that he would crucify them all. They took it laughingly; but they were all crucified later.

'Wouldn't you like to be — now?' He named the unhallowed name.

'Anything but that,' I mumbled, my mouth smothered by the gunman's back.

It dawned on me that maybe I was being taken for a hostage for the two men that were held prisoners in Dundalk jail. They had been executed that morning! It won't be a rest cure for me when the gunmen find that out.

To say the least of it, my position was precarious. One of the corner boys asked: 'Isn't it a fine thing to die to a flash?' 'Better,' I muttered, 'than to be that scoundrel.' But oh, what waste: my life for theirs! If and when I get out of their clutches, it will be my turn. This was little better than associating myself with Julius Caesar: but then there is no accounting for a mind distracted by fear.

We reached the last house by the Liffey bank – at the time vacant – where the river meets the first weir at Trinity College Boat House. Here at full tide the water can be nine feet deep.

I was bundled through the small gate in the wall.

'Can I tip the driver?' I asked. That made them all angry, the driver most of all.

I was taken into a dark cellar, evidently a coal cellar, and made to stand against the wall. Seven men in two ranks stood in front of the door. One of them began to strike matches. Those in the front row evidently did not trust him. He might claim that he had no hand in the shooting if they were caught. There was an altercation. 'How can I strike matches if I have to shoot?' he said.

Somebody struck another light. I could see the pistols wavering in the front row. I remember thinking that it was more for the sake of the firing squad than of their prisoner that they bind his eyes. Now I realised why a victim gave gold to the headsman to dispatch him quickly. The match went out. I took two steps to the side. When I tried to get back so as not to show the white feather to such little jackeens, my feet were stuck to the ground.

I have seen films where the crowd sticks to the ground and is unable to move. It must have been thought, and my contempt for the undisciplined rats, that made me able to stare them down.

The captain of the gunmen ordered, 'Soldiers, forward and seize prisoner. We are going for a lamp.' Five men came forward and led me out.

I noticed that the house was parallel to the river, which runs west to east. It was in the small cellar at the east end that I was stood against the wall. Now I was being taken to the west end of the house with the river not twenty yards away. The corner boys took me to what had evidently been a music room. Music books were scattered on the floor, which had been torn up along the wall. The torn-up planks and some of the music books were piled up to make a fire, for the night was very cold. The fire soon blazed; but the unheated chimney smoked.

'Is it a part of the Republican programme to gas a prisoner before shooting him?' I asked.

'What d'ye mean?'

'There's too much smoke in the room.'

'Ye won't notice it when they come back with the lamp.'

They were shivering from cold. I tried to lecture on small arms. 'Those automatics are dangerous. They have to have the lock drawn back before they will fire. Let me show you.' I reached for one of their guns; but there was nothing doing. With my ear on a stalk I listened for the return of the sedan with the lamp and the head gunman. Then I would be shot and my body thrown into the flooded river.

I bowed my head and groaned. 'You fellows have given me such a fright that I'll soon have diarrhoea.' I waited for the remark to soak in.

It is a vulgar notion that fright produces diarrhoea, whereas the fact is that all the secretions of the body are dried up.

Whether the remark had sunk in or not, I was terrified that the motor would return – 'Quick, a guard,' I said hurriedly. The fools seized me and stuck the gun into each side of my heavy coat. In the near darkness I slipped my arms out of the coat, while I remained inside it.

Up rushed the outside watchman, on whom I had not counted. 'What's all this?'

'He has to go out.'

It was dark outside but I feared that the eyes of the outside watchman would be accustomed to the dark. By the feel of gravel under my left foot and the smooth cement threshold about an inch above the gravel under my right, I knew that I was clear of the house. In a broken voice I said to the guards, 'Would you mind holding my coat?'

They were still holding the coat as I was going swiftly down the river with the current. The black water had swallowed me up.

Oh, how I rejoiced in spite of the shock. Now for the Caesar act! But I had some swimming to do and the river was icy cold. I tried to grasp overhanging willows but they passed through my numbed hands.

Cross to opposite bank? What a fool I would be! The gunmen would rush over there. It would take them only some minutes to cross the bridge at Liffey Bank and to break into the grounds that went beside the stream. I floated along and I vowed two swans to the river if it bore me safe to shore.

Our good Father Liffey received my gift duly.

The lights of the city began to appear, or were they the lights of the houses by the river? I was looking and wondering when all at once I felt that I could no longer breathe.

I am too young for a heart attack; and I can swim easily. What is the matter?

I pushed my face under and it came up clear. I could breathe freely now. What had happened? A cake of foam had choked my nose and mouth.

At last a submerged willow was directly in front of me. I put my arm round it and I was immediately swept under. For this I was ready. When I came up on the other side, I got my other arm along it and gradually moved ashore. After crawling slowly up the muddy bank I tried to stand up. At first I could feel only my knees; all was frozen from the knees down.

I made my way to a lighted house and looked through the window. Four women and a man were at supper. One of the women saw me and the table shook. Now all but the man were shaking and moaning. My mind was working like a dynamo. I must have looked a sorry sight, pale and with but one shirt sleeve, with blood trickling down my forehead.

'I am not dead,' I gasped.

The moaning ceased. I had been taken for a ghost. No one had ever come into that house from the river before.

They refused to give me help. Were they afraid of reprisals? Who knows or cares? The man said, 'Come along with me.' I did not tell him who I was. Maybe he guessed. Least said, soonest mended. He took me down the garden and opened a door in the wall. 'There is the depot across the Phoenix Park.'

I crossed the park and suddenly felt very weak. Suddenly I was caught in the glare of a searchlight. With my only sleeve raised, I walked along the beam. After a while I came to the depot railings. A sentry asked me who I was but I could not answer; I could only make hiccup-like noises.

Evidently the sentry feared a ruse; there must have been firing behind me. He would not let me in. Some officer came, and by this time I could speak: 'I am Senator Gogarty . . . I have been kidnapped . . . I have just escaped.' He caused the gate to be opened. The police surgeon, whom I knew, took me in charge and I was put to bed. Hot bottles and hot tea.

About two in the morning, after much telephoning and red tape, three armoured cars were sent for me. I rode in the middle one and passed in triumph through a city that saw me going to my death some hours ago.

Such are the vicissitudes of politics. I did not think of it in that way at the time. If I do so now, it is because I can regard the incident dispassionately.

I was taken to the Government Building and I was given Desmond Fitzgerald's bed, but I did not sleep for hours. I am afraid that planning retribution kept me awake. I remained in the Government Building for three weeks. Meanwhile, a telegram was sent to reassure my family. They returned to Dublin at once.

I used to slip out of my house, which was but a block and a half from the Government Building. When the ministers got to know of it, I was given a guard of eight men. The steed had been stolen but was found and guarded now!

My kidnapping would not have been believed had the government boys not found my coat. A few days later a man called with a bullet, evidently from a .38, its nose somewhat bent. It was dug out of the spine of the ringleader who had raided my house and carried me off. O'Leary was his name. He was a tram conductor on the Clonskea line. He had died 'to a flash', shrieking inappropriately under the wall of the Tranquilla Convent in Upper Rathmines. Later the others were caught.

I felt normal again. It was said of my father that his

enemies all came to a bad end, I had taken after him.

I did not know what the government thought of my arrest and escape. I did not like that proof which depended only on my coat. But when Senator Bagwell was taken from a house in Howth, there was no uncertainty. It was clear that an effort was being made to intimidate senators and so prevent any laws, punitive and otherwise, from being enacted. Promptly the government announced that twenty prisoners would be shot if Senator Bagwell was not released unharmed forthwith. He was 'allowed to escape'. That was the turning point: opposition was broken. Later, when I inquired why a similar proclamation had not been issued in my case, the Prime Minister said, smiling, 'You escaped?'

The newspapers did not share any scepticism that may have attended my escape. They were full of it. One of them published a photograph with an arrow pointing down the wall by which I fell into the water. To get it the photographer must have used a boat. One paper said that the gunmen might as well have expected to hold an electric eel as to hold me. That pleases me very much.

Credit must be given to men like Senator Bagwell, Jameson and Guinness, and Lord Mayo. Very easily they could have thrown in the sponge. They held on instead. Once they had resigned themselves to a change in the order of things, they set themselves to accept the Free State. They gritted their teeth. They did not turn tail even though they had been brought up with affinities for England, as indeed we all had, though with less to lose.

Renvyle House was burned, all but the rooms of the caretaker at the end of one wing. How the flames were controlled at all is a mystery; but it was no mystery to me to realise that the peasantry were hand-in-glove with those in the civil war for reasons far removed from 'patriotism' as far as the civil war was removed from it; the peasants wanted my land and they cared not how they came by it.

Lord Mayo's house was burned. Here there were pictures of historical import, all destroyed, together with evidences of a culture second to none in Europe. That is why I say that De Valera did more harm to Ireland than Cromwell; he had more to destroy. Compensate senators as the government later did, no compensation could restore these things.

Of all I lost in Renvyle House, I remember chiefly a self-portrait of my mother at sixteen with her auburn hair divided in the middle, her plain blue dress, and all-pervading air of sweetness and simplicity. No compensation can restore that.

As I have said, a guard of eight men and a sergeant was now assigned to me. The guard occupied a small room off the hall. One of them wounded himself and blew the leg off a Chippendale chair during his guardianship.

During odd evenings firing from the streets would break the drawing-room windows. The guard would reply after an interval, which I timed at nine minutes. Were they in collusion with the enemy? They might have been: everyone must live; or he thinks so, and does not always consider the means.

One man who disregarded the shots through the windows and the falling plaster was Æ, who came to see us every Friday night, rain or storm. So absorbed was he in affirming his own philosophy that he either did not hear, or ignored, such interruptions as shots through the windows and, nine minutes later, my guards' prompt reply. The ottoman on which the philosopher sat was removed out of the line of fire.

It is one thing to have a guard but another to have patients searched for arms. Neither makes for confidence, security or, in a doctor's case, practice. Luckily, I had enough patients in London and other parts of England to form the nucleus of a new practice.

With much reluctance I moved to London, where I was feted as a hero. I did not know that I was one. I thought that it was the hospitality that I might expect as one who had made a dramatic escape from De Valera's civil war. It took Seymour Leslie, a first cousin of Winston Churchill, to disabuse my dream. 'You arrived at just the right moment, when London had nothing better to do,' he said.

Every Wednesday I made it a point to cross to Dublin in order to take my place in the Senate. I would not give it to De Valera to say that his tactics had kept one voter from voting. For a while I was met at the boat by a guard in mufti. Of course, I could not know whether they were the enemy or not. It would have been easy for the enemy to masquerade as my guard and meet me at the mail boat and carry me off again. I had a Colt which I displayed as I sat on the back seat. Had the automobile gone by an indirect route, I intended to blow out the driver's brains and take the consequences. Luckily, nothing diverted the car. This, I think, goes to show that I was somewhat nervous and shaken by the kidnapping though I did not feel it in the excitement of escape.

It was harder to bear the confinement on the boat – I was forbidden to go on deck until the vessel docked at Holyhead and a representative of Scotland Yard met me. After a while I handed in my Colt to one of the big five in New Scotland Yard, which is directly over the Thames and looks across the river on St. Thomas's Hospital, where the son of the man who received my revolver was an intern. For all I know, it is still in the drawer in his office, though he himself is long ago departed. His name was Kearney, if my memory holds.

33 *'They Had Nothing Better To Do'*

The dislocation of my practice was compensated to some extent by the pleasure I got from meeting old friends in England. Compton Mackenzie edited and owned *The Gramophone*, a thriving magazine. Christopher Stone owned Field Place, Horsham; that was where Percy Bysshe

Shelley was born. I went down to Sussex to stay with him.

Dermot Freyer came in and out of his famous father's house in Harley Street, where there was a lift which his friend Tancred used to stop between two floors until the right word was found for whatever poem he was composing. I think that Sir Peter Freyer's patience was at last worn out by his son's friend. His son, too, may have fretted it somewhat, especially when he put under 'Amusements' in *Who's Who*, 'Trying to pass Half M.B. Examinations.' Perhaps the editors of *Who's Who* thought that it was the great surgeon they were listing and that he meant that his hobby was presiding at examinations.

Lady Leslie, the witty and vivacious, was my great friend. To her I owed introductions to people that I, in my walk of life, would never have met. She knew everybody. She it was who told me of Count Keyserling, gross and unkempt, who came for a week and stayed for three weeks until his hostess had to leave her town house to get rid of him. There I met Benjamin Guinness, the banker, who was restricted to three divorces by his bank!

At Lady Lavery's, in 5, Cromwell Place, and at George Moore's house, in Ebury Street, I often called. I had the misfortune one day of telling Moore that I had lunched with Lady Ebury, the wife of his landlord.

'She has the best cuisine in London. What did you eat?'

'To tell you the truth, I never noticed. I talk so much.'

He threw up his hands. 'You are a barbarian. Tell her to ask me.' But I was on no footing to advise Lady Ebury as to her guests. I was hardly a guest myself. Three weeks elapsed and no invitation came to George. He wrote a letter to *The Times* headed 121, Ebury Street, and beginning, 'From the long slum in which I live.'

I met the Duke of Connaught, the best-mannered man I ever knew. When he, with his hand to his ear, heard who I was, he told me that that morning he played eighteen holes of golf and spent two hours in the saddle and 'What do you think of that?'

'You are theatened with immortality, sir.'

Later, at lunch in his place, he remembered that and repeated it to Sir John Leslie, who was harder of hearing than the duke.

'What was that? Did he say "threatened with immortality"?'

In Lady Leslie's house in Great Cumberland Place I met two crown princesses of Greece. They were young girls, pink and white. 'Make a deeper bow than usual; and do not speak until they speak to you,' I was instructed. It seems that there are few themes to discuss with royalty. They must be born to be bored. If they spoke of the weather, one might be tempted to refer to 'Moving forever onward through most pellucid air', through which the Greeks of old went. But the Greek princesses probably had never been to Greece!

Yes, certainly I was feted even if 'London had nothing better to do'. Strange how susceptible I was to titles: Lady Leslie, Lady Leconfield, the Duke of Connaught, Crown Princesses; the Earl of Granard, Senator. It was rather amusing to find his house in Halkin Street with gates locked and guarded. It must have impressed the King, who dined there every second Friday. It did not impress me. Lord Granard's castle, at Castleforbes, had the hall blown in; but there was method in the madness of the bombardiers. Though they had orders from headquarters in Dublin to burn Senator the Earl of Granard's house, they only made a gesture. They did not want to be unemployed.

Much the same thing happened to Sir Hector McCalmont in County Kilkenny. He warned the locals that if his place were injured he would remove his racing stable elsewhere. Economics limited De Valera's policy of ruin: he could not bring civilisation altogether down, though he gave the country a lot of rubble.

My office was in Grosvenor Street, in the same street as Bruce Bruce-Porter – were there two spiders on his coat of arms? – and one of the mistresses of Edward VII.

I met Galloper Smith, who was now Lord Birkenhead.

His house was in Grosvenor Gardens down by the Victoria Station. I lunched there once or twice. I remember what a good mimic his daughter was. I must have forgotten the part he had played, for I kept thinking how Griffith took to him. Ah, it was because of the Galloper's admiration for Collins and not because of Griffith. The Galloper was a great rake. There have been many great rakes in English history; Charlie Fox was one. Wilkes another; and now comes Lord Birkenhead. I am wondering what Lord Birkenhead saw in me. Could it have been an affinity? I hope not.

Mrs Benjamin Guinness was a lavish hostess. Had it not been bad form to look a gift horse in the mouth, you might have wondered how expensive was the Guinness establishment. Many a lunch had I in Great Cumberland Place or Street. The evenings, too, had their entertainment. Nelson Keyes and Tallulah Bankhead combined to keep the boredom away. I remember laughing so much at Nelson Keyes that I forgot who it was he was impersonating! Whatever it was, laughter dissolved it. I remember being so amused that I secretly commended the bank for forbidding Benjamin to get rid of the third Mrs Guinness! Tallulah, raging on with hoarse voice and distorted features, was giving a parody of some prominent actress. Everyone laughed and I felt so indebted to Tallulah and our hostess that I invited them both to lunch at the Berkeley, which is a well-known hotel restaurant at the corner of Berkeley Street and Piccadilly. They came; but the spell was gone: it was day for one thing; and it was another for another.

When I wonder that I have forgotten what made me laugh so much at Nelson Keyes, I forget that the things that amuse so much can rarely be remembered. How often do you hear someone trying to tell a good story he heard overnight and failing utterly?

One morning as I walked down King's Road, Chelsea, I ran again into Seymour Leslie. 'I suppose we will meet at dinner to-night?' Now our hostess was reputed to be the biggest lion hunter in London. In fact an American girl who did not know the idiom once said to her, 'I hear that you are a great shot.'

For a moment which was, alas, too transient, I was filled with hope that I might appear to be 'a big shot' in the lady's eyes. Seymour quickly disabused all such vain misgivings when I asked the question, 'Who is her guest of honour?' 'The Unknown Soldier's widow.'

Our hostess, who often gave a tea party to Freyer and myself, one evening accosted us: 'You two are always laughing, standing over there in a corner. What are you laughing about?' I waited for the onus to fall on Freyer.

'About Tancred,' he said.

'Who is Tancred?'

Then I chipped in, 'Oh, he is a friend of Freyer's.'

'Well then, see that he comes to dinner here – let me see – oh, on this day week.' It was an order issued by 'She who must be obeyed.'

Freyer and I took counsel together. 'It will be rather difficult now that Tancred lives in a mild mental home,' Freyer said. 'But, as you are a doctor, the doctor in charge may let him out if you ask him as a favour. Surely Tancred is harmless.'

Dr Travers was very obliging. He would let Tancred out provided that I guaranteed to return him by midnight. A cinderella part!

It was Wednesday when Fryer and I turned up. Dinner was at eight-thirty but so far there was no Tancred. Perhaps he has got over-excited seeing that he is to be enlarged for the dinner. Perhaps Travers thought better of it and determined not to let him out after all. Perhaps Tancred is depressed. It was getting on for nine and everyone was restless, also hungry, when the door burst open and in rushed our friend.

'Well, well, well,' he said. 'It is awfully kind of you to invite me to dinner on the recommendation of those two oddities over there. You know I would never have been discourteous enough to come late but a very remarkable thing happened to me as I sat in the subway. By the way, I must tell you of a perfectly infallible method I have of judging character. It is quite infallible. Yes, quite ...' He broke off into a wild laugh.

Our hostess was too puzzled to be amazed. 'What is it?' she asked faintly.

'What is it? Let me explain. It is, like all great inventions, simple in the extreme: I simply judge people by the advertisements under which they sit. Now then, how came I to be late? I'll tell you. There was a lovely girl in a corner of the coach. She had a golden costume and stockings of light bronze. We were all alone. Now one would think that the social amenities would be somewhat relaxed three hundred feet under the earth's surface. Not a bit of it! She was sitting under Green and Black's tea, 'Used by all the big pots.' I at once realised that she was a big pot herself. But she took absolutely no notice of me. Why? Amazing! Surreptitiously I stole a glance at the advertisement under which I was sitting. SPARKLING MOSELLE! No wonder the poor child was frightened out of her wits.'

Our hostess did not appear to see any out-of-wits stuff in her guest. However, when at twelve, precisely, two quietly uniformed men without epaulets tapped our friend lightly on the shoulder, it may have occurred to her then. Probably it did, for neither Freyer nor I ever saw the interior of her house again.

I met an old friend, Lady Islington. Years back before taxis were used at all, she insisted on riding on a jaunting car in Dublin. The horse bolted, which showed unusual energy in a hackney. Her ladyship persisted in attributing the stopping of the runaway and the saving of her life to me although the exact fact is that the horse ran into a member of the Dublin Metropolitan Police and was 'taken into custody' with the jarvey.

Lady Islington was delighted with Dublin, which is the largest Georgian city extant, and it was this Georgianism that attracted her. She instructed me to buy Henrietta Street for her. Henrietta Street is a slum which, it was rumoured, Alderman Meade purchased for £900, which was then about the equivalent of £1400. Some of the finest examples of Georgian architecture were in Henrietta Street before the houses were denuded of mantels, stairways and doors; all except the two houses on the right as you approach the Inns of Court, which are now some sort of convent. For once in my life I was sufficiently businesslike to put the matter in the hands of – not a lawyer, oh no! – but an architect.

I chose Charles – I think that was his first name – O'Connor and asked him to get in touch with the man of business who represented Lady Islington. I cannot take much credit for this precaution because it arose, not from a knowledge of business, but from my knowledge of the transience of enthusiasms, especially the enthusiasms of ladies. I did not wish to be left with a slum on my hands and no answers to my letters of expostulation. O'Connor reported that, as a result of the habitation of slum dwellers for so long, the woodwork was impregnated with acrid odours which could not be got rid of, so the houses were useless for anything but tenements. Visions of fashion being revived, and of the north side of the city coming again into prominence, faded before the architect's report. So Lady Islington contented herself with her Adam house in one of the London squares, and with her moated house in the country.

It was to that house I was invited and in that house I stayed. I remember the tapestry which hung on the wall of my bedroom, and the house with its towers of rosy brick at the corners. The house rose from the moat; and the towers at the corners were capped with green bronze. That is all I remember. I cannot tell in what shire the house was, but I remember the long drive through the park and the oaks that stood with their branches out at right angles and not slanting upwards like the branches of quicker-growing trees. I remember Lord Islington's cigar after breakfast; as for the rest, it is harder to recall than a dream.

So ended my pleasant interlude in London, if you can call it an interlude where the fun was all on one side.

And then I went to south Sussex, to Petworth House. Petworth House is one of the greatest houses in England. It belongs to one of the largest landowners left in that country, Lord Leconfield. He ran his own pack of hounds, the Petworth Hounds, and they say often ran a fox to earth without leaving his own demesne. He had a disability or two: one was that he could not whisper. That was due probably to his having to shout across fields and spinneys as the hunt progressed.

To that house I was invited. I arrived about dinnertime; and, as there are no cocktails or other refreshments before dinner in a well-conducted English house, I felt somewhat depressed. This was not lessened by my being ushered into a small room where his lordship was seated with a blub-faced fellow beside him. The blub-faced fellow was Winston Churchill, who had loosed the Black and Tans on Ireland. Before I could speak to mine host, I was attacked by Churchill, who spoke as if he had a cleft palate: 'Gogarty, now that you have got your liberty, what are you going to do with it?' I took a very long count. When at last I pulled myself up, I answered very distinctly, 'Oh, we are going to use it to discriminate between our friends, *Mister* Churchill.' He gave a grunt, rose, and, as I thought, left the room. I turned to Lord Leconfield, 'Why is your guest so unamiable?' His shouted reply alarmed me: 'Don't you know? Nobody can trust the fellow. He crossed the Floor twice.' This was an allusion to the ratting of Winston, who was born a Conservative, then became a Liberal. On that occasion he suffered the greatest insult ever offered to a man in the House of Commons: when he entered with the Liberal party, the Conservatives rose to a man and left the House. Another grunt and this time Winston left the room.

Afterwards I met Winston as he was crackling up the stairs (his right knee emitted the rhetoric). 'Are you playing polo these days?' He did not answer. I was snubbed, ignored, brushed off. Doubtless he was going up to study *The Decline and Fall.*

And then I remembered Mrs John Jameson's request

when her brother was about to be sacked by Lloyd George. Probably Churchill thought the same, and in his opinion I had no right to be in Petworth House. And, if you are to judge by his host's distrust, neither had he. My mind went back to F. C. Crowley's theory of 'a popular' man.

34 *Politics And Palls*

'You must accept the governor-generalship. I won't have Healy, a man who betrayed Parnell.'

So spoke Griffith to me. I remember the incident well. We were walking along Nassau Street, passing a house with a large 8-in. gilt wood.

So I am not 'Down among the Dead Men' after all. In fact, in Arthur's opinion I am a better man than George Russell, Æ; and like Larry O'Neill and Nelson's Pillar, I stand where I did twenty years ago.

Now don't tell me that the mind cannot think of more than one thing at the same time. Mine thought of half a dozen things at once. The first was that Tim Healy had been working for the job and that pressure was being put on Griffith to accept him. What chance had I against Tim Healy? He had been in Parliament for more than thirty years and he had influence with those who were forming the Free State; and he probably was over in London now wire-pulling. Another thought that sprang up simultaneously was that the very fact that Healy had betrayed Parnell was in his favour. Parnell betrayed himself; but if Healy got the credit for it, it would help him now with the Church whose tool he was; and the Church was the real ruler of Ireland.

'When I wanted a place to meet certain emissaries from England, you risked all and lent me your house. When I asked . . . he hummed and hawed.' Griffith was referring to his meetings with Asquith and the disguised Lord Derby.

Politics has rewards out of all proportion to the merits of the subject, I thought. Then I thought, I cannot accept the job. I don't want the limelight. I am not a leader any more than Griffith is. Little did I think at the time that the post required little leadership, or character for that matter. Then, at the back of my mind there was the distinction to accept money from the nation; but this I could not say very well because Griffith was in receipt of a salary which he had earned by twenty years of hard work in grinding poverty. The post of governor-general was a sinecure. The governor was a mere rubber stamp or figurehead. Why should anybody take money for his convictions?

We walked on in silence while I pondered how to get out of the difficulty without offending Griffith, who was so well disposed towards me. I felt that, try as he might, he could not appoint anyone who would not be a nominee also of the Church; and I certainly was not likely to be one. Perhaps it was this thought, that Griffith could not 'deliver the goods', that made me so unenthusiastic.

Yes: I should be enthusiastic. I should thank Griffith. I was about to do that when luckily we sighted Jim Montgomery, who hailed us and pointed down Molesworth Street in the direction of the Bailey. For a while the crisis had passed. Jimmy's smile was meant for us both. To Griffith he said, 'Well you've certainly done it. You have taken England's hand off Ireland's throat and out of her pocket as you said you would.'

Griffith was silent; but he was pleased for all that. We entered the Bailey and went upstairs to the smoking room. The usual desultory talk. Griffith did not talk politics when there were people about. 'How are you making out, Jim, as a film censor?' 'Oh, between the Devil and the Holy See!' And so we walked on.

There was a call from the Government Building: Could I come at once to see the President, Arthur Griffith? He is far from well. I stopped whatever work was in hand and rushed down about two short blocks to see the President. I found him lying on a pallet in a small room at the back of the offices of the Minister for Justice on one of the higher floors. Seorsam McNicholl was in the room.

One glance and I asked for the telephone. It was necessary to get permission to move anybody from the Government Building, and for this permission Generals O'Murleigh and O'Sullivan had to be consulted.

'Where do you propose to take him?' I was asked.

'To the nuns' private hospital in 96, Lower Leeson Street.' I could not think of a place less likely to be raided than the nuns' private home.

The President was removed in an ambulance and the best room in 96, Lower Leeson Street was prepared. His blood pressure was very high. It is not necessary to go into details of his illness. When he was more or less conscious, he complained bitterly at having been removed from his work, particularly at such a time. However, his complaints failed to alter the fact that he was a very sick man and required both rest and isolation, especially from such friends as McNicholl.

A few days passed. I was not happy that I had to choose the nuns' home because of the fact that a member of the visiting staff of St Vincent's Hospital, which was round the corner in St Stephen's Green and in connection with which 96 was run, had the rather unprofessional idea that he could call without ceremony on any doctor's patient. Besides, there was no protection from nurses' gossip as there would have been had I sent the President to Elpis in Lower Mount Street. But this was regarded as a Protestant nursing home and, of course, was out of bounds for such a man as the Catholic President of the Irish Free State.

He remained in the nursing home for over a week. The last time I saw Arthur Griffith alive he was sitting uncomfortably in a chair in the middle of the room. On his knees were the day's papers. He could read them upside down as well as straight for he had been at one time a compositor.

'When will you let me out of this?' was his only question.

'When you are fit to leave.'

'I am fit.'

One morning there was a call from one of his nurses. Could I come at once? Mr Griffith was far from well. I took my time, for I thought that he was again giving trouble about being in a nursing home. I arrived to find him dead. He had never recovered from seeing, as he thought, his life's work ruined by treachery. George Washington beholding the devastation caused by Benedict Arnold on the property of the people is a case in point.

The funeral of Arthur Griffith went through historic College Green. The West Front of Trinity College looked out on the Bank of Ireland. Behind us in Grafton Street many shops continued to do business. Why did I not realise it then? While those of the people of Ireland who had not been split by the Splitter were in a state of emotion, business was being 'carried on as usual'. Economics stood while politics shook to its foundations. The Founder of the Irish Free State was being carried to his grave: 'The blood of some of the members of the Government' (*Irish Independent*, March 18, 1922) was waded through. The first victim was dead. The next was to follow within ten days. The Splitter and the Morrigas had spoken. Michael Collins was ambushed and killed in County Cork on August twenty-second. But there was business 'as usual' in Dublin. The Irish people could be as divided as possible so long as England had control of its markets.

I thought of the little man who lay dead before us. I had known him since 1899 or perhaps earlier, in the days of An Stad. Poverty did not shake his devotion. He was a poor man all his life, poor to the verge of starvation. Unbribable, firm, courageous, lovable, and fast to his friends. I remembered carrying his rifle as he marched through College Street. He was in the green uniform of the Volunteers. He was surrounded now by the soldiers in the green uniform of a state that was his own creation. They marched with his funeral cortege. My eyes were filled with tears.

Michael Collins was dead. Misfortune upon misfortune!

Behind and above the right ear of Michael Collins there was a small irregular wound in the bone of the skull. There was no exit wound. A ricochet evidently. He had been ambushed in his Lancia; not very far off from where De Valera was hiding. He died in the arms of Emmet Dalton and his body was brought to Dublin by boat from Cork because the railway viaduct had been blown up. Of the arrival of the boat with the body in the rainy darkness, I have written elsewhere.

For days he lay in state in the Town Hall, and Doyle-Jones, the sculptor, did a magnificent head of him in white bronze. Collins, who alone held Ireland together in the two years of the Black and Tan, Lloyd George and Hamar Greenwood outrages. There is a curse upon Ireland politically: she betrays her own children.

35 *'Trowle The Bonnie Bowl With Me'*

Going down Molesworth Street, I met Monty, the Film Censor. He was leaving his office and turning west, which is in the direction of the Bailey.

'Stepping westward, eh? A wildish destiny?'

He smiled as we crossed Duke Street together and went upstairs to our Parnassus in the Bailey.

George had come from the Brewery. Neil was there and, for a marvel, James Stephens. Neil was 'in possession' so Lewis took the orders.

Stephens spoke up: 'You know Neil has just published his poem about the wasp that got into the Rathmines bus, which was filled with sour-faced men and fat women. The bus was going citywards. How does it go, Neil?'

Neil would not say. Stephens remembered the admirable last line: 'That sunlight joined the sun again.'

George Redding moved his chair to make room for me.

In a low voice he told how he was summoned by the Board of the Brewery and asked if he were prepared to go to London. He answered that the interests of the Brewery were his interests. I was saddened at the thought of losing George.

Stephens had to be off and he left unobtrusively. He was an unobtrusive man. The most lyrical poet of them all when it came to lyricism, Yeats not excepted. But Stephens' flights were short and few.

I once asked James Stephens if he were ever sacked. 'No,' he said, 'but I sacked once myself. Macready's, a firm of attorneys, were paying me the enormous sum of 12/6 a week and a partner of the firm announced, "Owing to our policy of retrenchments" – one of them had just run off with a woman to Canada – "it will be necessary to reduce your salary to 10/-".' Stephens' answer was to take his hat and walk out.

He was by far the best scrivener and stenographer any firm ever had. He could do, and he often had to do, the work of three men. And after his gruelling day, he could write a lyric with the best; or compose *The Crock of Gold*, a 'best seller' of world acclaim.

'That short story of Stephens', "Hunger," is largely his own experience,' I said. 'Poverty ground the little man all through youth, but Poverty never got him down nor suffering either. When Lord Gray sent his lady friend a copy of *The Crock of Gold*, he wrote something like this – and it shows what a judge of character was Lord Gray:

> 'James Stephens is quite young, about twenty-seven, married ... He was hungry for weeks as a boy, slept in the parks, fought with the swans for a piece of bread. He lived on the kindness of poor people who liked the queer little fellow, and yet he has grown up with the most independent spirit. Nobody can get a whimper out of him ... He is small in stature but quite big inside, large and roomy.'

As far as my quotation went, it only bored the company. Neil was the first to show resentment.

'Oh, for God's sake!' he implored. 'It used to be dogs: now it is swans.' Neil was getting to his acerb state.

'There's a magnificent portrait of Stephens by Tuohy,' I remarked.

'I understand that the painter committed suicide,' Neil shot out.

'What's this about the telegram, "All is forgiven provided you don't come back"?' Monty asked.

My eulogy of Stephens had gone awry. Moral: You should never praise one Irishman to another Irishman.

> If I were as wise as they
> I would stray apart and brood;
> I would beat a hidden way
> Through the quiet heather spray
> To a sunny solitude.

I said to myself part of a poem by Stephens to the goats; and I beat a hidden way. I got out; no one protested at my departure but Monty followed. 'Time to go. Neil was getting sarcastic,' he said.

As we walked along, we spoke of Neil; he begins a drinking session in silence. Once the guilt feeling, or whatever it is, is drowned, he grows humorous and witty and then later on he becomes everyone's enemy. He sees an enemy in a friend.

'Half the trouble with Neil,' Monty informed me, 'is that he realises now that Arthur Griffith did not like him, and so he takes it out on any of Griffith's friends who survive.'

'You are taking Neil's politics seriously. Surely Griffith never cared what Neil thought?'

'You are wrong there. Griffith never forgave disloyalty to the cause and with disloyalty he had reason to associate Neil.'

'Why had he reason?' I asked; but Monty ran for his bus. As I watched his running figure, I realised that Monty, like Æ, would not say anything disagreeable about anybody. There was no doubt about Monty's loyalty. Had he not hidden Mulcahy when Mulcahy was head of the resistance movement?

Was I right about Æ? He could get indignant at times; and his indignation knew no bounds when he was informed about Neil's attitude to Griffith and the Treaty.

> Praise in your maudlin verse the men who died.
> Look black and bitter when their judges pass
> Who not to see your country glorified
> Would stop the drinking of a single glass.

Why is it that I like something imperfect even in a bar? It may be that I am afraid that perfection is too transient. It may be – awful thought – that I want to feel superior. Well, knowing myself as I think I do, although I do not dwell on it, I will venture to say that is not the answer. The probable reason is that I am afraid of perfection. My Eden requires a serpent.

I should have seen that something was brewing when Neil refused to help Stephens out when Stephens was praising and trying to quote Neil's poem about the wasp. Neil, of course, thought that Stephens was being superior, for what poet is not secretly jealous of another? Dublin's a bitter town. The country is not.

There was a time in pre-Christian Ireland when the Bard was the arbiter before even the king. Perhaps instinctively Neil remembers this and is forever acerb and discontented because of the fallen glory of the poets.

36 *Sir Horace And The Bearded Diphthong*

Sir Horace was dissatisfied with his own death which occurred without his being aware of it in Ireland while he was absent in the United States. Absenteeism could not be carried any further. Bad enough you would think but what was much worse: his obituary notice occupied only one-third of a column and most of that was taken up with a history of his family rather than of himself: not a word about the national purpose to which he had devoted his life! He resolved that such a thing would not happen again. With this in view he collected funds in the USA to found a paper of his own which would have at least a page describing his work for the country and black leads between the columns when he came finally to die. It was to be called, 'The Irish Statesman' (meaning Sir Horace). All that was wanted now was an editor, a man who would see eye to eye with him and give credit where credit was due.

Yeats who was fast to his friend could not have suggested a better editor than Æ (the first letters of aeon, that is the vicar of Hermes Trismegistus on earth). Was Æ not editor of *The Farmer's Gazette* – as you are doubtless well aware farmers are the backbone, etc.

The Irish Statesman would have a wider appeal: what do they know of Ireland that only Ireland know? Its leading articles would deal with problems that were not parochial but world wide. American sanitariums, not sanatoriums, catch cropping and the economic status of the pigmies of the Congo, British tonnage in foreign harbours, with a little poetry here and there. No; Sir Horace could not have had a better – not only an editor but co-adjutor than Æ.

Yeats if he were influenced at all must have remembered that when the National Theatre which afterwards became the Abbey, ran out of geniuses, Æ answered the SOS and contributed his 'Deirdre'.

Yes; Yeats never forgot how Æ had rallied to the call with his Deirdre, which was played in the Temperance Hall in Clarendon Street. 'Deirdre' with a name so weary that it deterred me from taking the least interest in her and her legend, was Æ's first and only play. Deirdre was a beautiful princess who was shut up by King Connor in a tower until she should be nubile. She fell in love with Naisi and ran off with him and his brothers to Glen Etive in Scotland. King Connor sent his battle champion, Fergus McRoy, to promise them safe conduct if they returned. Relying on the word of a king they returned only to have the king slay the brothers. Deirdre committed suicide and fell on her lover's corpse.

Æ could not bear suicide and murder on or off stage. He caused Manaanan McLir, god of the sea, to send an anaesthetic vapour which put them to sleep. The audience was not put to sleep because the bearded head, framed as if decapitated in the middle of the curtains announced in a cavernous and alarming voice, 'Manaanan McLir.' The god appeared *ex machina* and all was well. It put me in mind of the legend which makes Shakespeare play the ghost in his own play.

An invitation to lunch at Kilteragh, Sir Horace's new house in Foxrock, the fashionable suburb off the road to Bray. He has had it built with a revolving room on the roof in which he sleeps. There is a quotation from Kipling about an ashlar over the fire place and dadoes by Æ on the top of the library walls. These are the best paintings that Æ has ever done.

I think as I turn over the invitation what an escape I had when I forebore to be smart and uppish when answering his letter from the Royal Irish Automobile Club. And the hardest thing for a man of middle culture (and no family to brag about) is to refrain from smartness. It is worse than the fellow who begins his after dinner speech by being reminded of something. Such people never do anything: they are always 'reminded' of it. The only difference is that Sir Horace 'reminds' others. I shall have to put up with being a 'man of middling culture' as Marcel Arland, speaking of France said, 'Every man of middling culture has at some moment identified himself with Rimbaud.' I have never identified myself with Rimbaud. I left that for Joyce. Resent as I will being a man of middling culture what can I do? Go to lunch with Sir Horace. That's the first step. The second step is to listen to the people you will meet there. And don't butt in. Listen! There was a planted circle in front of Kilteragh with a rockery in its centre. Cars could drive round it when they entered and left.

The butler took my hat and gloves. I could hear voices and Sir Horace's voice that cackled with culture while it explained something in terms of something else. 'My dear fellow.' That must be Mahaffy; and so it was. Nobody stopped when I was announced. All the acolytes stood in a circle round Mahaffy while he stood head and shoulders over them all. He had a superior smirk or perhaps I should have said smile on his face. Mahaffy paused. The butler had a chance. 'Yes. Yes,' said Sir Horace. 'Won't you lead, Sir John?' So Sir John Pentland Mahaffy led us into the luncheon room. I was last man in; so I thought until someone came from somewhere and pushed me on. It was Anderson, one of Sir Horace's indispensable secretaries.

'I see your architect has scamped the cornice ornaments. No one can be expected to believe that they can support themselves on the corners without a hidden support. And hidden supports are quite contradictory to the principles of architecture.' Sir John smiled, inviting criticism. Sir Horace was talking to some English civil servant, probably the permanent under-secretary, an important person – there is always an important person at Sir Horace's. Anderson, who had pushed me into the room, sat opposite with his florid face. He increased his permanent and proprietary smile and answered officially for Sir Horace.

'You see, Sir John, we are newcomers. When Sir Horace found that his place was in Ireland he had to get a house and get it quickly.' That was the official answer and it contained the hidden flattery of 'found that his place was in Ireland'. Sir John, however, did not listen. In spite of the warning against monopolising the conversation contained in his 'Prolegomena to the Art of Conversation' he laid himself out to hold the table. At last he saw his chance. Sir Horace had paused in his explanation of the Irish question in its immediate application. 'Winchester I presume' Sir John said addressing the Englishman. The Englishman nodded without, however, withdrawing his attention from his host. Probably he made a mental note that if they were all as harmless as Sir Horace, the reports about the increasing realisation called Sein Fein could for the moment be discounted.

'I thought so,' Sir John said, and smiled his enigmatic smile. The Englishman was made to realise that Winchester was inferior to Eton.

Fr. Findlay was talking cheerfully about prospects. He was whole-heartedly in favour of them. Yes; indeed. Another harmless man for who would expect revolution from a Jesuit? Gill, whose beard had given George Moore such amusement, was tired. Overwork? Distinctly so. But remember it was all in an important cause, fresh, original, nascent, kinetic; and Sir Horace was at the helm.

'What's that you are eating?' Mahaffy asked.

'Yogurt,' Sir Horace said; and he too was overcome by weariness. Whether he got his weariness from Gill or Gill seeing that weariness in good cause was one of Sir Horace's attributes, reminded and reinfected Sir Horace somewhat in the way that a yawn spreads. The Englishman must have realised the enormity and importance of 'the national purpose'. I was in no position to tell: I was lunching for the first time with one of Ireland's regenerators with half a dozen secretaries. How could I decide which was wearier than the other?

'You are missing this excellent fish,' Mahaffy remarked.

(He was an authority on everything, cuisine included.) Now it was Æ's turn. Æ was busy forming agricultural banks all over the country. It was the most creditable of all Sir Horace's works. It failed to please Arthur Griffith however, He attacked Æ in a savage article entitled 'Down among the dead men,' evidence of Griffith's anger that a man of Æ's intelligence should be abstracted by Sir Horace from a direct attack upon England. Griffith failed to realise that, left to himself, Æ had little interest in politics, which he considered ephemeral compared to the eternity of philosophy and art.

The British Government possibly on the report of the important guest at lunch gave Sir Horace an ivory gavel, which he waved importantly at men of his own ilk as Chairman of the futile Convention. Griffith gave the country the Irish Free State which later became the Republic under the Prime Ministership of John Costello and not under de Valera, who had 15 years which included a civil war to declare it.

Arthur Griffith's miserably financed weekly, *The United Irishman* was, in spite of its poverty and the mockery of a more popular and vulgar periodical, waging a slowly eroding war with the greatest empire on earth. Griffith naturally could not bear to see genius wasted and misdirected, resented Æ's devotion to Sir Horace. When I expostulated with Griffith about his attack on Æ, he grunted and not speak as one who thought that I should not want an explanation. Anyhow the harm had been done. I felt that if I defended Æ more, I would be down among the dead men too. What Griffith wanted was Æ's loyalty to Ireland and not to an Anglo-Ireland which Sir Horace personified. Æ, who was not an extremist, was supposed to abandon his employer and to join the, to all appearances, down and out party. He was asked to choose between the dilettantism of the arts and the seriousness of politics. Had I but known it the aristocrat of the time was the enemy. It did not occur to me then. I sided with Griffith because hatred of injustice was engendered in me. And I hated humbug. I knew that Sir Horace was considered an ineffectual humbug or he would not have been chosen by that arch schemer and rogue, Lloyd George, Prime Minster of England, to act as Chairman (Sir Horace could not resist) of a Convention set up for no other purpose but to delay action. It sat appropriately enough behind the Trinity College clock. Of course, as was intended, the Convention could not agree even about its own terms of reference. It petered out. Sir Horace wrote to the papers regretting it.

Sir Horace got himself wrong with the extremists and was now through his Home Brighteners getting himself in wrong with the Hierarchy of the Catholic Church which dominates the country. The Catholic Church looks askance at any attempt to influence the mind of the peasant from without: 'This Summer intrusion of superior young men and women from English Universities coming over here in the guise of Home Brighteners weakens the National Idea and seeks to divert the minds of the people from the goal. They are all of them English Protestants. What can they know of Ireland who only England know? And what can they possibly know of our Holy Religion for which our forefathers bled and died?' This has the ring of the Emperor Chien Lung's answer to George III. Sir Horace failed to realise that there are times when religion identifies itself with patriotism and so becomes the only touchstone.

Mahaffy turned and strode across the lawn, with his left foot a little inwards, towards the summer house at the end of Sir Horace's very solid pergola. 'Who was that gumptionless fellow who talked about Siberia after an excellent lunch? That's the worst of lunching with Sir Horace, who seems bent on getting the most immiscible people together. It would be useless to talk to that limited fellow from Winchester whom Sir Horace invited over here to listen to his ideas. If he wished to hear facts about the country let him come to me. Meanwhile, this looks like an excellent cigar.' Mahaffy wandered on in search of Sir

Horace's summer house before lighting it because no one but a vulgarian smokes in the open air. Æ overtook him on the smooth lawn. 'Sir John' he panted. Mahaffy turned and asked with raised eyebrows, 'What is it, my good fellow?'

'Oh, Sir John we all want you to use your great influence. The Czar is knouting thousands and sending them to Siberia.'

'The Czar is knouting whom?' Æ was nonplussed for a moment but he came on again. 'Oh, the Russians. If you write to *The Times*.' Mahaffy looked at him, 'Get this into your head once for all: if the Czar does not knout them, they'll knout themselves.'

Oh, the wisdom of Mahaffy, 'if the Czar does not knout them, they'll knout themselves.' And that was many years before they knouted themselves and liquidated millions as well as sending whole nations to Siberia. Good Lord how right he was. When I say 'Good Lord' I am invoking the spirit of righteousness in man that has kept the idea of goodness before him and led him through the vicissitudes for thousands of years.

The butler came across the lawn and found me. 'Sir Horace would like to speak to you in the library.' I entered the house and was shown into the library. Sir Horace said, 'I want you to know that I laid the fellow who trailed the duck by the heels.' I knew it! Sir Horace himself ran over that duck!

37 *Confusion Compounded*

Let us prescind from the fantasy of Chief Secretary Short in the asylum near Drumcondra and proceed to consider Ireland as an open-air lunatic asylum.

I was the first to reject the sentimental symbolism of

Ireland under the sobriquets of Dark Rosaleen, Kathleen na Houlihan, or the silk of the Kine, females all, and substitute a man, one Endymion, a genial joker whom the Moon touched, seeing that she loved him – Endymion, a lunatic, maybe; but the typical Irishman, good-natured, humorous, cynical.

Who would I commit to my asylum which is in the open air for it includes the whole islands? I would commit Einstein because of his notoriety derived from an unthinking mob which pretends to understand him, and because of the fact that he does nothing to disillusion them. Once in, he would be constantly on the move and running round in circles, because, otherwise, as he himself might say, he might be measured. By the same token all measuring rods and rules would be kept out of sight because, if he found one, he would alter it.

And who would be the director of this open-air asylum? De Valera, of course. He would promise 'freedom' to all the loonies; and they would hail him as their deliverer. Of course he would not let them out! His job would be over if he did. How well he would get on with Bertie Einstein! They would have both politics and mathematics with which to confuse and confound themselves and each other if necessary; and those of the inmates who took themselves seriously.

Think of all the confusion implicit in Neo-Euclidean geometry. Why not? Remember that the whole country is more or less mad. There would be Relativity dished up as a discovery. Time would be mixed up with Space and called a time-space continuum. An equation would appear with *t* in it; that is 'time'. You might as well throw in colour; and noise. De Valera would be sure to add a spot of politics: 'the day is not far distant from the Republic continuum.' There would be the Fourth Dimension with Document Number II as its charter. Einstein would hide behind the Fifth Amendment. All this built upon the measurement of farms in Egypt after each inundation of the Nile!

Mystical mathematicians, who cannot express themselves clearly; though Truth is always clear. What do you call a fellow who tries to pull wool over your eyes and hides, if chased, like a cuttlefish in a roil of words? All right, call them that. Bertie doubts if there are twelve who understand him, and he is proud of the misunderstanding of the inmates. And yet it is not only in an asylum that one understands his jargon. That's why I have him in. He has learned the value of confusion; the other fellow was born confused.

Suppose that the loonies clamoured to be let out? That is unlikely, seeing that they do not know that they are in. If they shouted, De Valera would answer, 'Presently, as soon as you can appreciate the difference between liberty and true freedom.' Bertie would add, 'Don't disturb me. I am bringing the Cosmos into an equation.' Don't tell me that there is no positive value in a negotiation. Bertie and Eamon would get along famously.

'The swifter the river, the nearer the bridge.' Now what does that mean? I confess that it came to me in a dream. Bertie was expounding time-space while Eamon was spouting in an *ersatz* Limerick brogue about true freedom. He was very earnest about it. Politicians are always earnest, preoccupied and serious. Now where do they get that; and what do they take us for?

Why should not politicians be cheerful sometimes? Why should we be asked always to look ahead and always to be on our toes? Why should we not sit down and enjoy the blessings which we have? Oh no; that would never do! The tension between the goal and Man's inadequacy must be kept up. And Bertie and Eamon come from a race of experts at the game; the experts include Freud. The carrot must be held in front of the ass, or else stuck up his proctodaeum to give him an 'id'. In either case he would GO AHEAD. It would never do to have a contented public because there would be no place for politicians at all. So it begins to dawn on me why politicians must always be serious, solemn and even, like De Valera, lugubrious. He always looks lugubrious. It is his melancholy that makes him such a good politician.

It is somewhat the same with Bertie. That 'postulate' of mine about the river and the bridge will illustrate the nonsense Bertie spouts. And even though it is not political, it is stuff and nonsense all the same. If he were to be asked what connection there was between the swiftness of a river and a bridge, he would define both a river and a bridge; but leave the connection out; or, perhaps, put it in because it does not exist. It is something like De Valera's notion of a republic. That is why I have the two playboys, or rather melancholy humbugs, in the same house. Both are fiddlers with words and depend on the public's love of mystification. Einstein belabours the obvious; De Valera buries it under a tumulus of words.

Have you heard of the nitrous oxide or laughing gas experiment? 'No.' Let me tell it to you then. Some there are who under the influence of laughing gas are filled with a desire to solve the riddle of the universe and to tell it to all and sundry. When I was under gas, it seemed that I was beneath a sheet of ice and if I could only tell the skaters above me two words, all would be solved. Yeats had a similar experience, but he put it more poetically, 'Gogarty, I felt that the riddle of the universe could be written on a blade of grass.' And Einstein wants to reduce the indefinable cosmos to a formula, a laughing gas hallucination. That is why I have him in.

Absurd as the picture is, wouldn't it be more cheerful if De Valera were to dance – his black coat tails twirling – to the tune of Bertie's oral fiddle-faddle? It would be droller still if in his dancing he were to pettifog. Everyone would know that his *id* was speaking, and that it spoke the truth for he couldn't help himself.

Yes, it would be a wholesome and laughable thing if De Valera were to dance. How could he? you will ask. When did you see a great funny man? And De Valera is a great man if there is any truth in the remark attributed to Sir Joshua Reynolds, 'The greatest man is he who forms the taste of a nation, and the next greatest is he who corrupts it.' So how can you expect the next greatest man to play the Dancing Dervish?

Pettifogging would be too terse and too reflex to be effective. Especially as sight is more important than sound. This was borne in on me during some political campaign or other at which I spoke from the top of a limousine. I admit that the engine was kept running, for I never can be sure what the effect of my unvarnished oratory may be. There was another campaigner on the top of an adjoining car. He could not be heard for the cheering. He had worked himself up so effectively that his coat nearly fell off. His shirt sleeves were exposed by the emphasis of his harangue. The audience roared applause; and the applause was so loud that whatever I was saying was drowned in the shouting. Anyway, our man was returned, and not by the skin of his teeth, mark you.

It is passing strange that so few politicians, 'leaders' or dictators have been amusing. It would seem that wit has no place in politics. I am inclined to that opinion. There are exceptions: Lloyd George was a wit; so is Winston, if given time. Aneurin Bevan is a wit. So was J. H. Thomas, another Welshman who had to resign from the British Cabinet in disgrace. We all know how Lloyd George dealt in Marconis. 'Great wit and *dodging* sure are near allied.' Yet there have been honest men who were witty, Benjamin Franklin, for instance; in Ireland, Tim Healy, and his namesake, the priest. Wit and politics do not go together; therefore wits should not dabble in politics. And yet it is sinister to be devoid of humour. Savonarola, Stalin, Stafford Cripps and Hitler took themselves and everything else seriously. Look at the results!

38 *Renvyle Is Rebuilt*

The government were compensating those who had lost their houses in the civil war. In order to obtain compensation, an attorney had to be employed. I engaged the firm of Arthur Cox to obtain the monies to rebuild Renvyle. This was done expeditiously.

I did not like to interfere when it came to employing an architect. The one that Arthur Cox commissioned turned out to be an ecclesiastical architect, one accustomed to drawing plans for a church to seat six or eight hundred as the case might be. They were all barn-shaped with yellow pine seats and a window at the eastern end shaped like the gear wheel of a bicycle. That is why the new Renvyle House has Gothic fireplaces!

Apparently it had been a good fire; give them credit for that. China vases had been fused and had run down the walls. A great oaken beam had fallen into the well which was underneath the old house. So I was told. I had not the heart to visit the ruins. All I had by way of details was from the terse foreman of the Belfast builders.

There were certain restrictions on the compensation. For instance, pictures were left out. This prevented anyone from claiming that half a dozen Rembrandts had been burned. Antiques, too, and books.

The new house was intended for a hotel. As I could no longer afford to keep a country house I conceived the idea of making the country keep me. But it was not Ireland that rallied to the cause; most of the visitors came from England and the North. However, our friends could be franked.

Yeats and his bride spent part of their honeymoon in Renvyle. Yeats laid the Renvyle ghost which, in spite of the fire and in spite of the fact that the room it haunted had been turned into a ladies' toilet – a running stream they dare not cross – could be conjured still.

My wife built a four-roomed cottage in the grounds sixty yards from the hotel but hidden from it by a wood and hedges of dense fuchsia. There we could remain aloof from the visitors; but it was not as peaceful as the old house had been when it was private and Mahaffy came and sat outside it in the morning watching the mist rise from the lake and the mountain: 'I declare it is plum-blue.'

Meanwhile there was the house on the Island in Tully Lough, Freilaun. Freilaun means Heather Island. So does Innisfree, where Yeats lay for one whole night on the shore of Lough Gill, building through the midnight glow in his imagination his small cabin: 'I will arise and go now.' But it was never his luck as it was mine to live actually on a Heather Island.

There were eleven acres in the island and a house built by one of the Blakes who was a 'Sunday man', that is, a man who could only appear on Sundays when the King's writ could not be served. We added some rooms to the old house and lived there in blessed silence.

Outside, to the east, stood a five-branched plum tree. In a dell to the north was a plot where raspberries grew. The house was surrounded by great sycamore trees and plane trees. These made the island very warm, warmer than any of the houses on the mainland. In Tully Lough was another island called in English Half Moon Island. It is a heronry. I hope that my son-in-law, who owns Tully Lough now, will let the heronry alone. A third island was evidently a crannog, that is, a prehistorical island settlement. The ancients often built in lakes, doubtless to safeguard their children from the wolves and other wild animals that infested the land of old when it was nearly all one forest of great trees. I think that the Sunday man removed the surrounding stones that rimmed the crannog when he was building his four-room house on Freilaun.

There are otters in Tully Lough. I neither trapped nor shot them because nothing good comes of disturbing the balance of nature. It is a thing for which I was thankful: to be allowed to live in a lake and not to disturb the wild life around me.

How blessed is silence! In the raucous, shouting towns no one can hear the music of the spheres, which is silence. Noise is the loud laugh which bespeaks the empty mind, or, worse, the guilty mind that dare not be still. Here in the moonlight it is possible to decipher print if the moon is full. The only sound that breaks the silence of the night is lake water lapping and the bark of a distant dog. The noise of the bark is as necessary as the snake to Eden, so that the blessedness may be realised and felt.

The sea is only half a mile away. To get to it you must row over to the mainland and then go up and downhill. One of the British Government harbours is there; a rock at its entrance is covered at high tide. No place to bring in a fishing boat; but curraghs and sea gulls can make it and sometimes they do. The harbour has a purpose, at least I have found one for it; it makes a good place from which to dive and the shelter of its sea wall keeps the water more or less smooth.

At Renvyle the sea is closer, only a hundred yards from the house. There is a rock to which to swim. The rock stands up in the water and is more than forty yards off when the tide is in. When the tide is out some sand is exposed. So are the anemones and mussels, which cling to the rock. In front of Renvyle house is the lake of the Little Dark Wood and the little promontory that carries the wood. Ash trees bend back to touch the walls of the house and guard them from the Atlantic storms. When the sun is setting you can see its globe in the sky and in the lake at the same time. If you are lucky you may see the Green Glint. If you have not been lucky and see it you will be 'made up' for the rest of your born days.

What is the use of regretting one place when you are in another?

39 *The Again Coming Of Augustus*

A telegram from Wales. Augustus, on his way from Fryern Court in Hampshire, had run into a tar boiler. But he was on his way. When his car would be repaired he would be with us. He did not say when. (He never did say 'when'.) So I had to wait in daily expectation.

I hoped that Lord Howard de Walden, the peer who sponsored all Welsh geniuses, had not roped in Augustus again. You might think that once at Chirk Castle Augustus would never leave. But that would show that you did not know Augustus. He had not George Moore's satisfaction at being entertained by a peer of the realm. Augustus would not forget his suitcase deliberately at Chirk as George Moore told me he did, so that he might be invited again.

But suppose that a Welsh gloom, black as pitch – I am not thinking of the tar boiler – has enveloped Augustus, such a gloom as descended upon the table at that misassociated dinner party at Chirk. The tale I heard – I think Francis Macnamara was the narrator, was that in the middle of the silence the Bishop of Liverpool, who thought that a bishop should be 'all things to all men', tried a seemingly incontrovertible question of Augustus, who sat beside him dressed as a gypsy with an earring in one ear: 'Don't you think, sir, that every man should take unto himself a wife?'

'I have two!' Augustus boomed. The gloom deepened.

Days passed. Then came a rumour from Galway that Augustus had been seen. He had a commission to paint a beautiful American girl who had come to Galway with her husband all the way from Philadelphia to have her portrait painted. I hoped that there was truth in the rumour. It meant for one thing that the tar boiler had not daunted him. It also meant that he had not gone visiting, in spite of all temptation, in his native Wales.

I remembered his aversion to one castle. That was when he came as a Distinguished Guest of the Irish Nation, in 1928, to attend the Irish games. Many distinguished people helped the government to entertain. The Countess of Meath threw her house open. Dunsany put Augustus up at Dunsany Castle. In Dunsany Castle there is little self-indulgence, so somebody, perhaps it was I, must have spoken to his lordship about the idiosyncrasies of the artist. The result was that every room which he was likely to visit contained a siphon and its companionable decanter. There was a decanter everywhere except on the stairs. It was too much. Augustus blamed not the siphons but the castle, from which he fled unceremoniously.

At last he arrived. He had driven from Galway with one hand. And now he is at work on a portrait of the beautiful American and all is going well.

I believe that there are people who bring you luck. Just as I believe – only more so – that there are people whose very presence is a menace. This, you will say, is sheer superstition; but remember that I am Irish, and the Irish believed that their kings were half magical: one glance if it fell on you would make you lucky for life. Yeats in his unpublished poem *Crazy Jane and the King*, contrasting the Irish idea of kingship with the English store-dummy king, has a line, 'Saw the lucky eyeball shine.' And Augustus comes from wizard Wales. He is lucky.

Why do I take to the Welsh? It cannot be that they are amoral. It cannot be that they have the highest rate of illegitimacy in the Three Kingdoms. Nor can it be that they are free and easy and that they have 'no complaints'. I know: they do not have to be superior to everyone else. There are no cold, superior Welshmen. Yes, after much cogitation I have discovered why I am attracted by Welshmen. And their women are charming too. No one is afraid of them. No one is afraid to marry them.

There are few bachelors in Wales whereas in Ireland, with a population of less than four million, there are five hundred thousand bachelors. Why? Don't ask me. I am biassed; but this is certain: no one ever heard of a Welshman dying, as one of the ancient leaders of the Irish did, 'from an excess of women.'

Mrs Hope Scott is the sitter, a slender, sinuous, dark-haired beautiful woman and a great horsewoman. Her husband is a tall athletic man with a gift for turning a verse.

Talk of Penelope's web! I found Augustus early one morning undoing with turpentine the face he had painted the day before. And Scott had only two weeks' leave from the USA! It took six weeks, I think, before Augustus was satisfied. But is an artist ever satisfied?

I remembered how his long sinewy artist's hands had tugged at the ivy when we were both staying in the old house just after it had come to me. It was then I taught him to drive a car, or rather I was there when he drove off in a Ford, and could not stop until it had run out of gasoline, somewhere by the side of Lough Fee! I followed fearfully in another car and watched him take corner after corner full speed ahead. I have recorded the facts of that first drive of his and in that record I compared him to a Viking. 'Like a Viking who has steered, All blue eyes and yellow beard.' Now I find how right that was. In his book *Chiaroscuro*, he tells that Haverford, where he was born, had been a Norse settlement: Haverfjord. Sometimes you find the truth in a rhyme though you may be unaware of it.

One evening he came back late. He had been out in his car alone. He said that in the dark someone had sat behind him and had left him only when the lights of the house were seen. It was an eerie story that befitted an eerie time and place, midnight on the extreme shelf of Europe. He would sit for hours on a ridge overlooking Tully Lough painting on panels of sycamore wood where Croagh Patrick, far off, shot its cone into a niche of coloured sky. A Japanese battleship-builder bought the twelve panels that he painted while he was at Renvyle.

40 *The Hawk's Well*

Yeats and his wife came to stay with us and Augustus went to work on a portrait of Yeats. Where the original is now I do not know, but the portrait represents the poet in his old age. He is seated with a rug round his knees and his broad hat on his lap. His white hair is round his head like a nimbus and behind him the embroidered cloths of heaven are purple and silver. It is the last portrait of Yeats. It is reproduced in *As I Was Going Down Sackville Street*.

Poets require little entertainment. They can entertain themselves. If you want to entertain them therefore leave them alone. But something was in the wind. Yeats was in consultation with my wife and I was not invited to take part in their planning. At last the news broke: Players from the Abbey Theatre were coming to produce Yeats's *The Hawk's Well.*

An explanation of *The Hawk's Well* and similar plays is necessary. Yeats got his idea from the symbolic Noh plays of Japan. His imagination was excited; he saw a new mechanism, with the stage on the same level as the room. He could have a theatre wherever there was a large room that would hold forty or fifty persons. But the audience must be 'readers of poetry'. Did he mean to bring out at last his poetic plays, shelved for forty years? My wife said that he had, in his own words, 'attained a distance from life which can make credible strange events, elaborate words.' All this, mark you, was by way of explanation, or was it an apology for what was about to happen?

'He wants to show us the masks and costumes designed by his friend Edmund Dulac. He is tremendously excited. We have ample space in the large room.'

Indeed there was space enough, for the large room was larger than most drawing rooms. It was over forty feet long and it had a folding door that could be used for entrance and exit by the players.

I had not been consultd. Very well, this meant I was spared such obnoxious details as the reservation of the ground floor of the east wing for the Abbey Players.

It may not be all very well to be a poet – fifty per cent of them are distraught – but it must be very intense to be a dramatist. What I am coming to is this: there is Yeats in the loveliest spot on earth – it was Bob Flaherty who, having seen all the world, called Renvyle the loveliest spot on earth – and Yeats, instead of enjoying the place, is constrained to bring in help from without, to wit, his Abbey Players.

Lady Wellesley has remarked somewhere that Yeats never noticed natural scenery. That may be, but that he did at one time observe it narrowly is obvious from his poems, which never once bring in exotic or impossible scenes, but always things most apposite – the speckled eagle cock of Ballygauley Hill; the yew that has been green from time out of mind; the long grey pike that broods in Castle Dargan lake.

Well, he loves excitement; and there is this to be said in his favour: there is no way to give anyone an idea of a play you have written that compares to having it produced, acted and seen.

I had never seen *The Hawk's Well*, although it must have been on something during my frequent visits to the Abbey if there was any room for it between the plays that Yeats attributed to Lady Gregory and which were played *ad nauseam*. If I did see it, one thing is certain, I never saw it with Dulac's masks, head-dresses and costumes, nor did I hear his music.

It may be that all this shadow of an objection to having the peace of the place disturbed by players is an affectation of mine. I shall find myself pretending that I am so full of resources that I do not require any outside help to enjoy a holiday in a lovely place. Now I find myself looking forward to the play; so my attitude was all nonsense.

It is to be on after dinner, that is, about nine o'clock tonight. Yes, he is quite right, time hangs heavy after dinner, especially on those who do not indulge in the illiteracy of cards or, worse still, billiards.

Much more than forty people had come to see the play. Who told them? I had imagined, foolishly when you come to think of it, that a play and players can thrive privately. So that is what all the whispering was about: to get an audience. I thought that they must be 'readers of poetry'. Well, who would have thought that Mrs — and the ash-blonde daughter ever read poetry?

'Oliver!' It was the voice of Augustus. 'We have been looking for you everywhere. Come in! The play is beginning.'

Yeats was already speaking when I entered. I tried to sit in a back row. But the speaker paused until I went forward. His pause made my interruption more noticeable. He resumed at long last when I was seated. But where was Augustus John?

'As I was saying, I have found a form of drama that is at once aristocratic and distinguished . . . ' He is resuming the poetic drama that he reluctantly set aside when he found that a theatre, in order to support itself, had to stoop to the masses, I thought; but I was wrong. 'I have created an unpopular theatre, that is, a theatre which does not depend for existence on crowds and the box office. I have found a form that does its work by suggestion, by complexity of rhythm, colour, gesture, symbol, not by direct statement, I have not altered basically the Noh plays that were intended for nobles, but I have made them suitable to our conventions of aristocracy . . . '

How the audience must be flattered!

'I, as you will see shortly, have discovered the theatre's antiself.'

Should he explain? Perhaps not. Everybody will think that they require not intellect to appreciate his play but, what is rarer than intellect, understanding of symbolism;

and who can limit its wide suggestions? Every man for himself! Evidently the audience thinks that it is up to them to supply mystical emotions. They are all flattered. That's what the speaker wants; and . . .

'Perhaps I had better adumbrate the suggestions – not their significance, for that would be to limit them. The well, then, is the well of immortality or of wisdom, if you will. The hero approaches and find an old man seated there waiting for its bubbling. He has been there for fifty years.'

When the play was first written Yeats was fifty years of age.

'The well is guarded by a woman who is possessed by a hawk; call this woman intellect. She dances a magic dance which draws the hero off in pursuit and sheds sleep upon the old man. The song I have written for this play would suggest that the hero is Cuchulainn. I know well that you would not have me be explicit. Let it rest at that.'

> I call to the eye of the mind
> A well long choked up and dry
> And boughs long stripped by the wind,
> And I call to the mind's eye
> Pallor of an ivory face
> Its lofty dissolute air,
> A man climbing up to a place
> The salt sea wind has left bare.

Whatever sort of face Cuchulainn had, it was not an ivory face; but Yeats's face is the colour of ivory, and so was the face of Dante, who was 'Mocked by Guido for his lecherous life'.

Don't think that my thoughts distracted me from the speech. I remember it well.

'The masks, costumes and the music are by my friend, Edmund Dulac. Let us begin.'

Applause. Loud applause, all the greater in volume because of the room.

Thanks be to Heaven, Yeats at last is enjoying himself! Even the presence of a few old dames, to whom poetry – no matter how you use your imagination – can have no appeal, does nothing to diminish the poet's satisfaction. That I knew by the assured way in which he spoke. Often when he spoke he used his audiences for guinea-pigs as it were; using the audience to sound out the effects of his words. Now he had no need of such subterfuge. He was master of himself.

No, I had never seen *The Hawk's Well*. The Old Lady of the Abbey Theatre repelled me by continually inserting the few plays she was supposed to have written and attaching them to everyone else's work. Once I tackled Yeats about these so-called plays of Lady Gregory. 'You cannot tell me that she wrote *The Rising of the Moon*.' He, although he tried to be evasive, acknowledged this: 'We decided that whoever found a suitable title might have the words too.' As I suspected. Yeats, who had a fine sense of humour, did not want the comic to interfere with his fame as an outstanding poet who must, in conformity to the English idea, be totally lacking in humour, so he let Lady Gregory get away with the comics. That interchange actually took place. I do not remember the year, but I remember the conversation and how triumphant I felt when what I had long suspected from observation turned out to be correct. I have a sticky memory.

The Hawk's Well was played even as its author would have wished. It proved to be a supernatural presentation, the like of which has never been seen before on any stage. I know nothing of Japan, but they could not have produced anything as satisfying and as moving for Europeans as *The Hawk's Well*. The crisis faded into a magical dance. What a lovely thing Dulac made out of the human hawk woman!

I knew that Yeats was very well satisfied; but I also knew that to praise him would detract from the mystical impression he had produced. So I left him alone with his glory.

41 *Looking Back*

The sun was setting, a red ball over the vast sea. A thin strip of green divided the sea from the lake with its promontory, the Little Dark Wood, before me. Around the lawn on which I sat was a wall of fuchsia; and behind me the house.

The test of life, I thought, is, would you live it over again? Assuredly I would, and with little change and no 'apologia'.

Doctoring is not all. I went into politics with my eyes open. I never forgot Dr Kenny. At the same time I went on doctoring, and kept it up for thirty years. But politics gave me the opportunity to put into effect that which was borne in on me as of the first importance by my experience as a doctor – the abolition of slums.

A one-room tenement breeds twice as much tuberculosis as two rooms. Housing was the key not only to health but to morale. And politics offered a chance, if not to get slums abolished immediately, to point out the remedy.

There were many difficulties in the way of slum clearance. Not the least of these was the slum snob. 'Many a good man was born in a slum'; that I heard in the Senate. But why should a good man have to be born in a slum?

I promised to tell how Tom Kettle helped in the movement for better housing. He was giving evidence before one of the numerous committees. He said that he wanted to obtain entry to a typical slum, one situated in one of the old Georgian houses that had become derelict. Upper Dominick Street was selected because each side of the street was lined with houses of the best period, that had fallen into decay. The time was late at night. Tom, careless of how it might be construed against him, told how he was accosted by a whore and taken to a front room that had been the drawing room in better days. 'There was a family in each of the three corners; but as we approached the prostitute's corner we approached civilisation: there was a screen around her bed.'

I remember backing the Censor Bill. I knew that, when censorship was most active, literature was most alive.

What was the result of the passage of the Censor Bill? A gang of peeping Toms was let loose on every writer in the country; the censors smelled sex in every realistic literary creation; in one year they banned more books than the papal Index Expurgatorius had banned in fourteen years. They held up tourists at the ports of entry while they were searched to see if they carried any 'objectionable' book. By the way, the books which were objected to were not indicated. The censors had gotten out of hand. They were interfering with human liberty, not to mention the Tourist Industry. I should have foreseen to what extent lascivious old men in a Jansenistic country could go. I must acknowledge that my attitude towards censorship was wrong.

You may say that my experience of politics was an experience *in parvo*. But let me tell you that Irishmen are the most expert politicians in the world. The size of the country has nothing to do with its politics – there were three or four towns in ancient Greece each at the other's throat; and the Peloponnesos would fit into Ireland many times. Tammany, with the great city of New York surrounding it, is but a suburb of Dublin.

There is always this consolation in making mistakes: they prevent you from becoming complacent, self-satisfied and smug. I have another regret, but the circumstances were not altogether within my control. I might have purchased the Tower at Sandycove, where Joyce and I lived, from the British Government when it was clearing out of Ireland. I would now be the owner of it in fee simple. Why did I not jump at the chance? I did, but I was put off by a fellow, some little jack-in-office of a clerk in Dublin Castle, who wanted by delaying to impress me with the importance of the job he was doing for me.

Now when I think of the buildings that are close to the Tower, I am almost consoled. But that Tower was an ideal house. It could be locked up for a year with the utmost assurance of security; and when opened again it would be found to be dustless. The only things necessary to secure it against were pigeons, and they could be kept out by strong bars within the windows a few feet from the outer surface of the wall.

There is another form of consolation in the remark made by a public figure in one of his more idiotically inspired moments: 'History is useless because we do not know what might have happened had it gone the other way.' Or some such words that without the saving effect of a thorough Irish bull reveal a muddled head. Had history 'gone the other way', would it not still be history? I quote it to show how confused the mind of a 'leader' can be. However, I wish history had gone the other way just once and that I owned the Tower at Sandycove. De Valera could not have burned that.

Another regret I have is that I was not suspicious. This was not due to any magnanimity but because my head was in the clouds and, when it was not, I was too much inclined to leave responsibility to others. Thus it was that we were robbed of the estate which I made over to my mother by a deed of gift when I reached the age of twenty-one.

One day she said to me, 'Your father died intestate. Instead of putting the estate in Chancery, as legally I was bound to do, I spent the income on your education and the educations of your sister and brothers. Now you can put me in jail.' I found that a deed of gift to my mother would cover the situation, and made one accordingly. Had I inquired into the credentials of my mother's attorney I would have found that he had been struck off the Rolls, which is a rare disgrace for an attorney. Instead, I permitted him to make away with the whole property before my mother's death, which occurred within a few years of the deed of gift. Her attorney, or solicitor as they call them in Ireland, was an insinuating, bony-headed little scoundrel who had robbed his way to seeming prosperity. His supply of widows was limited only by his obscurity. He had met my mother at the altar rails, for he haunted the Jesuits' Church in Gardiner Street. That was enough for her. She had the uttermost confidence in the rogue. The result I have described. An automobile ran over him and his large head was fractured.

> Struck off the Rolls; Reinstated. Struck off a Rolls He
> broke his head; And now Dishonesty lies dead.

But the lines I wrote for his epitaph were little consolation.

Often I wonder, is the inherent tension between a raving moral maniac such as the biblical Jehovah and Man's inadequacy suitable for all nations? The Orientals have it not, yet they manage to live lives without dishonour. They cannot understand Original Sin. I can, not quite dogmatically perhaps, but the question is, Does the tension created by the attempts of poor humanity to appease a raving deity do any good? See what it has done to the Jews who started it.

Is it natural for Irishmen? What would they be without it? You may ask; but is that not like asking what is the use of history because we don't know what might have happened had it gone the other way? All I will say is that I am not the first Irishman to query the tension between Perfection and Inadequacy. Pelagius did it in the fifth century in the form in which it was presented to him – he said that there was no such thing as Original Sin. He had to be suppressed. It was either he or the sacraments. It comes to this: You cannot have a religion of suffering without Original Sin. In other words, man is not perfect. The Bishop of Hippo knew that; and it was he who fastened Original Sin on the innocent infant, who can only cry when being baptised.

The worship of Jehovah does not seem to have done the Jews much good. 'Suffering is the badge.' Take Cardinal Newman, for example. He was the son of Dutch bankers called Neumann, and wrote *Apologia pro Vita Sua*. That was in the '60s in Oxford.

What a place Oxford must have been then! Oxford Movement Number One. Tracts, sermons and dejections. Oxford must have been full of 'pi-jaws' then.

I must prefer to laugh at the tale of the absent-minded and undejected president of Trinity College, Oxford, who, when asked what the four statues on top of the church tower represented, said, 'The Holy Trinity.' 'But there are four,' the GI objected. 'Of course,' the president explained. 'Three Persons and one God.'

Think of it! I might have been saved! But, to reverse the problem, as Mahaffy said to the zealot who cornered him in a railway carriage and asked, 'Are you saved?': 'To tell you the truth, my good fellow, I am; but it was such a narrow squeak it does not bear talking about.'

From the Christian Brothers Primary School, where Brother Swan told me to chisel my words, to Dublin University there is an unpleasant lustrum. Dublin University, let us call it Trinity College, a name which is more often used, healed me and gave me of its best. The Divine Doctor, the Professor of Moral Philosophy, Henry Stewart Macran, whom I knew familiarly as Fafnir, one of the dragons of the ring; and the great John Pentland Mahaffy, one of the greatest intellects of a day that was full of outstanding men ... There the education was certainly classic and by no means scientific; and though we had a great scientist in the Engineering School, Professor Fitzgerald, one of the first men to experiment with a glider and the man who discovered wireless before Marconi, we kept him there. The Divine Doctor used to quote Plato whenever a mathematician was mentioned: 'I have hardly ever known a mathematician who was capable of reasoning.'

Often the thought strikes me, Have I ever left Dublin

University? Certainly I have never sought to improve on the universal outlook on life. With Lachesis I sang of the Past, with Clotho of the Present and, thus equipped, I can look, as I do now, at the Future with assurance.

The politician has to strike an average; he has to deal with a cross-section of humanity. He has to make allowances; this means that he has to treat men as inferiors. To succeed he has to be, as Tom Kettle said, somewhat of a mountebank. He has to cherish the Plain Man. He has to pretend that whatever he does is for the Plain Man's good, when in reality it is for his own aggrandisement. For me to pretend to be a Plain Man would be just a harlequinade. Someday I will get away from this humbug to where there is a genuine Republic.

Fairfield is gone that I thought was fixed forever. I like to imagine that it was there to fall back upon no matter how far I wandered. I would not like to be shut in it all the time because I could not tolerate eternity. But it was good to dream that some things did not change for all the flux.

> O grant me, Phoebus, calm content,
> Strength unimpaired, a mind entire,
> Old age without dishonour spent
> Nor unbefriended by the lyre.

My strength is unimpaired, my mind is entire, and as for being befriended by the lyre, Sir William Watson in his *Retrogressions* has these lines that notice me:

> Three Olivers before your time
> Were not unknown in prose and rhyme;
> One was the paladin or pal
> Of him who fought at Roncevalles;
> One gave Drogheda to pillage;
> And one wrote 'The Deserted Village';
> But sorra an Oliver ever was seen
> Compares with him of Stephen's Green.

I lived in Stephen's Green for three years beside the Shelbourne Hotel. My office that was is now a bar; appropriately, you may say. Now who is looking for symbols? But when all is said, and though the name of the book is *Retrogressions*, which means that he considered himself reverting to an inferior state, Ireland – remember that he suffered from melancholia – I feel greatly complimented, particularly since Sir William wrote some of his best lyrics while retrogressing in Ireland.

42 *Samain*

Lough Corrib, on the north, sends an arm due westward to meet a river that flows through the valley of the Joyce Country. In this water stands Caisleen na Circe, the Castle of the Hen. Legend has it that the husband of Grace O'Malley was besieged in that fortress and that she raised the siege. He was eke named, The Cock; and so to celebrate the story of how she came to his assistance, it is called the Castle of the Hen.

Another story goes that a magic hen laid an egg daily for each man of the garrison during a beleaguerment. The castle is in ruins now. The late Lord Ardilaun, one of the great family of Guinness, kept the ruin from falling down. To reach it, a boat is necessary.

The road from Cong skirts Lough Corrib until the Joyce Country is entered. The Joyces were a giant race. Each Joyce had six fingers and six toes. That is not unknown. In Ireland it is a mark of gigantism. The Hen's Castle and the giant Joyces and the unworldly atmosphere of the place make you feel that you are travelling through a legendary magic land.

One evening as dusk fell, I was driving along by the north of Lough Corrib to the west. It must have been in the autumn, for all the hillside to my right was covered by dull red fading fern, bracken and the dark green brambles of the withering blackberry. In that soft climate there is no winter, nor is there any loss of colour, though the colour be fuscous and subdued. The hillside was not bare. To the left the mountains hid the sun setting in vaporous light and here the gloaming lay without a gleam on water or on hill.

Suddenly, as if a backdrop came forward, the land seemed to open out, light shone on a fresh earth and bright grass; all figures moved in beauty, birds sang in blossoming apple trees.

I was gazing at the Delightful Plain, I was gazing at Mag Mell, and I gazed without astonishment, for what I saw seemed in the order of things.

Students of the ancient lore of Ireland know that Amairgin, the poet, gave to the Tuatha de Danaan the lower half of Ireland, that is, the territory under the earth and under the waters outside the garish light of day. The Sons of Mil received the upper part; and once a year on the last day of October and on the first day of November there is common territory between the upper and the lower parts. The Tuatha de Danaan are said to have come from the isles of northern Greece in time out of mind and to have brought their magic with them. They were well satisfied with their award, for were they not given Tir na nOc, the Land of Youth?

It was on the last day of October that I came to enter the Joyce Country on my way from Cong.

Magic! There is magic in the West; and it is everywhere. It is everywhere in the world only we do not recognise it. We call it Good Luck or Fortune, What does it do but show that there are outside powers that rule our lives?

In the West of Ireland it is understood, it is taken for granted. When I saw the Green Glint in the evening sky an old man told me that I was made up for life.

> Yesternight I saw in a vision
> Long-bodied Tuatha de Danaan;
> Iron men in a golden barge;
> Saw the eyes that never wink

Mirrored on the winking wave:
Eyes a righteous king should have . . .

And again, in the same (unpublished) poem, Yeats testified:

Saw the sages meet the king,
Seven fingers cautioning;
Saw the common people surge
Round a wave-wet landing stair,
Banging drum and tambourine;
Saw the lucky eyeball shine
On the lewd and learned there.

'Lucky eyeball'! Good Luck; it is magic all the same. I cannot explain it. Why should I? You know what I mean and why I was not astonished when I beheld the Delightful Plain full of fruit and flowers? All my life was a longing for it. Fools may call this longing, Thanatophilia, a Longing for Death; no, I long for immortality in Tir na nOc. There the monotony which I cannot sustain on earth would not be with me, for in Tir na nOc you escape from human time. Three hundred years there are but as a day in the upper half. There the denizens know nothing of old age; they have escaped from human Time. So have the dead, you will say; but the dead are not wakeful and aware as are those who dwell in Tir na nOc.

This longing for youth, this dislike of old age is pre-eminently an Irish trait. Blind Raftery, the poet, who was born in Mayo but spent his days in Galway town, his face to the wall (i.e., blind), playing his music 'to empty pockets', says in the last line of his famous poem, *The Country of Mayo*:

'Old age would never find me and I'd be young again.'

And in the twentieth century, Yeats in his *Seven Woods* tells how the squirrels rejoiced: 'As if they had been hidden in green boughs Where old age cannot find them.'

The ancient Irish had no Valhalla in the heavens. They had their Land of Youth in their own country, under the earth and under the waves. No one made the earth. When it came to making such things, that was a blacksmith's business. Under the earth and under the water there was an idyllic life where even eternity could not bore you. This means very much to me because even beauty, if dwelt on too long, begins to pall. But in Mag Mell, the Delightful Plain, it is otherwise: Mag Mell . . . why not call it Fairfield? That was the delight of my youth and in Tir na nOc I will see it again. I'll be young again in Tir na nOc.

In the West of Ireland there is magic everywhere. It is behind religion, for what is religion but the supernatural regulated? Reason cannot affect it, for reason was given us for a safe-conduct through our daily life; but magic deals with eternal values.

Some day, on the first of November perhaps, the earth will be opened and I shall enter into no strange realm but the realm of youth renewed.

Boys! O Boys!

MUSIC FOR CHAMELEONS

new writings by Truman Capote

This extraordinary book of reminiscences, conversational portraits and stories contains the now-famous piece, *Handcarved Coffins: A Nonfiction Account of An American Crime*, in which Capote once again focuses on the study of murder. It also includes *A Beautiful Child*, a touching and perceptive account of a day with Marilyn Monroe and *A Day's Work* when he accompanies a Manhattan cleaning lady on her rounds . . .

'Capote is an extraordinary writer and his latest offering, a cool, sparkling collection of 14 mainly non-fiction pieces, sometimes written like film scripts, is the most scintillating, original, fertile and stimulating book I have read for a very long time'

Sunday Express

GENERAL FICTION **0 7221 2243 8** **£1.50**

Also by Truman Capote in Sphere Books:
IN COLD BLOOD